Ancient Civilization:
4000 B.C.–400 A.D.

The Structure of European History
studies and interpretations

⋄§§⋄

NORMAN F. CANTOR and MICHAEL S. WERTHMAN, Editors

Ancient Civilization: 4000 B.C.-400 A.D.

Second Edition

edited by NORMAN F. CANTOR

State University of New York at Binghamton

and MICHAEL S. WERTHMAN

Thomas Y. Crowell Company   *New York*

ESTABLISHED 1834

ACKNOWLEDGMENTS: The editors wish to express their gratitude to the following publishers and individuals for permission to quote selections from the works designated:

R. R. Bolgar, *The Classical Heritage and Its Beneficiaries*. Reprinted by permission of Cambridge University Press, New York.

Rudolf Bultmann, *Primitive Christianity in its Contemporary Setting*, translated by Reverend R. H. Fuller. Copyright © 1956 by Rudolf Bultmann. Reprinted by permission of The World Publishing Company.

R. G. Collingwood, *The Idea of History*. Reprinted by permission of The Clarendon Press, Oxford.

Glyn Daniel. From *The First Civilizations* by Glyn Daniel. Copyright © 1968 by Glyn Daniel. Reprinted with permission of the Publisher, Thomas Y. Crowell Company, Inc.

M. I. Finley, *The Ancient Greeks*. Copyright © 1963 by M. I. Finley. All rights reserved. Reprinted by permission of The Viking Press, Inc.

Finley Hooper, *Greek Realities*. Copyright © 1967 by Finley Hooper. Reprinted by permission of Charles Scribner's Sons.

Michael Rostovtzeff, *History of the Ancient World*. Volume II: *Rome*, translated by J. D. Duff. Reprinted by permission of The Clarendon Press, Oxford.

Michael Rostovtzeff, *Social and Economic History of the Roman Empire*, Volume I, 2d ed., translated by P. M. Fraser. Reprinted by permission of The Clarendon Press, Oxford.

Ronald Syme, *The Roman Revolution*. Reprinted by permission of The Clarendon Press, Oxford.

Preface

〜§〜 *The Structure of European History* is a six-volume anthology series whose purpose is to present to the undergraduate and lay reader leading interpretations of fundamental political, economic, social, and intellectual change in European history from the advent of civilization to the present day. The six volumes are devoted to the following eras of European history:

    I. Ancient Civilization: 4000 B.C.–400 A.D.
    II. Medieval Society: 400–1450
  III. Renaissance, Reformation, and Absolutism: 1450–1650
  IV. The Fulfillment and Collapse of the Old Regime: 1650–1815
    V. The Making of the Modern World: 1815–1914
  VI. The Twentieth Century: 1914 to the Present

Every volume consists of eight relatively long selections, each of which is preceded by an editors' introduction that outlines the problem, identifies the author, defines his methods and assumptions, and establishes his interpretation within the historiography of the subject. A brief list of additional important books on the same subject or on related subjects follows each selection. Each volume contains a brief introduction to the period as a whole that delineates the leading themes by which modern scholarship has illuminated the era.

Almost all of the forty-eight selections in the six volumes were written in the past forty years and the majority since 1940. In recent decades historians of Europe have sought to extrapolate broad movements of historical change from the vast amount of data that modern research has built up. There has been a general tendency in modern scholarship to bridge the conventional compartmentalization of politi-

cal, economic, social, and intellectual history and to analyze a movement or event which falls primarily in one of these categories within
the context of a total view of social and cultural change. Historians
more and more attempt to present a picture of the past as rich, as
complex, and as full as human experience itself. The intertwining and
mutual involvement of many kinds of aspirations and achievements are
now seen to be the basic existential facts shaping previous societies
just as they shape social conditions in our own time.

We have sought in these six volumes to present to the student and
lay reader examples of this comprehensive and total approach to the
understanding of European history. In making our selections we have
been governed by the criterion of choosing interpretations which view
critical movements and trends in the history of Western civilization in
as broad and as many-faceted a context as possible. We have also aimed
to make selections which are distinguished by a clear and forceful style
and which can be easily comprehended by students in a freshman
survey course and by the college-educated lay reader.

Most of the selections in each of the six volumes of this series are the
original, seminal theses presented by distinguished scholars after many
years of research and reflection. In a few instances the criterion of com-
prehension by the novice student and lay reader has led us to take an
extract from a work of synthesis and high vulgarization which in turn
is based on very important monographic studies.

N.F.C.
M.S.W.

Contents

Introduction

꧁꧂ Less than fifty years ago it was widely believed that as an ongoing field of research ancient history was almost finished. It was assumed that our knowledge of the structure of ancient civilization was rapidly reaching its ultimate limits. More than a century of assiduous mining of the fragmentary primary sources had elicited all possible meaning and significance from this material, it was held, and the pattern of ancient history, with the exception of a very few aspects, mostly in the area of the ancient Near East, had taken on a definitive form in modern scholarship.

In recent decades these assumptions have been proved grossly premature, and in the past twenty years no other era of European history has been subjected to more searching revision and more fundamental reinterpretation than that of the ancient world. Almost every important general theme regarded as virtually definitive forty years ago has been undermined, challenged, and in many instances persuasively negated or revised by recent research.

This reinterpretation of ancient history has occurred for three main reasons. In the first place, far from the primary materials being exhausted, as was commonly assumed some forty years ago, a very substantial amount of new material has been uncovered in the way of archaeological digs and the finding of papyrus rolls, and more discoveries of this kind of material are made every year. It will be several years and perhaps decades before scholars have exhaustively studied and analyzed this new information and thor-

oughly evaluated its significance. Secondly, in recent decades, the study of ancient history, along with the historiography of other eras of Western civilization, has been
strongly influenced by the concepts of the social and be-
havioral sciences, particularly sociology, economic theory,
comparative religion, and anthropology, and this has led to
revolutionary new insights into data that was well known
four decades ago and to the achievement of novel and profound general interpretations. Thirdly, new insights have
been derived from studying ancient Mediterranean civilization as a whole instead of isolating the various centers of
the ancient world from each other. Thereby the cultural,
religious, and economic interaction of various parts of ancient Mediterranean civilization has been perceived, and
general patterns of change are coming into focus whose
existence was not even suspected by early twentieth-century scholars.

This volume presents eight of the most important themes
in the recent historiography of ancient civilization. Leading
historians assess the way in which civilization emerged
in the ancient Near East; the origins of Greek civilization, the precise nature of its debt to Minoan (Cretan)
and Near Eastern cultures, and the social and political organization and ideals of Homeric Greece; the nature of the
Greek city-state and the causes of its achievements and
failures; the process of transition from the Roman Republic to the Roman Empire; the actual doctrines Jesus
preached, the nature of the original Christian gospel, and
the influence of the contemporary setting in which primitive Christianity developed; the institutional structure and
the causes of the breakdown of the Roman world; the
foundations of historical thought in the work of Greco-
Roman and early Christian writers; and the character of
the classical tradition and the manner of its preservation
and transmission to succeeding generations.

Other leading themes with which modern scholarship on
the ancient world has been primarily concerned are the
social and intellectual origins of Judaism and the pattern
of development of Judaic thought down to the Christian
era; the institutions of the Hellenistic world of the third

and second centuries B.C. and the extent of the impact of the Hellenistic heritage on later Judaism, early Christianity, and the culture of the Roman Empire in general; and the development of the Christian Church into a universal, institutionalized religion.

GLYN DANIEL

The Advent of Civilization

◆§◈◈ European history begins with a paradox: what we
regard as indispensable preconditions for Western civilization first appeared not within the geographical confines of
Europe but in the Near East, in Mesopotamia and Egypt,
between 4000 and 3000 B.C. The societies that developed
here are the first that a hundred years of archaeological
investigation have shown to have had efficient food production, urbanization, a systematic use of metallurgy, recogniz-
able governmental and legal institutions of the state, a common moral and judicial order imposed over a large area,
public works, a universal religion marked by a hierarchical
priesthood and commonly observed rites and liturgy, and
finally, forms of literacy. In other words, there was civilization.

We can view these Near Eastern societies of the post-
neolithic era as the starting point for European history even
though it was not until after 1450 B.C. that a society any-
where approximating this level of civilization appeared
within the geographical limits of Europe, namely in the
southern part of mainland Greece. European civilization is
not simply a geographical term but rather a congeries of
ideals, social institutions, and cultural practices. If we seek
to identify the time and place of the advent of civilization,
we are searching for the origins of an organized and specialized way of life which ultimately took hold in western

FROM Glyn Daniel, *The First Civilizations* (New York:
Thomas Y. Crowell Company, 1968), pp. 15–34, 69–82.

4

Europe, even if its first manifestations were elsewhere. European history until the fifth century A.D. is in fact part of the history of the Mediterranean world, and European culture is an outgrowth of ancient Mediterranean civilization which had its birthplace in the fourth millennium B.C. in Mesopotamia.

Preeminent among the scholars who in the first half of the twentieth century tried to determine the causes of the rise of civilization in the ancient Near East was V. Gordon Childe, a tough-minded, indefatigably hard-working, completely independent and inner-directed Australian who for more than three decades from the late 1920's was professor of prehistoric archaeology first at the University of Edinburgh and then at the University of London. With the clarity and precision of his literary style, unusual among writers in this field, Childe pressed his solution to the first great problem in European history in several books, one of which, *What Happened in History*, published in 1942, was addressed to the general reader and is probably the most widely read serious work on prehistory published in the twentieth century.

It is significant that there is no question mark at the end of the title *What Happened in History*. Childe, a doctrinaire Marxist, was certain he knew what happened: the advent of civilization was based on what he called "the urban revolution," and this urbanization with its attendant specialization made possible entirely new moral, religious, and aesthetic potentialities. The urban revolution of the Near East was the consequence of a technological-economic change, the use of metal and the development of metallurgy that liberated a part of the populace from the soil and produced a group of artisan craftsmen who were specialists. The urban revolution also produced the first economic surplus, which in Mesopotamia and Egypt was concentrated in the hands of priestly and despotic rulers. No longer tied to the soil for the barest necessity of food, the peasant was subjugated to a human master, and the craftsmen became the exploited hirelings of the state. In Childe's view the dawn of civilization was also the beginning of the exploitation of the masses.

Childe's interpretation of the advent of civilization in Mesopotamia will stand as one of the great historiographical achievements of the twentieth century. But as with all monumental historical interpretations, it has been challenged by the discovery of new evidence (in this case archaeological), by the resifting of already known facts, and by new perspectives stemming from the intellectual currents of the historians' own day. Generally, scholars have become disenchanted with the traditional division of prehistory in accordance with stone and metal artifacts, and this has undermined Childe's emphasis on metallurgical change as the key to "the urban revolution." Accordingly, the distinguished American archaeologist, Robert Braidwood, perhaps Childe's most trenchant critic, has focused on agricultural rather than metallurgical change as the key to the advent of civilized society in Mesopotamia. Braidwood argues that in Mesopotamia between about 5000 B.C. and 3200 B.C. there was a shift in cultivation from the sides of hills to the river valleys. This change necessitated irrigation which could be undertaken only on a large scale, and this in turn brought about extensive social and political organization—the precondition for other facets of civilization. Childe's materialism has, perhaps inevitably, also been found unpalatable by subsequent interpreters of this great moment in human history; a deeply felt need to consider the human side has influenced Samuel Kramer who in his study of Sumer, the first Mesopotamian civilization, stresses "the psychological factor" behind the great change of the fourth millennium B.C. Similarly Robert Redfield, a great American anthropologist and prehistorian who did not share Childe's Marxist predilections, has posed the question whether some change in human consciousness, some deepseated shift in moral values, might not have given the men of the fourth millennium B.C. a glimpse of a new horizon, a glimmer of a new way of life.

Glyn Daniel, professor of prehistoric archaeology at Cambridge University, is the scholar who comes closest to Childe in achieving for a later generation of students a breadth of view and a skill in communicating very complex material in a succinct and easily comprehensible way. In the

following admirable study he begins by surveying the early
development of prehistoric historiography, explaining how
the now outmoded and even, in some cases, treacherous
interpretations fashionable fifty years ago emerged, and
then reexamines Childe's thesis in the light of recent research and interpretation.

ক্ষ্ণ

   In a recent article in *The Spectator* ["The Science of Rubbish"],
Professor Stuart Piggott referred to archaeology as 'the science of rubbish'. He was indicating that archaeology is the study of what material
has been left behind, of the minor monuments that time 'which anti-
quates antiquities, and hath an art to make dust of all things, hath yet
spared', of the dead bones which have 'quietly rested under the drums
and tramplings of three conquests', to quote Sir Thomas Browne. Do
you also remember Francis Bacon's definition of what archaeology was
concerned with? 'Antiquities', he said, 'are history defaced or some remnants of history which have casually escaped the shipwreck of time.'
   It is with these remnants of history, this rubbish that has escaped the
shipwreck of time, that [we are] concerned. When I saw the title of Professor Piggott's article I was immediately reminded of the fine condemnation of archaeology once uttered by that most amusing American Professor of Anthropology, the late Ernest Alfred Hooton. 'Archaeology',
he said, 'implies an interest in the obsolete paraphernalia of the past,
which to the multitude stigmatizes its students as unregardful of the
necessities of the present—the senile playboys of science rooting in the
rubbish heaps of antiquity.' I am one of these senile playboys and I am
asking you to root in the rubbish heaps of antiquity with me: let us dig
archaeology together to find what light it throws on what I regard as
one of the most important historical problems—the problem of the beginnings of the ancient civilizations of man. Our theme, then, is what
archaeology, the study of the material remains of the human past, tells
us about the origin of the civilized societies of antiquity, about the origin of the earliest and first civilized societies—that is to say about the
origins of civilization itself. . . .
   The first book that studied the origins of civilization from evidence of
archaeology was published almost a hundred years ago: it was called
The Origins of Civilization. It was written by the banker, politician,
scholar, Member of Parliament who was born to the name John Lub-

bock, became Sir John Lubbock, Bart, and was raised to the peerage as Lord Avebury—someone said cynically at the time of his elevation: 'And how long shall we have to wait until he becomes Viscount Stonehenge?' . . .

Lubbock's *The Origins of Civilization* . . . was the work of an archaeologist and natural scientist studying a problem for which the sources were part material, that is to say, archaeological; and part literary, that is to say, historical in the narrow sense of written history, history *sensu stricto*. We realize today that written sources can tell us next to nothing about the origins of the first civilized societies: the problem is an archaeological one. Many—too many—who have written about the origins of civilization since Lubbock's time have failed to appreciate this fact: the literature abounds in geographical, historical and philosophical generalizations. Here we have little use for these: the problem is archaeological, and our concern is with the hard facts of archaeology. . . .

*   *   *   *   *

Until Lubbock's time man's history was conventionally divided into modern, medieval and ancient. Lubbock defined the fourth division, that of prehistory—a kind of misnomer: it really means pre-written history. Writing is an achievement which came late in man's cultural development: the earliest surviving writing comes from Egypt and Mesopotamia and is not earlier than about 3000 B.C. Writing, then, is a skill which is some five thousand years old. Man may have come into existence, perhaps in Africa, one to one and a half million years ago. *Homo sapiens* was certainly in existence thirty to forty thousand years ago, and possibly much earlier. At a very conservative estimate the pre-literate, prehistoric past of *homo sapiens* is ten times as long as written history, and the prehistoric past of man as a genus *Homo* very much longer. It is the final stages of the long pre-literate past that concern us here, and it is the testimony of the spade, and not the testimony of the written word, that suggests to us the views we should now take about the origins of civilized societies. By the time writing has arrived and recorded history is upon us, civilized societies have already been born.

There is a difficulty here, a difficulty of method and approach. The historian proper is suspicious of the historian improper, if I may so call the archaeologist who copes with the science of prehistoric 'rubbish', the scholar who deals with pots and pans and ruins, and invents names for the people who created non-literate cultures. And on his side the archaeologist is suspicious of the broad approaches made by the historian and philosopher of history and often retreats to his taxonomy and typology and takes refuge in the minutiae of ancient material culture. This is why the problem we are studying here is so fascinating and so fraught with dangers and pitfalls, for it needs archaeological knowledge and a breadth of historical thinking. We may not achieve the union of these, but let us try.

Our picture of man's remote past is derived from archaeology, with all its associated scientific disciplines such as, for example, human palaeontology, geochronology, and the study of faunal and floral remains. The relative values of the material and literary sources for reconstructing the past of man vary from the beginnings to the present day. In prehistory, as we have said, archaeology is paramount; indeed prehistory *is* prehistoric archaeology. In ancient history archaeology is of very great importance, and sometimes much of it is referred to as proto-history. We cannot solve or begin to see our way towards a solution of the fascinating problem of man's emergence from savagery through illiterate barbarism to literate civilization until and unless we appreciate what archaeology has to say; how much it has to say, and sometimes how little. . . . The limitations of the written sources, on the other hand, are more obvious: they just do not exist before 3000 B.C. in the Near East. The antiquity of man's first civilizations is buried in the pre-literate past and it is what archaeology tells about the last stages of that pre-literate past as it emerges via proto-history into history that is our concern.

The word 'civilization' is by no means a very old one in the English language. Boswell reports that in 1772 he urged Dr. Johnson to insert the word in his Dictionary, but the Doctor declined: he preferred the older word 'civility', and this, like the word 'urbanity' reflected the culture of the townsman in *urbs* or *civitas* as distinct from that of the barbarian—the agricultural rustic. It was of course an invidious term: here we use civilization and urbanization as objective and specific terms—terms without the overtones which we associate with the words civility and urbanity. We do not suggest that the people of the first civilizations, the literate town-dwellers of Ur and Mohenjo-daro and Anyang, were necessarily civil or urbane. But they were literate and lived in towns and were the first people to do so in the long process of man's cultural and social evolution from the darkest savagery of the early Palaeolithic.

I have already used the words culture and civilization several times: the best way to define them is to quote what the late Professor A. L.

Kroeber said. Kroeber (1876–1960) was one of the great pioneer American anthropologists. From 1957 onwards he began to set down in outline material for a book he never finished: it was called *A Roster of Civilizations and Culture,* and this is what he wrote on a sheet found after his death in his files for this book:

The terms civilization and culture are used here not contrastively and exclusively, but inclusively as essential synonyms of sometimes varying accent. There is no difference of principle between the two words, they denote somewhat distinguishable grades of degree of the same thing. Civilization currently carries an overtone of high development of a society: culture has become the customary term of universal denotation in this range, applicable alike to high or low products and heritages of societies. Every human society has its culture, complex or simple . . . for the larger and richer cultures the term civilization has current usage, and need not be quarrelled with, on the understanding that no distinctions of kind between civilization and culture are implied.

In my view this definition cannot be bettered for clearness and correctness. There are no implied distinctions of kind or value involved. I might add just one thing to make clearer the difference between the archaeological/anthropological use of the words culture and civilization, and the ordinary descriptive use of these words with value-judgements. All men by definition have culture, but all men by practice are not necessarily cultivated. Most men these days belong in whole or in part to a civilization—that is to say to a particular pattern of culture—but many others, the so-called primitives, still live in a society that has not attained to this complexity. And all men who are part of a civilization are not necessarily civilized or civil.

Lubbock, though he was an archaeologist—among many other things —was writing at a time before many of the great archaeological discoveries of man's earliest civilizations had been made. He wrote, too, at a time when, though Charles Darwin had disturbed complacent people by the publication of his *The Origin of Species* in 1859, and Charles Lyell and John Evans had further disturbed people by their acceptance, in that very same *annus mirabilis,* of the great antiquity of man, there was a fairly clear and a fairly comfortable idea as to what civilization was. It was Western Europe, and the Victorian age was the proud pinnacle of that edifice, Western Civilization. We all of us, in a wide variety of ways, still use this tag phrase, Western Civilization. We are proud of it, ashamed of it, it is the great glory of democracy and Christianity, it is bourgeois capitalism, we are ready to die for it, it is effete and al-

ready dying on its feet: it all depends on how you look at it. And in
many a place we still encounter the traditional history book picture of
the evolution and the components of Western Civilization—the three
components from Athens and Rome and Jerusalem. Athens gave Western Civilization its intellectual and artistic heritage, Rome the practical
achievement of Government and law, and Jerusalem its faith and
morals. Viewed thus it is all as simple as that, and the notion is often
repeated in this simplistic form.

But even in the nineteenth century this over-simple story of the three
civilizations which lay behind the medieval and modern West—Greek,
Roman and Hebrew—was obviously not a complete and full story.
The humanist and the Christian, even without detailed archaeological
sources, and relying on the dubious historicity of the Bible, and the
more accurate observations and descriptions of men like Herodotus,
knew of Egyptians and Assyrians and Babylonians, and of Medes and
Persians. Most scholars had forgotten, or had chosen to forget, that in
the period between 1492 and 1530, the period from Columbus to Ame-
rigo Vespucci, civilizations had been discovered and in part destroyed
by the Spanish conquistadors in Central America. . . .

But if the Victorians thought little about what lay behind Greece and
Rome and the Medes and the Persians, and paid little attention to Central America, they had some vague ideas of the antiquity of civilized life
in India and China. Had not China invented paper and gunpowder, and
were there not sahibs and *quai hais* who had seen some damned interesting old remains in the jungles of India, and was there not among a
few a feeling that, rope-tricks and sword-swallowing fakirs apart, there
was some very ancient wisdom in the East? We were in the nineteenth
century and many of us still are occidentocentric. As the late Professor
Ralph Linton said in *The Tree of Culture,* itself a very valuable introduction to the cultural evolution of man, 'It has been said that the battle
of Waterloo was won on the playing fields of Eton, and one might add
that Singapore was lost in its classrooms.'

The revolution through archaeology in our knowledge of man's
earliest civilizations took place in the seventy-five years that succeeded
The Origin of Species and Lubbock's *Prehistoric Times.* In 1877 Ernest
de Sarzec, the French consul at Basra, began digging at a place called
Telloh, where stone statuettes had been found; and, during the next
quarter century, he found the Sumerians through archaeology. In 1871
Heinrich Schliemann began digging at Hissarlik in western Turkey and
found Troy. On and off he dug until his death in 1890, and in between

his four archaeological campaigns in Troy, he excavated at Mycenae and Tiryns and revealed to the world a new civilization, that of the Mycenaeans. Schliemann was negotiating for permission to dig in Crete when he died: in 1899 Arthur Evans began excavations at Knossos, and in nine weeks uncovered a vast building which he identified as the palace of Minos. The next year he announced the existence of an early civilization which he labelled the Minoan.

In the first volume of *The Cambridge History of India* which was published in 1922, Sir John Marshall wrote: 'It is the misfortune of Indian history that its earliest and most obscure pages derive little light from contemporary antiquities.' Two years later, in 1924, in *The Illustrated London News* he was announcing that excavations at Mohenjo-daro and Harappa, in what is now Pakistan, had revealed a new prehistoric civilization, that now usually referred to as the Indus or Harappan civilization. During the last few decades of the nineteenth century farmers tilling their fields near Anyang in north China found curious bits of decorated bones, the so-called oracle-bones. In 1928 the Academica Sinica and the Smithsonian Institution began to dig at Anyang and revealed the prehistoric Bronze Age civilization of China, now firmly identified with the Shang dynasty of the Chinese historians.

And from China to Peru. The last thirty to forty years of reconnaissance and excavation in Middle America and Peru has revealed the origin and growth of the Nuclear American civilizations. So that we are now in a very different position from Lubbock's when he set out to write his *Origins of Civilization* in 1870. We now believe that we know from archaeology the whereabouts and the whenabouts of the first civilizations of man—in southern Mesopotamia, in Egypt, in the Indus Valley, in the Yellow River in China, in the Valley of Mexico, in the jungles of Guatemala and Honduras and in the coastlands and highlands of Peru. In these seven areas the first civilizations came into existence. We will not call them primary civilizations because this makes it difficult to refer to Crete, Mycenae, the Hittites, and Greece and Rome as other than secondary civilizations, and this term 'secondary' seems to have a pejorative meaning. We shall talk rather of the first, the earliest civilizations, and of later civilizations.

* * * * *

Kroeber's definition was that civilization was a particular pattern of culture. Gordon Childe, in his books *Man Makes Himself* and *What Happened in History*, listed the elements which he thought made up the pattern of the urban civilized communities of the ancient Near East—

the plough, the wheeled cart, traction animals, the sailing boat, the smelting of copper ores, the solar calendar, writing, processes of reckoning, standards of measurement, irrigation, specialized craftsmen, city-life, a surplus of foodstuffs available to support those members of the community who are no longer themselves producing their own food. Certainly the common features in the subsistence of the early civilizations are these: first, the existence of a surplus from the soil to meet and support new economic classes; second, a complex subsistence pattern —not one based on a single crop—and some degree of intensive land use of which irrigation was one technique. Childe's list is mainly one of material things. Redfield, in his analysis of civilization, stresses in addition four things: one, the value placed upon the central accumulation of capital collected through tribute or taxation; two, special privileges to the ruling class; three, the high value accorded to 'the State'; four, the rise of national religions, priestly classes, god-rulers or god-priests and ceremonial-bureaucratic centres.

In 1958 the Oriental Institute of the University of Chicago held a symposium on the origins of civilization in the Near East: the papers prepared for the symposium and the lectures and discussions that took place were published in 1960 in a book entitled *City Invincible*. Quite naturally, many who took part in this invaluable symposium produced their own definitions of civilization. The late Professor Clyde Kluckhohn said that a society to be called civilized must have two of the following: towns upward of 5,000 people, a written language, and monumental ceremonial centres. Gelb argued that you could not have civilization without writing. 'I have reached the conclusion,' he said, 'that writing is of such importance that civilization cannot exist without it, and, conversely, that writing cannot exist except in a civilization.' Professor Robert Adams's definition of a civilization was a society with a functionally interrelated set of social institutions which he listed as:

1. class stratification marked by highly different degrees of ownership of control of the main productive resources;
2. political and religious hierarchies complementing each other in the administration of territorially organized states; and
3. complex division of labour with full-time craftsmen, servants, soldiers, and officials alongside the great mass of primary peasant producers.

One other definition, this time not from the Chicago conference, but by Professor Stuart Piggott, from his Preface to Professor Max Mallowan's recently published *Early Mesopotamia and Iran*:

We should surely not be far from the mark if we thought of civilized societies as those which worked out a solution to the problem of living in a relatively permanent community, at a level of technological and societal development above that of the hunting band, the family farm-stead, the rustic self-sufficient village or the pastoral tribe, and with a capacity for storing information in the form of written documents or their equivalent. Civilization, like all human culture at whatsoever level, is something artificial and man-made, the result of making tools (phys-ical and conceptual) of increasing complexity in response to the enlarg-ing concepts of community life developing in men's minds.

When we speak, then, of the origins of civilization we mean the origins of the first literate town-dwellers; we are discussing what Gordon Childe called the Urban Revolution—but we shall see that what I prefer to call the process of synoecism was not a revolution but an evolution, and one that took place in several parts of the world. Our problem is how and why and where and when barbarian societies made this leap forward into literate town-dwelling communities. And here is the nub of the question: did this forward leap take place once only, or did it take place many times? . . .

We have already begged another question by referring over and over again to barbarism. The Greeks knew what they meant by barbarians: they called them *barbaroi* which is the same thing as *barbarophonoi*, that is to say the people who spoke a foreign or barbarian language— the people who went *'bar! bar!'* The Greeks met these people on the frontiers of the civilized world and had names for them such as Sarma-tians and Scythians and Celts and Ligurians. Herodotus gave an ac-count of a people living in a lake village in Greece, and here he was writing an ethnographical account of what we nowadays would call a Neolithic or Bronze Age community. The barbarians whom the Greeks met had many things in common—they were illiterate, they didn't live in towns, some of them were nomadic and drank mare's milk, and some of them, surprisingly, wore trousers. But their worst crime was that they didn't speak Greek—and that showed clearly how barbarian they were!

Yet the barbarians, although they had no towns or writing or litera-ture, were accomplished in many arts and crafts. They had domesticated animals—indeed many of them were horse-riders—and they cultivated grain. Some of them, like the Celts and Scythians, had developed a re-markable style of art. They were indeed near-civilized, or so thought the Greeks.

The Greeks did not often meet people who were not agriculturists or herders; they did not have many dealings with those human beings whom from the Middle Ages onwards we have been calling savages: *silvaticus* from *silva* a wood or forest. Savages were the people of the woods and forests—the uncultivated ones, and they certainly did not know the cultivation of grains: even in 1588 the word was being used for uncivilized people living in the lowest state of culture—people in a state of nature: and you may remember Tennyson's phrase: 'I will take some savage woman, she shall rear my dusky race.'

By the late eighteenth century there was a clear awareness among some scholars at least, of savages, barbarians and civilized people as the three stages in man's social and cultural evolution. Governor Pownall—he was Governor of Massachusetts—wrote in Volume II of *Archaeologia* in 1773:

This globe of earth hath, according to the process of its nature, existed under a successive change of forms, and been inhabited by various species of mankind, living under various modes of life, suited to that particular state of the earth in which they existed. The face of the earth being originally everywhere covered with wood, except where water prevailed, the first human beings of it were *Woodland-Men* living on the fruits, fish and game of the forest. To these the land-worker succeeded. He *settled* on the land, became a fixed inhabitant and increased and multiplied. Where-ever the land-worker came, he, as at this day, ate out the scattered race of Wood-men.

In the late eighteenth century there was speculation about the succession: Woodland-men, the men of *silva*, the salvages or savages; then the Land-Workers—the settled people, the barbarians of the Greeks—and finally, civilization. This was the threefold sequence of food-gatherers, primitive agriculturists and herders, civilization; in a word, or rather in three words—Savagery, Barbarism, and Civilization. Sven Nilsson, Professor of Zoology at Lund University in Sweden, set out these views in his *Skandinaviska Nordens Urinvånåre*, the first edition of which was published in Lund in 1838–43. The second edition was translated into English—actually by John Lubbock—and appeared in 1868 under the title of *The Primitive Inhabitants of Scandinavia*. Here Nilsson sets out a classification of man's past based on the mode of subsistence. First there was the *savage* state—the childhood of the race—when man was a hunter, fisher and collector of berries and fruits. Secondly, the *herdsman* or *nomad* stage, when hunting was an occasional occupation but man subsisted mainly on the products of his herds. The third stage was the *agricultural*, and the fourth *civilization*, which, incidentally, Nilsson defined on the basis of coined money, writing and the division of labour. His idea of a herding or pastoral stage between food-gathering and agriculture lingered on long, and it is rather curious to find the poet Coleridge saying in 1836 that 'the progress from savagery to civilization is evidently first from the hunting to the pastoral stage.'

The anthropologists and ethnographers of the nineteenth century who were beginning to interest the world in existing primitive societies and the fascinating problems of their interrelationships with the past of modern societies—was it progress and development or retrogression and decay?—did not necessarily accept the four-stage model of Nilsson, namely, savage food-gatherer, herdsman-nomad, agriculturist and civilized man, but they did accept in general the model of savagery, barbarism and civilization, and this has been with us ever since. I have no complaint about it in its thoroughly general way. Its first clear formal statement was in Edward Tylor's *Anthropology: An Introduction to the Study of Man and Civilization*, published in 1881. Tylor became the first Reader in Anthropology in Britain, and then the first Professor, at Oxford. . . . Tylor proposed formally to distinguish three stages in human history: savagery; barbarism, which he defined as beginning with agriculture; and civilization, which he began with writing.

The American anthropologist Lewis H. Morgan, in his *Ancient Society: or Researches in the Lines of Human Progress from Savagery through Barbarism to Civilization* (1877), proceeded to define these terms more exactly according to the enlargement of man's sources of subsistence. He distinguished seven periods—seven ethnic periods as he called them. The first six were:

1. *Lower Savagery,* from the emergence of man to the discovery of fire;
2. *Middle Savagery,* from the discovery of fire to the discovery of the bow and arrow;
3. *Upper Savagery,* from the discovery of the bow and arrow to the discovery of pottery;
4. *Lower Barbarism,* this stage began with the discovery of pottery (which, to Morgan, was the dividing line between Savagery and Barbarism) and ended with the domestication of animals;
5. *Middle Barbarism,* from the domestication of animals to the smelting of iron ore;
6. *Upper Barbarism,* from the discovery of iron to the invention of the phonetic alphabet.

Finally, the seventh period was civilization with writing and the alphabet.

These schemes of Tylor and Morgan were of course theoretical ones; they were models of the past like the simpler models of Pownall and Nilsson. At the same time as Nilsson was writing, another model was being developed, mainly in Denmark: it was a technological model and saw man's past in three stages or ages of Stone, Bronze and Iron. C. J. Thomsen, the first Curator of the Danish National Museum at Copenhagen, opened this museum to the public in 1819 with its exhibits classified in this way. His assistant and eventual successor, J. J. A. Worsaae, demonstrated that these three successive technologies were not merely a theoretical model, but were the proven and observed fact of excavations. It was the great contribution of Worsaae to show in his digging in the Danish peat bogs and the barrows of Jutland that man had once lived in a stone age, and then had become metal-using, but only knew copper and its alloy with tin, namely bronze; and that only late in his evolution—we know now that it was not before 1500 B.C. in Anatolia and much later in other parts of the world—500 B.C. in [Britain]—man became iron-using.

It was soon realized that there were several stages of the Stone Age, and it was Lubbock, a hundred years ago, who produced the terms 'Palaeolithic' and 'Neolithic' for the Old and New Stone Ages. A Mesolithic was added later, and by some an Eolithic, and all the five ages— Palaeolithic, Mesolithic, Neolithic, Bronze Age and Iron Age—were divided into epochs and periods reflecting in their turn various patterns of material culture and various groupings of artifacts.

Two people at least tried to marry together the two models. One was the late Gordon Childe, the other J. G. D. Clark, at present Disney Professor of Archaeology in Cambridge. If you look at Childe's classic *What Happened in History*, first published in 1942, you will find chapters labelled Palaeolithic Savagery, Neolithic Barbarism, the Higher Barbarism of the Copper Age, Early Bronze Age Civilization, and so on. To me these marriages of the two models are not very helpful; indeed, as I have myself been advocating for years, the technological model, which served us so well for so long—and without which perhaps archaeology would never have developed as a discipline—can now happily be abandoned in general parlance, though it will for long be used taxonomically, and we shall all see on museum labels for the rest of our days tags like Upper Palaeolithic, Middle Neolithic and so on.

It is, incidentally, particularly interesting that in the development of pre-Columbian American archaeology . . . after a period of using the old neo-Grecist labels, American archaeology has devised a terminology of its own, with phrases like Lithic, Archaic, Formative, Classic and post-Classic. . . . The Classic phase is the phase of early American civilization in Mexico, Yucatán and Peru.

You may well ask why this is a suitable moment for re-discussing the whole problem of the origins of that special pattern of culture which we have agreed to label civilization: what has happened, if you like to put it this way, since the last war to bring these wide issues again to the forefront? My answer to this is threefold: first, there have been new excavations and new discoveries of far-reaching kinds—the discovery of Eridu in Mesopotamia, for example, claimed, and surely correctly, as the oldest of all cities; the re-excavation of Mohenjo-daro and Harappa with the fresh light it has thrown on these Indus cities; the discovery of many new Indus sites; the excavations in China which have taken us back to the origins of the Shang civilization; and then, endless work in Mesoamerica and Peru culminating in the discovery of the origins of American agriculture.

First then, discovery, fresh facts. But secondly, the dating of these facts. It has always been difficult and often defeating to find accurate dates for events before the invention of writing in Mesopotamia five thousand years ago; and dates for barbarian cultures and civilizations that were completely outside the range of contact with the early chronologies of the ancient Near East. Archaeology has for long badly needed a technique of dating independent of man and writing. The first geochronological techniques were dendrochronology, developed in America and able to take pre-Columbian American cultures back fifteen hundred years before Columbus, to about the time of the birth of Christ; and geochronology in the narrow sense of the word, that is to say, counting of clay varves—the thin layer of clay left behind by the melt waters of the retreating glaciers—which enabled the Swedish geologist Baron de Geer to calculate a date for the end of the last Ice Age and to provide a geochronology of the last twelve thousand years. The interrelation of the study of pollens with the dated clay varves has brought about a tremendous extension of geochronology and the provision of a time-table of the post-glacial vegetational and climatic phases.

But the great breakthrough, perhaps the greatest breakthrough in the development of archaeology, came as a result of research in nuclear physics in the last war. Professor Willard F. Libby, then Professor of Physics in Chicago and now Professor of Chemistry in California—the first Nobel prizeman in archaeology, as he has been described—discovered that it was possible to date absolutely organic objects from the

past, such as bone and charcoal, because when an organism died its
Carbon 12 content remained constant but its Carbon 14 content dis-
integrated at a fixed rate. There are now over seventy laboratories all
over the world engaged in producing these radiocarbon dates.

It is because of this revolutionary geochronological technique that
we can now state as historical facts that:

1. The savages of the Upper Palaeolithic in southern France and northern Spain who lived by hunting and fishing and collecting fruit and
   berries, whose cultures have names like Aurignacian, Solutrean and
   Magdalenian, and who produced the cave art of Lascaux, Niaux and
   Altamira, lived from around about 35,000 to 10,000 B.C.;
2. The beginnings of the domestication of animals and the cultivation
   of grain first took place in the ancient Near East about ten thousand
   years ago. The great American orientalist James Breasted invented
   the phrase 'the Fertile Crescent' for the grassland hill-slopes that
   existed from Egypt through Palestine to northern Mesopotamia and
   western Iran, and it is here that, as he guessed, the first farmers came
   into existence. This was a region which had wild wheat and barley
   and wild sheep and goats. Our first farmers occur in northern Mesopotamia and Palestine but also in a third area outside the Fertile
   Crescent of Breasted—in southern Anatolia;
3. Civilization in the sense in which we are using the word did not
   develop in the foothills of the Zagros Mountains or in Palestine or in
   southern Anatolia—did not in fact develop in the Fertile Crescent or
   where the first peasant farmers flourished. It developed in southern
   Mesopotamia. . . . Professor Samuel Kramer wrote a book about
   early Mesopotamia called *History begins at Sumer*—a fine, catch-
   penny title, but also true; man did first achieve civilization on the
   flood plains of the twin rivers, the Tigris and Euphrates.

*   *   *   *   *

It was, then, some five thousand years ago that civilization began in
southern Mesopotamia. . . . By the fourth Uruk phase (Uruk IV), somewhere between 3200 and 3100 B.C., we were without any doubt dealing
with a society that was civilized according to the definitions of civilization which we are adopting in this book. There were cities, specialized
craftsmen, co-operative irrigation works, ceremonial centres, writing—
and many more things which make the proto-literate society of Uruk
and Jemdet Nasr civilized in the meaningful historical and archaeological use of that word. And that civilization, which in terms of archaeological levels and periods is Uruk IV and Jemdet Nasr, is Sumerian.

The Early Dynastic period of Sumer covers the part of the third millennium from 2800 to 2400 B.C. and ends with the conquest of Sumer by a Semitic king of the North, Sargon I of Akkad. Then there was a Sumerian 'Renaissance' from 2120 B.C. until Ur was destroyed at the end of the third millennium B.C. This was certainly not the end of Sumerian civilization but it was the end of Sumer as an independent ruling nation. So, when we talk of the first civilization of man, the Sumerian civilization, we mean that civilized society, that highly developed and sophisticated culture which flourished in southern Mesopotamia from the second half of the fourth millennium B.C. to the end of the third millennium.

Let us go over the basic characteristics of this first civilized society. First, the Sumerians were city dwellers. Their cities were surrounded by brick walls and a ditch and dominated by temples and ziggurats set on high platforms. Outside the walls were gardens, fields, dykes, canals and harbours. The walls of Erech encompassed two square miles, and Lagash is reported as having thirty-six thousand males, probably adult males, so that it might well have been a town or city of eighty to a hundred thousand people—approximately the size of the modern English towns of Oxford or Cambridge or Norwich. It has been estimated that at the height of its expansion half a million people lived within the four square miles of Ur, and that Kish, Eridu, Lagash and Nippur at their greatest moments might have had comparable populations.

Each city was the centre of a little city-state: Sumer was organized on the basis of fifteen to twenty small city-states each politically autonomous, but all economically interdependent. Each city-state in turn tried to get control of others, or of the whole federation: inter-city-state wars occurred but they were not major affairs and were usually about administrative matters like the ownership of land or irrigation rights.

The Sumerian cities or large towns were based on a flourishing agriculture; barley was the main crop, but wheat, emmer, millet and sesame were also grown, and, of course the date-palm, 'its feet in the water and its head in the scorching sun'. There were fruits and vegetables, and domesticated cattle and sheep. It should be borne in mind that at the present day the plain watered by the Tigris and Euphrates is a rich farming land and that it was much richer before extensive salination took place. The whole population of the area could easily live on the produce of the land and barter the surplus for what they wanted from abroad. It is important to remember too that this was no subsistence agriculture; it was a well organized agriculture with a complex system of irrigation canals. Irrigation and drainage involved complicated and co-operative efforts requiring control, organization and a centralized society.

In Sumerian, and for that matter Akkadian, there seems to be no distinction between the words that we in English apply to different sizes of settlements—city, town, village, hamlet. *Uru* and *alu* are all these things although the villages grouped around a city were called *uru barra*. In the settlement there were specialized craftsmen in their workshops, as well as granaries and magazines. There were smiths, glaziers, jewellers and seal-cutters. The so-called Royal Graves of Ur give us a picture of Sumerian art and craftsmanship between 3000 and 2800 B.C., and show that at that time the Sumerians were masters of metallurgy, stone-carving, glass-working, filigree work and carpentry.

One of their main crafts was metallurgy. Native copper worked cold is attested at Çatal Hüyük in Anatolia in the seventh millennium B.C. In the 'Ubaid period of Mesopotamia, that is to say certainly from 4400 to 4300 B.C., metal was common and cast axes of copper were being made at least in the north of the country, and objects of gold make their first appearance. From at least the beginnings of Dynastic times the Sumerian smith knew how to alloy copper and tin to produce bronze, and the first discovery of this alloy—so important in the late prehistoric and proto-historic world—may well have been due to Sumerian smiths. They certainly understood the closed mould and the *cire-perdue* method of casting, which they probably invented. The earliest certain example of *cire-perdue* casting is the elaborate model of a car or chariot drawn by four onagers from Tell Agrab: this dates from Early Dynastic II, that is to say, about the middle of the third millennium B.C. It also seems likely that it was the metallurgical expertise of the Sumerians that included the invention of the socket. They had been using gold since 'Ubaid times: they also used silver and lead, and from 3000 B.C. onwards occasional objects of iron appear. The Sumerian smiths were clearly experimenting in metallurgy.

There was no native metal in Mesopotamia: metal-working and many another craft involved extensive trade relations. The Sumerians got tin from eastern Iran, from Asia Minor and Syria, and perhaps, although we cannot be certain about this, from Europe. They got gold from Elam, Cappadocia and the region of Antioch, while silver and lead came from the Taurus mountains and from Elam. Copper they obtained from Oman in the south of the Persian Gulf, and perhaps from the Caucasus as well. Oman was also the source of stone for querns and door-sockets and statues. Lapis lazuli came from Persia and Afghanistan, mother of pearl from the Persian Gulf, sank (or chank) shells from India, cedar and pine from the Lebanon Mountains of Syria and the Zagros Mountains of Iran. Thus the trade relations of the Sumerians were very wide from Asia Minor to India, and we know something about how this trade was carried out. By 2500 B.C. a colony, or a factory if you prefer the word, of Sumerians existed at Kanesh in Asia Minor, and this commercial and colonial outpost of the people of south Mesopotamia was arranging for the export of copper and silver and lead from mines in Anatolia. And . . . there were certainly commercial relations with the Indus cities to the east and with Egypt to the west.

Next in our list of the Sumerian contributions to the civilized world is the wheel. The Sumerians invented the wheel. First it was a potter's wheel: they made fine pottery on the wheel and baked it in complicated ovens and they knew the art of glazing, and incidentally we should mention here that the first glass also was Sumerian. Before 3000 B.C. they had used the wheel as a rotary device to make vehicles more mobile: they had heavy four-wheeled working waggons and lighter two-wheeled carts which might have been used as battle cars or chariots; all these were solid-wheeled vehicles.

The Sumerian towns had ceremonial centres of distinction and importance. At the end of the Uruk phase at Erech, the *tell*—the accumulation of the settlements that had gone before—was as much as 60 feet high, and there was a gigantic temple dedicated to the goddess E-anna. This temple measured 245 feet by 100 and behind it was the ziggurat 35 feet high with a flight of steps leading to the summit, where there was a platform covered with asphalt on which was a smaller temple 73 feet long by 57 feet 6 inches. As Gordon Childe put it vividly, 'One is no longer standing in a village green but in the square of a cathedral city.'

These ceremonial centres and other places were served by a fine architecture. In dynastic times the Sumerians used plano-convex or pincushion-shaped bricks. It was the Sumerian architects who invented the brick column; theirs were the oldest columns in the world, inspired directly by the trunk of the date palm.

The centres of the Sumerian city-states were these ceremonial areas, the *temenos*, the citadel with the temples of the gods. Each city seems to have had a patron god, and among the Sumerian pantheon was a group of goddesses, all perhaps representing different aspects of the earth-mother goddess, one of the first and earliest of goddesses in human history. It was on the ziggurat, the staged tower or artificial mountain, that each year the Sumerians celebrated their most sacred ritual: at the new year a young priest and a young priestess were led to the ziggurat where in the presence of an officiating priest they consummated the symbolical union which according to Sumerian religion assured the success of the new season's crops. This done, they were killed and buried.

Contemporary with the great temples of Uruk IV we find the earliest evidence of writing. This writing was on clay tablets. There are 500 to 600 clay tablets or fragments of such tablets from Uruk IV, III and II, and this is the largest and earliest stratified collection of writing known to us. At first the signs were of objects, animate and inanimate, which were, we assume, important in the lives of the Sumerians—sheep, cows, cereals, temples, milk-pails, agricultural implements. They are mainly pictograms but there are exceptions, and in some instances the significance of the signs is still unknown. The writing of the Sumerians, their cuneiform or wedge-shaped writing, was done with a reed. The development of a syllabic script was the achievement of the Babylonians, and . . . a shrewd scholar like Oppert was certain that Babylonian writing could not have been devised by a Semitic-speaking people but had been borrowed from earlier non-Semitic speakers—the Sumerians.

The earliest written documents of the Sumerians are not literature: they are not sagas, or legends of creation. They are domestic or commercial documents such as lists of deliveries of bread and beer to various people, ration lists, and lists of items delivered to temple and other officials. The first written documents of about 3500 B.C. are memos and receipts for cattle, milk, corn, sheep.

The Sumerians made many more inventions than we have space to enumerate, but there is one aspect of their inventive genius that must be mentioned briefly, namely their mathematics. They had a system of calendars and a well-thought-out system of mathematics, and had made many and accurate astronomical observations. The debt of Western Civilization to the Sumerians is large, and in our list we should not omit positional numeration and the sexagesimal system by which we still divide our clocks and the circle. And, curiously enough, there are even a few Sumerian words that we still use in English—cane, alcohol, dragoman, gypsum, myrrh, saffron and naphtha.

All these things and much besides certainly add up to a civilization, and, what is more, to the first civilization. So many things started among the cities of southern Mesopotamia that it is no surprise to find Kramer saying that Sumer had almost too many firsts. Certainly the vital contribution made by the Sumerians to the development of civilized life must be considered one of the greatest early achievements of man. We have some idea of what the Sumerians looked like and of their ordinary life. They were short in stature and had large curved noses. In their statues they represent themselves as bullet-headed people with big dark heads, long beards, but no moustaches. They dressed themselves in sheepskins or garments of woven wool, and wore skirts with flounces. At their banquets they sat in groups and drank a sort of beer: a jar of this beer stood on the floor between them and they drank it through long metal tubes. They made music on harps of various kinds and shapes. For their amusements they wrestled and boxed, they hunted, and they raced in light two-wheeled carts or chariots to which four onagers, or wild asses, were yoked.

Who were the Sumerians and where did they come from? There has been, not unnaturally, a very great deal of discussion of this problem, and it is of course not merely the problem of where did the Sumerians come from, but the problem of whence came the people who created man's first civilization. I quote . . . from *Genesis*, xi: 'And it came to pass, as they journeyed from the east, that they found a plain in the land of Shinar, and they dwelt there.' Berosus, writing in the fourth/third century B.C., described a race of monsters, half-men and half-fish which, led by one Oannes, came out of the Persian Gulf, and, settling in the coast towns of Sumer, introduced the arts of writing, of agriculture and of working in metal. 'All the things that make for the amelioration of life were bequeathed to men by Oannes, and since that time no further inventions have been made.'

We should at once remember three things in discussing this problem of Sumerian origins: first, that the earliest building style of the Sumerians was based on a tradition of working in timber; secondly, that the Sumerian gods are always represented as standing on mountains— the ziggurat is an artificial mountain. But in the third place we must bear in mind that archaeology can now tell us that the earliest settlements in southern Mesopotamia do not, probably, go further back than 5000 B.C. at the most and that the first agriculturists and the first village life was earlier than this in areas outside the land of the twin rivers, for example in the north of Mesopotamia, in Iran, in Jordan and in Turkey.

It was groups of these earlier and earliest agriculturists who settled in the flood plain of the Tigris-Euphrates, and, to use Robert Braidwood's evocative phrase, 'fingered their way' down the rivers to the Persian Gulf. I think that no one would now challenge this very general statement, namely that the 'Ubaid people came into southern Mesopotamia from outside, although they would disagree about which area these people came from, and they might want to argue for fresh outside influences between the first villages and Uruk IV. Naturally, it is not possible to be dogmatic in this matter and say that the people who were in southern Mesopotamia before 3500 B.C. were definitely Sumerians. We cannot label people with a historical name before that name occurs in writing. But let me put this another way: the Sumerians are the people who lived in southern Mesopotamia probably from 5000 B.C. onwards. When the light of history shines on them, that is to say the light of written history provided by the records in cuneiform writing which they had themselves invented, they were calling themselves Sumerians.

Let us go back again to *Genesis*, and this time to the Creation story as told in *Genesis*, i:

In the beginning God created the heaven and the earth. And the earth was without form, and void; and darkness was upon the face of the deep. And the Spirit of God moved upon the face of the waters. And God said, Let there be light: and there was light . . . And God said, Let there be a firmament in the midst of the waters, and let it divide the waters from the waters. And God made the firmament, and divided the waters which were under the firmament from the waters which were above the firmament: and it was so . . . And God said, Let the waters under the heaven be gathered together unto one place, and let the dry land appear: and it was so. And God called the dry land Earth; and the gathering together of the waters called he Seas . . . And God said, Let the earth bring forth grass, the herb yielding seed, and the fruit tree yielding fruit after his kind, . . .

We are here concerned with the affairs of this third day—admittedly a notional day, a stage in the evolution of man and the world, if you like to put it that way. For many centuries, of course, theologians and others thought that this was a correct account of prehistoric origins, in that it had been inspired by a supernatural being and had supernatural authority. I do not think that at the present day any but the most rabid fundamentalists still hold this untenable view. From 1876 onwards Babylonian accounts of the Creation have been published which reveal the origin of the *Genesis* account. The longest of these is known as *Enuma Elish* from its two first words which mean 'when on high', and was written in the early part of the second millennium B.C. It survives almost complete on seven cuneiform tablets. There is another account written both in Babylonian and Sumerian on a tablet discovered at Sippar dating from the sixth century B.C. I quote a few sentences from it:

All lands were sea
Then there was a movement on the midst of the sea;
At that time Eridu was made. . . .
Marduk laid a reed on the face of the waters,
He formed dust and poured it out beside the reed
That he might cause the gods to dwell in the dwelling of their
  hearts' desire
He formed mankind
With him the goddess Aruru created the seed of mankind.
The beasts of the field and living things in the field he formed
The Tigris and Euphrates he created and established them in
  their place:
Their name he proclaimed in goodly manner
The grass, the rush of the marsh, the reed and the forest he
  created,
The lands, the marshes and the swamps;
The wild cow and her young, the lamb of the fold,
Orchards and forests;
The he-goat and the mountain-goat . . .
The Lord Marduk built a dam beside the sea . . .
Reeds he formed, trees he created;
Bricks he laid, buildings he erected;
Houses he made, cities he built . . .
Erech he made . . .

There is only one comment I wish to add here to this fascinating Mesopotamian epic of creation which is the source of the *Genesis* creation legend, and that was a remark of Gordon Childe's. It was no divine being, he said, who brought dry land out of the waters, established the Tigris and Euphrates in their places, created fields and orchards and forests: it was the hard-working proto-Sumerians.

We must, then, substitute the proto-Sumerians for Yahweh or Marduk; and we know what they did and when they did it, namely in southern Mesopotamia they created for the first time in human history a civilization where before there had only been villages. They created an urban literate society; they created the first civilization. We know the answers to the questions what and when and where; but we also want to know how and why civilization was created in Mesopotamia.

You will not be surprised to be told that a great number of theories have been put forward to explain the how and the why of Sumerian civilization. The first group of theories may be called the geographical explanations, and among these we may list the so-called propinquity theory of Brooks. This theory argued that everything was so lovely in the garden—to put it crudely, and, incidentally, I think Brooks unconsciously meant the Garden of Eden—that it was all bound to happen. Here in Mesopotamia were wild wheat and barley, wild sheep and goats and a fertile river delta; given all these things together, and civilization was inevitable. But Brooks was conflating thousands of years of human history: he was conflating the origins of agriculture in the Near East as a whole with the origins of civilization in Sumer. The same conflation has been made by those such as Arnold Toynbee, who like to think of a similar simple explanation accounting for the origins of Egyptian and Mesopotamian civilization, viewed in terms of the end of the Ice Age.

The simplest account of the geographical origins of civilization in the ancient Near East has often been set out: as the ice sheets retreated across Europe and the rain belt that was over the Sahara moved north, the hunters and food-gatherers who had been happy to live in the Saharan grasslands were forced to migrate, south into Africa, north following the retreating ice to Europe; or to settle in the river valleys of the Nile and the Tigris-Euphrates, turn into agriculturists, and so, encouraged by the fertility of these river valleys, to prosper and lay the basis of civilization. Put in this bald fashion the story sounds improbable and grossly over-simplified; and in any case, it was not, as we now know, in the river valleys of Egypt and Mesopotamia that incipient agriculture and the beginnings of village life took place.

But, even so, we shall have to agree that the river valleys and the floods had something to do with the development of higher barbarian culture into what we term civilization. It cannot be an accident that the four ancient civilizations of the Old World are based on the Tigris-Euphrates, the Nile, the Indus and the Yellow River. To say this is not to hint at any form of geographical determinism, but to say that the geographical environment of these river valleys and alluvial plains was an important factor in the genesis of the civilizations: it provided possibilities. Echoing Herodotus's famous sentence that 'Egypt is the gift of the Nile', George Roux declares that 'in many respects it can also be said of Mesopotamia that it is a gift of the twin river.'

The scholar who has written most in English about the particular problem of the origins of civilization and archaeology is Vere Gordon Childe, and he was certainly one of the most formative and important figures in the historical development of thought about archaeological facts and the light they throw on the beginnings of civilized societies. In 1936 Childe wrote a small book entitled *Man Makes Himself,* and he followed this up six years later with *What Happened in History,* a title which was deliberately provoking to the ordinary historian with a restricted perspective of the past because it ends with Byzantium—indeed the last chapter is called 'The Decline and Fall of the Ancient World.'

Childe argued that there had been three great revolutions in human history, the first two of these he called the Neolithic and Urban Revolutions, while the third was the Industrial Revolution. In many ways what he was propounding in the thirties and early forties of this century is still true, but we would now want to modify it in several ways, largely owing to the increase of our archaeological knowledge since his death: and it is a quarter of a century since Childe wrote *What Happened in History.* The first modification is that these processes were not revolutionary: revolution suggests something that happened quickly and purposefully. The changes from food-gathering to food-producing and from self-sufficient village life to literate towns were evolutionary rather than revolutionary changes: they took long periods of time and they were not so much purposeful as the practical application of discoveries and inventions that were often made accidentally. To say this, of course, is in no way to belittle the importance of these changes. Secondly, I do not like the use of the words Neolithic and Urban to describe these great changes. The term Neolithic was invented by Sir John Lubbock for what was conceived, a hundred years ago, as the second half of the Stone Age, and it was still being defined in the archaeological textbooks of the first quarter of this century as a stage of human culture distinguished by polished stone axes, pottery, domesticated animals and the cultivation of grain—this was the quadrivium of the Neolithic. We now know so much more about the period 10,000 to 4000 B.C. in the Near East and from 5000 to 1000 B.C. in America, and we have found societies evolving from food-gathering and hunter-fisher groups into societies with only one, or two, or three, of these four diagnostic features. The result of this, incidentally, has been the creation of strange and unnecessary phrases like 'Pre-Pottery Neolithic' and 'Aceramic Neolithic.' The truth is that the word Neolithic can no longer be defined in a sensible or meaningful way.

The trouble with the word Urban, and with referring as Childe did to the Urban Revolution, is that this word is to most people overlaid with ideas of conurbations, skyscrapers, factories, underground railways and double-decker buses, with commuters and big business. I would prefer to use the English version of the Greek word *synoecismus* which was used by Thucydides and meant the union of several towns and villages under one capital city. Garner in 1902 spoke of the time 'when the town was first formed by the synoecism of the neighbouring villages.'

My third objection to Childe's general thesis lies in the model of prehistory which was informing his thought and writing. It was a model which, while eschewing the extravagant hyper-diffusionism of the Egyptocentrics like Elliot, Smith and Perry, and Sumerocentrics like Raglan, nevertheless had at the back of it the idea that there was only one Neolithic Revolution and only one Urban Revolution and that both of them took place in the most ancient Near East. . . .

In addition to his general thesis, Childe gave his specific reasons why the urban civilization of Sumer came into existence, and these we can consider quite apart from any general idea of the number of times that urbanization or the *synoecismus*-process took place in human history. Childe did not propound a geographical determinism, but a materialist determinism. He was quite sure that the origin of Sumerian civilization was due to a series of technological discoveries. He wrote: 'Metallurgy, the wheel, the ox-cart, the pack-ass, and the sailing ship provided the foundations for a new organization. Without it the new materials would remain luxuries, the new crafts would not function, the new devices would be just conveniences.' And yet he was uncertain about allowing the whole process of the birth of the first civilization to be explained by a catalogue of technological inventions and discoveries, and conceded that 'the alluvial valleys of the great rivers offered a more exacting environment.'

It seems to me that the alluvial plain of the Tigris and Euphrates offered an exciting as well as an exacting environment. The groups of people who fingered their way down from the higher lands where incipient agriculture had developed and the first villages came into existence found themselves in a very rich micro-environment and one that was liable to floods and which needed irrigation by canals, and cooperative

enterprises. Out of this fertility and this cooperation the villages prospered and grew, and the miracle of the first civilization happened: the
Sumerian synoecism took place. But it was not the environment that
caused this first civilization in human history to happen; it was the Sumerians themselves. In 1932 Lucien Febvre published his *Geographical
Introduction to History,* and in that very important book he criticizes
with wit and good humour the excesses of the geographical determi-
nists. What the physical environment provides, he argued, was possibilities, and it is in terms of this possibilism that we should envisage
the emergence of the Sumerian civilization. The Sumerians, or, if you
like, the proto-Sumerians, settled in the environment provided by the
Tigris-Euphrates deltaic plain and took advantage of the possibilities of
that environment to grow and prosper. But we must not delude ourselves into thinking that all one has to do is to produce possibilities and
they will automatically be accepted and used. . . . There were many
areas of possibilities existing in the world that did not in fact produce
civilizations.

The genius of the people must be seen against the background of the
possibilities of their geographical environment. It was, as Childe said,
not God but the hard-working Sumerians who created the land between
the two rivers. It was the genius of the Sumerians that invented the
wheel, glass, bronze, writing, the calendar and the city. It may have
been something special in their make-up, and I cannot do better than
end . . . with a sentence from Kramer: 'The psychological factor responsible to no little extent for both the material and cultural achievements
of the Sumerians was an all-pervading and deeply ingrained drive for
pre-eminence and prestige, for victory and success.'

Suggestions for Further Reading

BRAIDWOOD, ROBERT, *The Near East and the Foundations for Civilization.*
    Eugene, Ore.: Oregon State System of Higher Education, 1952.
CERAM, C. W., *Gods, Graves, and Scholars,* translated by E. B. Garside.
    New York: Alfred A. Knopf, 1951.
CHILDE, V. GORDON, *The Prehistory of European Civilization.* Harmonds-
    worth, Middlesex: Penguin Books, Ltd., 1958.
CHILDE, V. GORDON, *What Happened in History.* Harmondsworth,
    Middlesex: Penguin Books, Ltd., 1942.

FRANKFORT, HENRI, et al., *Before Philosophy*. Harmondsworth, Middle-
    sex: Penguin Books, Ltd., 1949.
HAWKES, JACQUETTA, ed., *The World of the Past*, 2 vols. New York:
    Alfred A. Knopf, 1963.
PIGGOTT, STUART, *Ancient Europe from the Beginnings of Agriculture to
    Classical Antiquity*. Edinburgh: University Press, 1965.
REDFIELD, ROBERT, *The Primitive World and Its Transformations*. Ithaca,
    N.Y.: Cornell University Press, 1953.

FINLEY HOOPER

Minoan and Mycenaean Civilization

◆§◈◈ In the second millennium B.C. Near Eastern civilization was diffused into Greece from the flourishing society
of Minoan Crete. Cretan society was a direct perpetuation
of the Near Eastern pattern; its only possible difference was
that its elite was even narrower and aristocratic control over
the resources of the society even tighter and more authoritarian. The civilization that appeared in mainland Greece
—between 1400 and 1000 B.C.—derived a good deal of its
culture, its values, its literature, and its art from Minoan
civilization.

The first Hellenic civilization, which we now know as
Mycenaean, arose from the confluence on the Greek mainland of Near Eastern civilization imported by itinerant
Cretans and a new warrior people who came down from the
north in successive waves and established themselves in
Greece. The great monuments to this Mycenaean Greek
civilization are the Homeric poems, which may have been
written as late as 800 B.C. but reflect substantially the stage
of development that we find in the late second millennium
B.C. The higher culture of the Mycenaean Greek civilization
was borrowed from the Near East through Crete, but the
social structure established in this first period of Greek history differed markedly from that of the ancient Near East
and of Crete; it owed a great deal to the warrior-tribal
society of the Greek invaders from the north.

FROM Finley Hooper, *Greek Realities* (New York:
Charles Scribner's Sons, 1967), pp. 23–55, 60–62.

Mycenaean Greece, as described in the *Iliad* and the *Odyssey*, was a society in its Heroic Age—a stage that appears again among the Germanic peoples who invaded Europe in the fifth and sixth centuries A.D. This is a primitive society in which the basic social units—the tribe, the family, and the king—have been somewhat weakened during a period of migration and conquest, and a great military chieftain or hero has become the center of the social structure. There is a fairly large mass of free men, and most people are roughly social equals. There are some slaves, but the free men, who engage in war, agriculture, and industrial pursuits, characterize the society. It is not a wealthy society; there is a small surplus, but the houses of even the wealthiest men are quite modest. The society can only gain wealth through foreign conquest. Such an attack upon a wealthy city is described in the *Iliad* in which an expedition of Greek warrior-chiefs attack and sack Troy, a rich city on the west coast of Asia Minor.

In the society described in the *Iliad* there were a few great warriors who had won more booty than anyone else. They had more land and larger houses than the other warriors, but they were very different from the self-perpetuating, authoritarian, narrow, and exclusive aristocracy of the ancient Near East. The Greek warrior aristocracy attained its position largely through individual prowess; it was consequently fluid in membership, since any strong man who appeared among the ranks of ordinary free men could very rapidly become a military hero. Ruling or dominant families perpetuated themselves, but because no family had enormous wealth or extensive lands and because the basis of leadership was skill in war, the leading families were likely to shift from generation to generation. One might say, therefore, that the basis for social leadership was an extremely pragmatic one depending on military skill or leadership in battle and thus quite unlike the self-perpetuating elitism of the Near East.

One of the great warriors, through long success in military leadership, could establish himself as king. He then had a bigger house, and his family was likely to continue ruling, but incompetent descendants were not tolerated as

kings. Society had to live; the social group had to protect
its members—ordinary free men—and preserve its ability
to gain wealth through booty and conquest. If the king
was not of minimal competence, then even though his
father had been a great warrior, he was not king for very
long. The people found a new king and a new leader.

Aside from its warrior character, the social structure and
economic organization of Mycenaean Greece were conditioned by its geographical environment. Greece is not a
fertile land; it is a semi-arid country in which a great deal
of land is taken up by limestone hills. These were heavily
forested in ancient times, but were unsuitable for anything
but wood lots. There are also very high hills, or mountains, which break up the country into small valleys. A factor in the large-scale social organization of the Near East
was its long river valleys that provided large geographical
units. These did not exist in Greece, and it was inevitable
therefore that the political units would be small. Greek
kingdoms extended over a valley, or a couple of valleys if
the hills between were not too formidable. There was a
maze of small kingdoms, small chieftaincies, and at best the
loose domination of a single great warrior over several
valleys—but his real control was not very extensive. Under
these conditions, the aristocrats were bound to be men of
limited wealth, whose domains and areas of influence were
confined to relatively small areas. Greece was inescapably
very different from the large centralized states of the ancient Near East, where the aristocrats controlled river valleys that extended five hundred or a thousand miles and
took in vast numbers of people.

Sometime after 1000 B.C., Mycenaean civilization declined; its culture, wealth, and artistic style were all impoverished. Historians are not exactly sure why this happened. The incursions of new waves of invaders from the
north—the Dorian Greeks—undoubtedly were an important factor, but probably not the only cause. Greece entered
a so-called "Dark Ages," "dark" because they seem rather
barbarian and savage, but also because we do not know
very much about what happened. After about 600 B.C.,
Greece entered a third and distinct phase of history. The

first was the Mycenaean, which we have described; the second was the "Dark Ages," of which we know very little. The third phase was immensely important; it is the era that historians and humanists generally envision when they think of Greek history—namely, the era of the classical poets, philosophers, and the city-state [see the M. I. Finley selection in this volume].

The history of Minoan and Mycenaean cultures has only become known during the past sixty years as a vast amount of archaeological evidence has been discovered and matched with the insights provided by the Homeric literature. Much of the writing on Mycenaean civilization is still highly technical and very difficult for the layman and student. The following study by the American scholar Finley Hooper, while based upon an authoritative knowledge of recent archaeological work, is yet a remarkably clear analysis of what is known about the nature, origins, and impact of Mycenaean civilization. Hooper's book, *Greek Realities*, from which this selection is taken, is generally a splendid synthesis of Greek history.

CRETAN PROSPERITY

During the Bronze Age, the island of Crete achieved a bountiful economic and artistic life earlier than the other parts of the Aegean world. The exchange of goods with Egypt began sooner in Crete and this communication with an established center of civilization has always supplied a ready explanation for an early blossoming. The Cretans may also have learned about the usefulness of metals before their neighbors. Certainly they had advanced techniques of seamanship. Whatever the advantages of these islanders, they made the most of them. The distribution of their pottery and the widespread influence of Minoan [after Crete's fabulous, and maybe fabled, King Minos] motifs have shown how extensively they traveled in all parts of the surrounding waters.

The wealth and power accruing to Crete from its own resources and from overseas ventures have prompted the tag "little England" as a likely analogy. In a romantic sense this may have been true but, to be realistic, how far can commerce develop without a coinage? Cretan prosperity must have depended on the successful barter of items then current in international trade. Presumably their ships carried special items like ivory and obsidian as well as cargoes of skins, olive oil, wine and timber. Archaeologists have found ingots of copper stored on the island. In the absence of any evidence to the contrary, it has been assumed that these slabs of metal weighing sixty pounds or more were used for balance of trade payments. At least the guess seems logical.

Ingots of this type are on display in the Archaeological Museum of Heraclion, the modern city near the ancient site of Knossos. This spacious museum houses the lion's share of the materials which have been recovered in Crete. Currency ingots are also exhibited at Bodrum, the Turkish town situated where ancient Halicarnassus once stood. The small, but up-to-date museum at this place has a special interest because it displays some of the finds from the recent underwater archaeological expeditions conducted off the coast of Turkey. Apparently not all of the payments reached their destination.

The memory of Cretan power in the eastern Mediterranean has been preserved in the story of the Athenian hero Theseus defeating the Minotaur (half man, half bull). According to the legend, the Athenians had been required each year to send a payment of seven youths and seven maidens to Crete. Theseus with the help of Minos' daughter Ariadne finally ended this disgraceful subservience. Were there any historical clues hidden amid the romance of this myth? It has been suggested that Theseus was actually seeking to end the impressment of Athenian youths into the Cretan navy. If so, the myth bore witness to a naval power which at one time or another dominated the Aegean Sea. Archaeologists have been more exact. Their evidence shows that Crete was enjoying her greatest days during the period designated as Middle Minoan III and Late Minoan I—roughly the three hundred years between 1750 and 1450 [B.C.].

The excavations of Cretan palaces have supplied the best evidence of the life and times of this period. Attention usually centers on the principal city Knossos and the second city Phaistos, but there have also been informative finds in less pretentious palaces such as the one at Mallia. At these sites the problem has not been merely to recover a single structure which had been built and later buried; archaeologists have found remains of buildings reconstructed at various times along with the evidence of changes made in between.

Earthquakes during the Bronze Age were hard on Cretan architecture. They still are. In examining the effects of an earthquake on a Minoan palace in the sixteenth century B.C. or on a house shattered as recently as A.D. 1935, the cracks in partly demolished walls are seen to run the same way, diagonally upward toward the south.

Atop the primary Neolithic material at Knossos was evidence of a palace which had been damaged by an earthquake about 1700 B.C. Studies showed that this building and others at Phaistos and Mallia were later repaired and enlarged and then toppled by another catastrophe in the sixteenth century. At Knossos, there followed a much grander palace which extended over and included the previously used space. The rapidity with which this residence was rebuilt attests to the continuing prosperity of the Cretans at the time.

The time of building of this last great palace of the Cretan civilization has served archaeologists as a dividing point between the Middle Minoan III period and Late Minoan I. But the construction was not so much a peak as it was a significant point in the plateau from 1750 to 1450. Before this prosperous period there was a slow development; not long afterwards, a decline.

Although the king at Knossos needed and could afford a larger establishment than was necessary at Phaistos, the palaces at these major centers were much alike. Both were multi-level complexes with rooms of all sizes, including an unusual variety of large and small halls for state meetings and receptions. At Knossos, in the rebuilding after 1700, the grand staircase which so often appears in photographs of the palace was added. It began at the Hall of Colonnades and led up to the second and third floors, where most of the space was given over to living quarters with some rooms apparently grouped together as apartments. Among the other facilities of the palace were a variety of "service" rooms including workshops where furniture might be made or repaired. Storerooms were everywhere and the containers once used for storing wine and grain are still to be seen.

For all its surprising complexity, the palace at Knossos was still not in a class with Louis XIV's Versailles although the idea was similar. The king kept an eye on his relatives and nobles by having them live on the premises. Because of the many internal rooms it was necessary to build light wells here and there, just as in modern apartment structures. But the real surprise of the living quarters were the bathrooms served by drains and an extensive sewerage system. A small room in the palace at Knossos, which has been dubbed the Queen's Lavatory, was equipped with a flush toilet, an extraordinarily refined accommodation for so early a date. The use of metals had indeed revolutionized society. In the earlier Neolithic period there were of course houses, at least for tribal leaders, but many families were still living in caves. Zeus, so says the myth, was born in one.

Gaily colored plants and animals were the chief subjects in the imaginative frescoes which decorated the rooms and hallways at Knossos. The paintings now seen *in situ* at the palace are copies. The fragments of the originals which have survived are exhibited in splendid fashion in Room K, the Hall of the Minoan Frescoes, in the Archaeological Museum of Heraclion. Among them are the remarkable *La Parisienne* and the *Cup-bearer* which bring to mind Picasso and an ancient Egyptian stylist both at once.

The Cretan artists who hurriedly but skillfully dashed paint on the wet plaster at Knossos remain nameless, even though their naturalism and *joie de vivre* delight us so today. Their interest in nature for its own sake was strikingly secular. Missing were the usual foreboding solemnities so typical of other early societies.

The popularity of exported Minoan pottery is understandable in view of its attractiveness. Surviving examples exhibit flowers in pastel shades of pink and blue and orange. There was also a willingness to borrow ideas from abroad, as seen in the frequent ingenuous displays of the papyrus plant indigenous to Egypt. This was part of a continuing search for novelty evident in fresh designs combining rocks, seaweed and fish. Lively spirals were everywhere a useful decoration in the ancient world, and the Cretan artists used them too, but they also delighted to think of variations. Why not, for example, substitute the curling tentacles of octopuses?

Cretan artists showed an extraordinary boldness in the use of colors. In their frescoes, if they wanted to paint a monkey blue they did, and so added brightness of accent to match the agility of the animals which enlivened the wall of some dimly lit room.

The occasional frescoes which show dancers, soldiers or athletes are among the best-known works by these Cretan painters. Especially famous is a bull-leaping scene in which trim young men and girls are engaged in gymnastic exercises over the backs of bulls. This so-called "Toreador" fresco and the frequent scenes of boxers show the Cretans to have been forerunners of the Greeks in their stress on athletics.

The colorful art and its display of a lively sociability between men and women in Crete gives an impression of modernity. In religion, although the dominance of the female had not changed since the Neolithic period, the Cretan conception of their chief deity had been updated. At the height of the Bronze Age she was still a nature goddess, but her appearance had been radically altered. In contrast with the earlier fetish-like appearance, she had become a graceful figure dressed in the fashion of the day. The extant statuettes from the Middle Minoan period display full skirts touching the ground. The short-sleeved blouses are tightly bodiced at the waist, but open at the front with the breasts entirely exposed. The costume was typical of the times and only the symbols of divinity marked the goddess. She was frequently adorned with snakes. One might be placed around her neck and then entwined around her arms. In another example she is shown with arms outstretched holding a snake in each hand.

The snake was a familiar symbol in ancient times and there could scarcely have been a more ambivalent one. The Cretans, however, seem to have regarded serpents more with reverence than with fear. On the household level, the snake was popularly considered a "good luck" charm. As an attribute of the goddess the snake appeared as a symbol of her protective care for the community. The deity also had her special bird and was frequently shown with a dove perched on her head.

If the stream of Cretan religious life ran back in time to the East, in the future it was to extend its influence northward to the mainland. The Athenians as late as the seventh century B.C. sent to Crete for a purifier when their city became "polluted" from blood shed on holy ground. A plausible conclusion would be that the arts of divination had spread from Crete northward and that in time of serious trouble the mainlanders sought an expert at the source.

No temples were built during the Bronze Age as in later classical times. State rites were conducted in the palace. Archaeologists have designated certain rooms as shrines wherein Cretan kings, like the rulers in earlier Near Eastern kingdoms, served as chief priests and conducted rites for the welfare of all. On the walls at Knossos were prominent drawings of the double axe sacred to the chief goddess. Interestingly enough, the Greeks who borrowed the term *labrys* for double axe from the Lydians later referred to the palace in their myths as the labyrinth.

Ordinary men worshipped at small household altars or perhaps more frequently out-of-doors. In Crete, the adoration of pillars and the worship of trees and streams foreshadowed a day when the olive tree became sacred to Athena and it was said that a brook at Delphi carried the voice of Apollo.

At Knossos, a simple, straight-back, armless stone throne identifies the Throne Room. The stone benches around the wall suggest the sitting of a council or perhaps a court. A sunken area, called a lustral basin, partially partitioned off at one side, was undoubtedly used for ritual bathing. In view of the civil and religious powers held by the king, there can be little argument against the notion that proceedings of an official character began with sacred ceremonials.

When visiting this low-pitched and small, somewhat mysterious chamber, a visitor's attention is easily diverted from the question of its possible uses by the colorful murals so generously added by modern restorers. The extant portions of the original frescoes served to inspire the present decoration of the room. Evans found the remains of a couchant wingless griffin on either side of a doorway in the west wall. During the subsequent restoration work, a similar pattern of matching griffins (with considerable elaboration) was painted on the wall behind the throne. The bright reds, yellows and blues in these paintings give the room a rather startling appearance but, as previously noted, there is ample evidence at Knossos and elsewhere to show that the Cretans overcame drabness in their palaces with brilliantly painted columns and walls. The degree of satisfaction which the modern work affords varies with the individual beholder. The tourist enjoys the spirit of the restoration. It means there is something to see. The specialist focuses a critical eye on the figures themselves. For instance, it has been suggested that bulls, symbolic of the king as the hero-consort of the Cretan goddess, might have been the original guardians of the throne. However, a crucial fragment from this wall supports the decision by Evans to place these griffins where they are. Does this mean that the throne actually belonged to a Priestess of the Mother Goddess and not to the king? Interested scholars continue to exchange opinions about such questions.

Either griffins or bulls in the Throne Room at Knossos add another link to the eastern Mediterranean where such designs were frequently represented in paint and stone. Nowhere, however, could they have guarded a throne so self-confidently secure as the one in Crete. The palace was not fortified, nor were there walls around the houses and shops grouped nearby. The absence of a citadel may be taken to mean that the rulers of this wealthy capital were sufficiently concerned about the welfare of all the Cretans so as to insure a tranquil loyalty. Communications over the connecting roads of the island must have been good and the allegiance of the ruler at Phaistos seems to have been assumed without force. Whether a king in his own right or a loyal baron, he would appear not to have felt abused. In brief, the king at Knossos guaranteed prosperity to the island and furnished a navy to guard its shores. These were the weapons of internal peace.

STRANGE APPEARING TABLETS

. . . Sir Arthur Evans' original purpose in going to Crete was to look for evidence of prehistoric writing. He did not have far to search. Native women on the island were using as charms small seal-stones which had been found in the countryside, relics of the distant past. The signs on these stones were hieroglyphs—pictures used as words for the objects represented. In Egypt and elsewhere in the Near East, writing had begun in the same simple way.

In March, 1900, within a week after Evans began his excavations at Knossos, he discovered clay tablets bearing a more complex system of writing. The find was not unexpected. The rudimentary markings of the seal-stones were obviously not equal to the task of keeping records during the commercially advanced Bronze Age.

Storerooms in the palace at Knossos suggest that inventories had been kept—on *papyri* (paper) and on clay tablets. *Papyri*, however, have only rarely been preserved away from the dry and saving sands of Egypt. The records Evans found were written on clay and at that only kept by chance. Customarily, tablets were not baked; they were only dried, since the same clay was reused again and again. In later days, when consuming fires destroyed the palace, some tablets were by ill-fortune baked and so by good fortune preserved. They are, however, fragile "documents" and now and then a few have been lost when left absentmindedly in the rain.

The tablets found at Knossos and later at other sites in Crete range in size from one inch to one foot in width. They exhibit a variety of strange appearing symbols written from left to right, with some pictographs and obvious ciphers (e.g., III = three) mixed in. We know now that the symbols represent a shift from pictures to syllables. It was a momentous step. Assume, for example, that the writer had already a picture of a "bee" and a picture of a "leaf." He could combine the two pictures (now using the symbols phonetically) and so write the word "belief" for which there was no picture. The alternative would have been to invent pictures for words like "belief" arbitrarily and thus to write as the Chinese still do with a vast number of pictographs. The syllabic system is easier. And the later alphabetic device of using a limited number of letters to form syllables is even simpler.

To the non-specialist the tablets recovered in Crete look much alike. Close examination by Evans and his staff, however, revealed that they were actually of two types and it was apparent that one script had been derived from the other. Since neither could be identified with any known system of writing, Evans, for convenience sake, called the earlier script Linear A and the later "derived script" Linear B. Linear A was found at various sites in Crete, but Linear B only at Knossos.

It was observed at the outset that the records written in these curious scripts were primarily inventories, probably accounts of royal wealth or payments due the palace. Obviously they were not literary pieces in which the scribes revealed either their own thoughts or those of the rulers whom they served. So, even if easily read, the tablets would not have provided an historical account to explain why Linear A was replaced at Knossos by Linear B.

Evans has been generously praised for recovering the evidence of three stages of writing in Crete: the early hieroglyphic type which yielded to Linear A about 1650 (although hieroglyphs continued to be used for sacred writings) and finally Linear B which came into use at Knossos about 1450. Unfortunately, for almost forty years this noted archaeologist's preoccupation with the architecture of the palace at Knossos and his unpraiseworthy reluctance to release the tablets to others hampered further investigation of the subject.

Nevertheless, since preliminary studies had shown that nearly half of the signs used in Linear B had been carried over from Linear A, it was assumed that both scripts were used for writing the same Minoan tongue (although what language the Minoans were speaking remained unknown). The fact that Linear B was found at Knossos and nowhere else in Crete was explained by the assumption that only in a busy capital would any variant be needed. This hypothesis held up until Professor Blegen discovered Linear B tablets at Pylos on the mainland in 1939. In 1952, Professor Alan B. Wace had similar good fortune at Mycenae. Tablets continue to be recovered. The most recent finds have been at Thebes [in Greece].

The discovery by Blegen offered a better explanation for the mystery of the two scripts at Knossos. It seemed apparent that since Linear B belonged to the mainlanders they must have captured Knossos about 1450. Yet the invaders had not brought this script with them; rather they had first found a need for writing after they reached Crete. At Knossos they became the new owners of abundant and various kinds of property, including storerooms of chariot chassis and separate stores of wheels. They needed written inventories of their own. Linear B was therefore an adaptation of Linear A to a new language altogether. The mainlanders carried this method of writing home with them, as a convenient device by which to record their mounting wealth. These later tablets are the ones now being recovered.

Ironically the new discovery created more darkness than light. If Linear B was not "Minoan" what was it? Schliemann [1822–1890, discoverer of Troy] had brought Homer's Achaeans into the light of day. Now these strange looking tablets made them a mystery people. Who in fact were the builders of Mycenae, Tiryns and Pylos?

It was not until 1952 that Linear B was deciphered. Michael Ventris, a young English architect, found these curious signs intriguing and unforgettable. This was fortunate for he kept working on the problem and finally made the tablets talk. More experienced scholars had busied themselves studying the tablets from the "outside" by looking for parallels elsewhere. The classical Cypriot script seemed particularly inviting. Ventris carefully considered the various possible affinities, but it was his decision to work from "inside" Linear B that lead to his eventual triumph.

Some of the symbols in Linear B looked alike, but about eighty-nine of them were sufficiently different to form a list. A publication of the Pylos tablets by Professor Emmett L. Bennett of the University of Wisconsin helped immeasurably with this count. Because the eighty-nine symbols were too few for a pictographic system of writing and too many for an alphabetic one, it was apparent that they were syllables. Ventris tried various approaches in his effort to learn how these syllables "behaved," and so to discover the pattern of the language which they represented. The usefulness of probability in breaking an enemy code was borrowed from cryptography. On a given page of English it is to be expected that words such as "and" or "the" will have a high rate of frequency. As it happened, Ventris discovered that in the Linear B script "and" was a syllable which occurred frequently at the end of one word as a connective with the next. Unfortunately the problem of decipherment involved many more difficulties than this simple illustration would indicate.

To determine what possible relationships the syllables held to one another, Ventris charted the history of each symbol (syllable). How many times did it appear at the beginning of a word, in the middle or at the end? Which symbols appeared together most often and what was their position when they did? He was aided in this direction by the work of the late Alice Kober, an American scholar who had concluded that the language of Linear B was inflected (i.e., word endings changed according to case, gender and number, as in Latin).

Ventris' "grids" on which he pictorially worked out the behavior of the symbols appear bewilderingly complex to the layman. Nor should we be surprised that much of this young Englishman's success has been attributed to his amazing powers of visual memory. In brief, the decipherment of Linear B was a game of many moves. Ventris had a good head for it. He eventually saw how the syllables were behaving. To his amazement he was not looking at a new pattern, but simply recognizing an old one. Linear B was an archaic form of Greek. Ventris had discovered that the Mycenaeans had borrowed Linear A which the Minoans used to write their language (whatever it may have been) and adapted it to suit the Greek tongue. Centuries later, the Greeks of Homer's day would represent their syllables with alphabetic letters rather than those odd signs, but they would be saying the same thing.

By a series of brilliant deductions a "dead" language had been brought to life in one of the major coups of modern scholarship. A triumph all the more astounding for having crowned so brief a career. In 1956 Michael Ventris was killed in an automobile accident at the age of thirty-four.

An account of the complexities involved in the decipherment of Linear B has been written by John Chadwick who was among the first to accept Ventris' hypothesis. He later became his collaborator and then in a sense his heir. His discussion of linguistic problems, while lucid, may have a limited appeal. On the other hand even a non-specialist can appreciate the difficulty of reading obscure signs in various hands. The scribes were not writing for later researchers but for each other. They found it easier to recognize a carelessly written symbol than a modern reader who must stop and ask himself if a peculiar looking sign is something new. Even mistakes may at times be helpful. Chadwick points out the usefulness of erasures. Here and there a symbol on a tablet had been partially rubbed out and a new one put in its place. Since men usually confuse signs or sounds which are much alike, these careless mistakes became valuable clues, contributions to modern scholarship from scribes dead for three thousand years.

The news that the Mycenaeans were Greeks was welcomed in the scholarly world which had long awaited a solution to this perplexing problem. Heinrich Schliemann would not have been so surprised. He knew the Mycenaeans spoke Greek. Homer said so.

Almost everybody now accepts the Ventris decipherment of Linear B. There are only variant expert opinions about Linear A. The use of syllables and ciphers is plain. The language which the Minoans may have been using is not. The best known of the proposals about Linear A is the suggestion of Semitic (Akkadian) affinities advanced in 1957 by Professor Cyrus Gordon of Brandeis University. Other scholars have found more comfort by working back from the Greek of Linear B with the expectation that the substitution of known values from the later script may provide valuable clues to the earlier one.

As Chadwick remarks, there is no evidence that Mycenaean scribes attempted complicated or even long sentences. As Evans had surmised, the deciphered Linear B tablets are primarily inventories and so provide no more of an explanation why the capital city of Crete was taken over by the Achaeans about 1450 [B.C.] than would the Linear A records.

Had success alone invited trouble? Perhaps Knossos became a decadent plum, ripe for picking by the more militant mainlanders. Nobody knows what happened. Nevertheless, according to the tradition which Evans established, the great days of the island were numbered. A scant fifty years later, about 1400, all of Crete was laid waste by some catastrophe. It has been postulated that the earlier Mycenaean attack had triggered a softening of Cretan defenses and morale. Then an invading coalition of old enemies successfully put this long-time sea power to rest. Other scholars have argued that a native rebellion accounted for the widespread destruction, and still others say the holocaust was ordered by the Mycenaean overlords grown impatient with the problems of the island. A more radical approach delays the end until 1200 and attributes it to the later Dorian invasions which also devastated the mainland.

Almost everybody seems to agree that the Greeks did invade Crete and rule at Knossos for a period of fifty or maybe two hundred and fifty years. Also, the greater number of Mycenaean wares than Cretan products found in Egypt for the period after about 1500 shows that the mainland had far outstripped Crete in exports. The historical embroidery which interested scholars have sewn around these two points has been torn with controversy. And it will continue to be. Recent geological studies have prompted the eminent Greek archaeologist Spyridon Marinatos to hypothesize that the great Minoan catastrophe actually occurred before 1450 B.C. and was caused by the effects of volcanic eruptions on the nearby island of Thera.

MYCENAEAN CIVILIZATION

The Greeks are so often remembered as hapless victims of the heavy-footed Romans that it seems strange to find them as seafaring invaders. They have been remembered best for their later cultural achievements and until the archaeological work of the past century there was little else to consider. The early history of the land was unknown. It is still by no means a complete and clear, or even continuous, story but a few points at least seem well established.

As in Crete, the Neolithic period on the mainland stretched back before 3000 B.C. Traces of the earliest settlements suggest (again as in Crete) that they were initiated by migrants from the East. During the shadowy period of the third millennium, 3000 to 2000 B.C., other peoples arrived, among them the carriers of copper and bronze. The arrival of these newcomers is also associated by archaeologists with the appearance of better-made pottery carrying novel designs. The earlier Neolithic arrivals and these later invaders spoke languages related to Minoan and were presumably part of the same migratory movements in which waves of settlers moved westward from Asia Minor and Syria.

It was also during the third millennium (about 2600 B.C.) that Greek-speaking tribes began to move down from the north into the Balkan peninsula. They did not, however, continue all the way south, but settled in the northern reaches of Macedonia and Epirus where they then remained for several centuries. Their language tied them to a family of peoples who during this same period were moving in different directions from a common, albeit vast, homeland. Presumably they all came from somewhere north of the Danube, between the Baltic and Black Seas. Today, the similarities of basic words in the Germanic, Italic, Greek and Sanskrit languages argue that in the remote past the ancestors of these peoples, now scattered from England to India, were once neighbors. They were the possessors of Indo-European tongues to be distinguished, for instance, from the Semitic group.

No one knows why these people began to move or took the various directions they did. It is certain, however, that it was a very long time before they became settled where we now know them to be. Significantly, it was perhaps a thousand years or more after Greek-speaking

tribes first arrived in the Balkans before their descendants fully possessed the southernmost region which became their historic homeland.
Far from bringing new skills with them, they had actually less advanced
techniques than those of the Neolithic folk settled in the northern regions where they first intruded. At the time the sounds of a different
language would have easily identified the newcomers. Modern excavators must spot their presence at various sites by the sudden appearance
of a new kind of dwelling, a rectangular building with a porch at the
front supported by two posts. Apparently the classical temples were
distantly descended from this rudimentary *megaron* structure.

The Greek-speaking tribes did not begin to move from the outlying
regions of northern Macedonia and Epirus into the southernmost part
of the Balkan peninsula until about 1900 B.C. Archaeological charts
show that after that date (and at least one expert thinks that it should
be set earlier at 2100), burials of taller "Nordic" skeletons began to
appear more to the south than they had previously. Other skeletal remains show that these northerners were bringing horses with them,
perhaps only as pack animals or for a Hun-style cavalry. The day of
charioteering as a part of warfare and games was a long way off. Yet
the future was foreshadowed in other ways. The votive deities found
among the remains of their settlements indicate a shift toward the masculine side of religion. Wherever these new people settled, phallic figures rivaled the established fertility goddesses. At a later day, to be sure,
the Father Zeus would reign on Olympus. Did classical myth sanctify
the succession by ascribing his birth to an older nature goddess of
Crete?

The historical distribution of place names in Greece supports the
archaeological thesis of a southerly migration. Among names older than
memory, those with pre-Greek endings dominate in the south where
they are expected. Town names with Greek endings are concentrated in
the north.

The arrival of the Greek-speaking tribes in central Greece and the
Peloponnesus was not a peaceful operation. At various sites a level of
burnt brick offers wordless testimony of a violent attack. The frequency
of this evidence in the years following 1900 shows the scope and se-
riousness of the new invasions. Yet the cultural evolution of Helladic
[Bronze Age Greek] civilization was not interrupted in the sense that
there was a Dark Age. On the contrary, the invaders whose descendants
became Homer's "fair-haired Achaeans" assimilated the advanced
agricultural skills and craftsmanship of the "pre-Greek" population.

Furthermore, fair-haired or not, these descendants would be a mixture of both Nordic and Mediterranean physical types although in the long run the short, dark characteristics of the south became predominant. In brief, the Mycenaeans were Greeks in the same way that the Angles and Saxons who conquered the Britons were Englishmen.

Again, as with the Angles and Saxons, the speech of the Greek-speaking invaders tended to absorb and drown out other sounds. Yet not altogether. In classical times the survival of isolated pockets of non-Greek languages, such as Pelasgian, offered the last echoes of the pre-Greek peoples who had once dominated the land.

During the long period in which the Greeks remained settled in the northern regions, Macedonia, Thessaly, and Epirus, they had developed different dialects. When members of each of these regions moved into Greece they stayed with their own. Those speaking the Ionic dialect eventually settled in Attica and were the forefathers of the Athenians. The Aeolic dialect prevailed in central and northeastern Greece while the Arcadian became predominant in the Peloponnesus.

Historians have borrowed the term Achaean from Homer and the term Mycenaean from archaeologists. Both names have been used more or less interchangeably to refer to all the Greeks of the Bronze Age. To be more exact, however, they pertain to the Arcadian and Aeolian Greeks rather than to the Ionians. The main centers of the Mycenaean civilization which flourished from about 1600 B.C. to about 1150 B.C. were in the Peloponnesus and central Greece. "Mycenaean" materials have been found in Ionian Attica and in outposts in the eastern Aegean, but they are secondary to the finds in the heartland which stretched from Pylos through the Argolid to Thebes. The *Iliad* offers corroborative evidence. The host assembled for the attack on Troy was gathered primarily from that heartland region. Moreover, Homer used the term Danaan as well as Achaean to refer to the Mycenaeans, and both names have been recognized as the sea-raiders who are mentioned in surviving inscriptions of the Hittites and Egyptians. Only the citadels built by the Arcadians and Aeolians show either the wealth or strength which could have won such international attention.

THE WAY THEY FIND THEM

It is not known exactly when Mycenae began its career as the major center of the earliest Greek civilization. Obviously its acropolis offered an excellent defensive position which enabled those who held it to command respect in the Argolid plain. Today, the visitor to this lofty citadel looks out across the countryside for miles around. It is apparent that no one could approach unnoticed.

The acropolis at Mycenae, like the more famous site at Athens, was occupied from Neolithic times onward. The first clear evidence of power and prosperity at this place has been found in twenty-four graves which have been dated to about 1700 B.C., or maybe somewhat later. Men who have possessed exalted power and wealth have frequently used a large share of both to provide themselves with impressive entombments. The pyramids of Egypt are the best example. Never for a moment have those Pharaonic monuments allowed the memory of their builders to lapse. The rulers of Mycenae were not so fortunate. Until Schliemann began their restoration to history they had slipped back into myth. In lieu of other evidence, the types of burials which these rulers provided for themselves have become important. Archaeologists, prosaically but honestly, label the Mycenaean kings the way they find them. The earliest, those found in the graves dated to about 1700, have been called the First Shaft Dynasty. The later burials which Schliemann found have been designated as those of the Second Shaft Dynasty. There followed under different arrangements a Tholos Tomb Dynasty.

Shaft graves were cut vertically into ground composed of more rock than earth. They were marked by sculptured *stelae*, corresponding to modern tombstones. In the earliest graves, the skeletons (some singly, but in one instance four together) belonged to descendants of tall people from the north, not the short Mediterranean men. Very likely they were the first Greek-speaking rulers of Mycenae. In any event they seem to have been too busy establishing their power locally to have had any "international" relations. The weaponry and jewelry in their tombs cannot easily be equated to Minoan objects of the same time. Nor at this early date need there have been any contact with Crete.

The shaft graves which Schliemann discovered offer a different story. They belonged to a line of rulers who reigned from about 1600 to 1500. In this later era, the golden articles deposited in the burials show Cretan influence in both technique and motif. Of special interest are the many pieces of jewelry shaped like octopuses.

How much of a spell Crete cast over the budding Mycenaean civilization has become a controversial question. At one time the arts of the mainland were considered to be little more than an offshoot of the more advanced Minoan culture. Because Evans had placed the evolution of the Cretan civilization well in advance of the Mycenaean achievement, that viewpoint seemed plausible. Furthermore, critics observed that the Mycenaean possessions appeared less tasteful than those of the Minoan kings. There seemed to be too much gold added, a gaudiness which was to be expected from late-comers.

In spite of these arguments, there has always been some speculation about the traditional chronology which Evans established. However, it has only come under heavy attack in recent years. The ever increasing fund of information about the Mycenaean civilization has encouraged certain observers like L. R. Palmer, Professor of Comparative Philology in Oxford University, to suggest revisions in chronology which would tend to downgrade Cretan precedence and by the same process give more credit to native initiative on the mainland.

The painters at Mycenae, Pylos and Tiryns served local patrons whose tastes and interest inspired a tradition different from that of Crete. Thus, scenes of war and hunting at Mycenae offer a contrast to the idyllic flora and fauna of Knossos. Nor should the emphasis on warfare be unexpected. The Mycenaeans were settled in independent kingdoms and apparently spent their time battling each other when not united against an outsider. Under these conditions their presumed lack of taste has been happily described as the warrior's love of splendor.

Even accepting the arguments for greater Mycenaean independence, a consensus remains that the Bronze Age reached a climax earlier in Crete than elsewhere in the Aegean world. The excellence of Mycenaean works in the sixteenth century might still, in part, have been attributable to Cretan craftsmen who journeyed northward. Without question Minoan motifs were borrowed by mainlanders to decorate their palace walls. In fact, by good fortune, it has been possible to restore the so-called "shield fresco" in the palace at Knossos because a smaller copy of the original has survived on the mainland in the palace of Tiryns.

In Late Minoan times realistic Mycenaean scenes of hunting and warfare appeared with increasing frequency in Crete. Obviously the borrowing went both ways. Therefore it might be concluded that in the beginning the tide flowed mostly from Crete northward and afterwards there was a mixture of Minoan and Mycenaean styles. It is a simple statement. Yet on the subject of artistic dependency there is always room for argument since most answers are probably as good as the question.

The perpetuation of ancestral custom has always been a means to stability and continuity. In the custom-conscious ancient world it was unlikely that the members of a royal family would depart from the ways of their forefathers, especially in the matter of burials. Accordingly the introduction of a new type of tomb at Mycenae about 1500 has been used by scholars to mark the beginning of a new dynasty. The shaft grave gave way to the more elaborate *tholos* tomb made by cutting a beehive-type chamber in the side of a hill. A passageway was cut leading to the portal where the rise of the hill was sufficient to allow for the height of the tomb. When this corridor was lined with large blocks of stone it offered a formal entrance way. The most famous of the beehive chambers measures over forty-six feet in diameter and reaches a height in the center of better than forty-three feet. It has been called the "Treasury of Atreus" because it was assumed by excavators that such an elaborate facility must have housed the wealth of the father of Agamemnon. Off the main chamber, a small, low-ceiling room seems to have been designed expressly for that purpose. However, this was not common and only one other tomb is known to have had one. What treasure the largest of the *tholos* tombs actually contained must remain unknown for they were conspicuous on the landscape and a monumental temptation to grave robbers. The size and finish of these tombs marked them as belonging to royalty. As in life, so in death their noble associates were nearby, resting in less elaborate rooms. These smaller entombments had unlined entrance ways and were in fact crude chambers cut out of the hillside with even the interior left unfinished. At Dendra, about seven miles southeast of Mycenae, a minor *tholos* tomb was discovered intact in 1926 and its gold and silver treasures, now in the National Museum in Athens, are a clue to the valuables which the widespread *tholoi* once contained.

During the time that the Tholos Tomb Dynasty ruled at Mycenae, Knossos was captured by the mainlanders. Included in the evidence of foreign domination at the Cretan capital is the introduction of beehive tombs. The eclipse of Cretan power was coincident with the rise of the ambitious mainland centers. Pylos, Tiryns, and especially Mycenae, saw their best days in the two centuries and a half between 1400 and 1150 B.C. At Mycenae two lions (to be exact, lionesses) carved on a triangular stone stood guard above the main entrance to the citadel. And they are still there, although now headless, to mark the "Lion Gate" through which rode the kings who lived in the palace and were buried in the great *tholos* tombs on the plain below. The palace itself was actually a group of buildings surrounding large and small courtyards. There were occasional ceremonial halls, shrines, bedrooms and bathrooms similar to those in the complex at Knossos, but on a much smaller scale.

The remains of other palaces and *tholos* tombs elsewhere in the Peloponnesus mark the location of rival dynasties. Everywhere there were riches. The golden cups discovered in a *tholos* tomb at little known Vaphio, near Sparta, are among the most publicized articles yet found in Greece. These matching cups, showing embossed scenes of a wild boar hunt, were perhaps the work of a craftsman who traveled from court to court, a busy restless Cellini of his time. Were the cups sent as a gift to a neighboring ruler? In Homer, the honor of receiving a precious artistic piece could be heightened by the announcement of the notables who had once possessed it.

A FAMILIAR PYRAMID OF CLASSES

The rulers of these Achaean kingdoms may have had wealth to rival that of the earlier kings at Knossos, but they do not seem to have known the same sense of security—except possibly at Pylos where neither Nestor nor his predecessors felt any need for walled fortifications. About 1350 B.C., a wall of huge stones to a width of twenty-three feet was built to guard the acropolis at Mycenae. At Tiryns, the walls of a later date were even more impressive. These stone fortresses may be taken as a fair measure of the anxiety which so often accompanies the accumulation of wealth. They also conjure up a thought of the Middle Ages. And with good reason for the earliest Greek society was similar in certain respects to that of Medieval Europe. Significantly, in each of these small Achaean kingdoms there was a familiar pyramid of classes. We have no eye-witness accounts, to be sure, but that is the picture supplied by archaeological finds, by the Linear B tablets and the writings of Homer.

Homer's epics were of course not contemporary writings, nor were they intended to describe or explain the Achaean world. Homer knew little enough about those times himself. In fact, he could not avoid some anachronisms. Here and there he mentions iron which had been introduced long before his own era, but was presumably missing in the Achaean Age. He also thought that cremation was as common a practice in Mycenaean times as in his own. The *tholos* tombs have yielded evidence of some cremations but they are exceptional. There are other difficulties—a sufficient number to allow some scholars to doubt that the Homeric epics retain a reliable memory of Mycenaean times. The Linear B records suggest a highly bureaucratical society akin to that of earlier

Near Eastern states and out of tenor with Homer's stories. Yet the view from a great distance cannot be expected to be the same as one close-up. Nor are the interests of a poet the same as those of a scribe. Broadly speaking, the tales which Homer retold centuries later did correctly reflect a society of rank and custom.

At the apex of the pyramid stood the king and his well-born friends. These aristocrats, born and raised to predatory habits, occupied themselves in accumulating wealth and defending what they owned. In the *Iliad,* they talked much of honor and were known by their armor and weapons. Achaean warriors customarily wore leather helmets with metal pieces attached, but Homer mentions a helmet decorated with boars' teeth and a colorful fresco dated to the period shows a man wearing one. Other Mycenaean paintings depict warriors with plated corselets and carrying shields shaped like figure "eights," large enough to cover them from head to toe. In contrast, on a vase from Mycenae there are shown fighters who have only small round shields for protection. These men carry the familiar bronze-tipped spears. Elsewhere warriors are seen armed with two-edged swords and short daggers similar to those which have been found in Mycenaean tombs. The Achaean warriors may not have been so attached to their weapons as was the medieval knight Roland, who named his sword Durendal, but they did live by them and they were buried with them.

The son of an aristocrat was trained in his father's image. He grew up familiar with palace life and skilled in handling a chariot, the class symbol of those who rode to the hunt and to war (by this time chariots were being used in actual combat). As usual, even those who possessed the most felt the urge for something extra. While the detachable wheels of most chariots were made of wood, some have been found made partly of bronze or rimmed in bronze. Those with silver were surely used for ceremonial purposes and perhaps only by the king.

The dominant position of the aristocrats was secure. Artisans, bards, seers and scribes served them and were dependent on their good will. Even the making and trading of pottery seems to have been a royal monopoly. These clients did not constitute an independent bourgeoisie who might muster the support of the peasantry to challenge the political power of the well-born. Their power was not in fact political at all. By custom, men of every class accepted the fact that they should live the way their ancestors had lived. Status was fixed by the amount of land owned; and a given family remained on the same property, be it large or small, generation after generation. The internal peace and order of such societies have always seemed to sanctify them as being right. What always was, would always be. The danger to the king and his companions would not be from below but from each other and from outside forces.

In the *Iliad*, Agamemnon appears as a king among kings, the first among equals. Like the early Capetian monarchs in France, he ruled a strategic area of land and managed by his wealth and his position to dominate his neighbors. In turn, he won allegiance, even if it were grudging, from more distant rulers. Yet domination of the Argolid plain did not mean absolute power. The thickness of the walls at Tiryns testified to that. As in Medieval times, various kingdoms quarreled incessantly and yet joined together in the crusades, so too, in Homer's account of the Trojan War, there were contingents of only six ships allied with others up to one hundred. Agamemnon may have been the leader of this host which sailed for Troy, but the *Iliad* shows that he could not make Achilles obey him after they arrived. Moreover, the *Odyssey* makes it clear that a king could have trouble with his own native nobility. The spirited Odysseus, like a later lion-hearted Richard, might well have wondered what was happening during his absence from home.

In Homer's description of the local scene at Ithaca, the landholders seem less like romantic knights and more like patriarchal ranchers of our own Old West—ranchers who were not above rustling each other's cattle.

Family loyalty was all important. When a son married, he brought his wife into an established household ruled by his father. The produce of the estate was kept in common storerooms and the family treasure remained intact until the father died. The surviving sons then set up their own households. And so it went from generation to generation. A man's identity was not established by his own name, but by the names of his ancestors. Genealogies were often recited and family ties were rarely broken. Brothers fought together. Whoever offended one offended the other. So it was that Agamemnon brought more ships to Troy than any other king for the abducted Helen was his brother's wife.

The intensity of these blood ties led to great respect for those who were kinsmen and little regard for those who were not. There were vendettas, raids on neighboring estates, and the unwelcome intrusion of free-loaders if a master happened to be absent from his household. So it was that Odysseus returned to face the obstreperous suitors who had served themselves from his well-stocked storerooms and thrown fear into his wife and family. When these suitors arrived in Hades it was apparently not unexpected that Agamemnon would ask them if they had been slain stealing sheep or women.

If piracy was a pastime with the Achaeans, so was hospitality. Then, as now, the year of a vintage was important and the best wine was saved for an occasion. Homer also recounts how the nobles generously bestowed their captured booty on one another with all the aplomb of robber-barons. In the *Odyssey* there are frequent references to gifts exchanged between friends and strangers alike. No guest, invited or in passing, should leave empty-handed.

Tacitus (*circa 55–circa 117 A.D.*), a Roman historian, describes in the *Germania* the same contrasting roles of violence and generosity among the early Germans. According to his account, the Germans too found a quiet life boring and lived in an uproarious routine of blood and plunder. Yet he calls these restless warriors the most hospitable of all men. Like Homer's Achaeans they seemed never to have been merely eating, much less dining, but always enjoying a feast.

The Mycenaeans were restless on land among themselves and a bane by sea to others, including the Hittites. These were an Indo-European people who moved into Asia Minor about the same time as the Greeks were arriving in the southern Balkans. Although their empire centered in the hinterland, it extended westward toward the Aegean Sea. Apparently they had contacts with the outposts which the Mycenaeans established in Melos, Rhodes, Cyprus, and at Miletus on the coast of Asia Minor. Hittite records which are dated between the fourteenth and twelfth centuries B.C. mention the kings and the land of Ahhiyava, which for the time and place could only mean the Achaeans. These documents describe the customary exchange of gifts, and also show how Achaean carelessness about other people's property put a severe strain on diplomatic relations. The same was true in Egypt where inscriptions of the thirteenth and twelfth centuries B.C. tell of the defeat of marauders from the north including the Akaiwasha (Achaeans) and the Denyen (Danaans).

Against this historical background the epic assault on Troy has been put into better perspective. Helen's face may have launched a few ships but the rest were on a more practical mission. The famed walls of Troy were a clue to the city's importance. This fortress city guarded the approaches to the Hellespont (Dardanelles) and held sway over the other towns in the Hellespontine region which comprised the northwest sector of Asia Minor. Rich from tolls and tribute, Troy was also the place to be taken if raiders were to pass inland. The Trojan episode therefore appears to have been another campaign by which the Achaeans sought to enrich themselves at the expense of their affluent neighbors. The date for the fall of Troy has been much disputed. The traditional year is 1184. Modern authorities like 1260 better.

The warrior class of the Achaeans could afford the entertainment of bards who sang tales about their exploits and in the process lifted these piratical excursions out of the ordinary into the realm of heroic adventure. Ever since the time when Homer retold these same stories centuries later, Achilles and Odysseus have been the stout-hearted yet tender-hearted prototypes of folk heroes. Either of these warriors could have fought alongside Roland and his Frankish knights on that marvelous and bloody day at Roncesvalles. Such is the gift of poetry.

Since the reconstruction of Achaean society has been based on inferences it must be offered cautiously. If a detailed report of "how things really were" happened to be available, it might include some surprises.

Throughout ancient times the vast majority of men were busy in the production of food. The same is true in underdeveloped areas today. Call them peasants, serfs, or tenant farmers, they comprise the broad base of any pyramid. In the Classical Age, a thousand years after the Mycenaean period, there were fewer trees on the Greek horizon, but the herders of goats and sheep and the farmers gathering grain were everlastingly the same. In Achaean times, these men, along with those who grew olives or kept bees, lived in villages which dotted the countryside. For them life was local and routine. Few men knew how to keep records. Nor did they need to. Scribes of the king kept their accounts for them, and for tax purposes. The Linear B tablets say that much. They also offer a sufficient variety of official titles to suggest that there was a hierarchy of bureaucrats although they do not say exactly what these persons might have been doing, if anything.

Neither does the available evidence offer a clear picture of the intricacies of landholding. Still, enough is known to avoid the temptation of filling in the story by borrowing too much from the better documented Middle Ages. The comparison cannot be stretched to include all the complexities of feudalism. The *aristoi*, the noble companions who fought alongside the king, were to be sure large landowners and their wealth and privileges were held by hereditary right. But they do not seem to have been "dukes" and "counts" who stood between the sovereign and his subjects. Although there may have been some tenancy and even debt peonage, the majority of small herders and farmers appear to have been yeomen, free and responsible only to the king. Responsible, probably, for hard labor on his walls, roads and fortifications.

Archaeologists have found an amazing array of objects produced by men who belonged neither to the small warrior class which Homer described, nor to the peasantry whose pigs were so carefully listed on the Linear B tablets. Marble tables inlaid with gold, fancy footstools inlaid with ivory, and jewelry of sparkling originality represent an artisan class quite apart from the usual weavers and armor makers. If specialization offers a clue to the level of a civilization, then the Mycenaean society was well along. Here again, archaeological findings have shown that Homer was misinformed. Despite his knowledge about Mycenaean wealth, he did not realize what a brilliant artistic season this city had had. He assumed that fine jewelry and articles of rare craftsmanship were brought to Greece by the Phoenicians, just as in his own day. Subsequent to Schliemann's time, archaeological discoveries from Sicily to Palestine, and at sites far up the Nile in Egypt, have shown that the Mycenaeans were exporters of an extra fine pottery which appears as a luxury item alongside the native wares of the overseas buyers.

Below the skilled craftsmen who served the king and his court was a large group of personal attendants. They included the usual palace contingent of valets, maids, nurses, and cooks. Furthermore, according to Homer, it was customary for the king and his friends to be accompanied by a retinue of servants on their campaigns. Remaining at home were the hired hands who worked the fields and tended the flocks of their wealthy employers.

Off the social scale altogether were the slaves. They were mostly women, for men were killed as they expected to be if they lost a battle. The women, however, were carted off as booty to become the cleaning women of the wives of the conquerors. Or, if young and attractive, to serve the pleasure of the warriors themselves. Maybe. Homer mentions at least one wife who refused to tolerate it.

The *Iliad* and the *Odyssey* have been relied upon to patch together the history of Achaean Greece. The survival of these epics has made them valuable source material; and yet using them for this purpose is akin to writing a history of the American Civil War from the works of Walt Whitman. Events and places are incidental to a poet, even if he notes them correctly. The poet is not after facts; he searches for the mystery of life. And he often finds it locked inside old stories, for they

are the best stories and never really old at all. True, they may describe
how particular men behaved according to the customs of their times,
but more importantly they speak of emotions which have always been
the same. The historical value of Homer's epics have not accounted for
their survival. They meant much more than mere history to the Greeks
of classical times, and to those who have read them since.

*   *   *   *   *

CONDITIONS WHICH MEN CANNOT CHANGE

The Homeric epics were as important to ancient Greek society as the
Bible is to our own. Perhaps more so, for the *Iliad* and the *Odyssey*
were the primers of Greek education. They still are. To the credit of
the Greeks, their children have always learned to read and write by
examples from the very best in native literature. A child may not go
far with his schooling, but if he learns to read and write he knows
Homer. When Socrates made his famous appeal to a large jury in
Athens in 399 B.C. he quoted from the *Iliad*. Here at least was common
ground.

Homer's writings did not comprise scripture in the sense that they
were the "revealed word of God." Yet, as in the Bible, there were woven
into these epics three persistent themes of human interest: the nature
of the supernatural, the intervention of the supernatural in human
events, and acute observations about the behavior of men toward one
another.

The epics describe the province of each of the twelve Olympian gods.
Nearly all of them were named in the Linear B tablets. Homer writes
about the same deities as the Mycenaeans had actually worshipped. Yet
the tablets mention other gods and not all of them have been clearly
identified. Perhaps some of these represent the cruder aspects of religious practices, snake cults and fertility rites which Homer ignores.
When the poet limited the number of gods to be given preference, he
introduced order and a degree of sophistication into a highly confusing,
often interchangeable, list of deities.

In the remote past, sticks and stones had been considered divine, but
Homer spoke for an age when supernatural powers were personified as
men and women, larger than life, living forever on special food. They
acted according to the same passions and prejudices of men, even as the
Hebrew Yahweh who walked and talked in the cool of the evening, and
described himself as a jealous God.

The nature of God is not a matter which historians need to decide for others, but the various ways in which men have conceived of the divine is a matter of historical interest. It may be observed that although a few Greek philosophers spoke of a single creative principle, the overwhelming majority of the Greeks throughout ancient times accounted for events according to the wishes of these anthropomorphic gods which Homer describes.

In the *Iliad*, Homer makes it plain how this happened. It is Apollo who demands that Agamemnon return the captured maid Chryseis to her father. When he refuses the god sends a plague to show his displeasure. How else could the sudden deaths of so many Achaeans be explained? Finally, Agamemnon is forced to accede to the god's wishes. It is then that he takes Briseis from Achilles. In turn, Achilles' mother, Thetis, appeals to Zeus for revenge and according to the god's promise matters do appear to go hard for the Achaeans. Later, when Hector goes out to meet Achilles, it is Athena who disguises herself and tricks him into believing that she is his brother and will give him another spear if his first throw misses. It is Athena too who grabs Hector's well-aimed missile and saves Achilles from being struck. Why else would this most skilled of all Trojan warriors have missed? Yet even these well-intended favors for Achilles do not really decide the issue. There are matters beyond the gods themselves. Homer tells how Zeus, the Father, held the scales. At first they were balanced. Then they tipped against Hector. As he is dying, Hector voices a plaint which would echo again and again in Greek literature: "At last my fate has found me." Achilles says, "Let me too die as nobly as this man when my time comes." Ancient man lived a shorter, far less comfortable life than his modern counterpart. He was preoccupied with how best to face adversity. By contrast, modern man, studying to improve himself, paddling his own canoe, seeks to make his own fate and so avoid adversity altogether.

Only on one occasion does Zeus point a finger at man. In the *Odyssey* he asks: "Why do men so often rage against the will of the gods when it is the wickedness of their own hearts which brings them woe?" This idea was not popularized before the time of the renowned secularists Euripides and Thucydides in the late fifth century, yet there was no reason why this notion should not appear in Homer. He was telling stories. The explanations why things happened in the way they did were not more contradictory than life itself. Each suited a particular circumstance and a different way in which a man might look at destiny.

Homer's epics do not offer an evolutionary development toward a higher concept of God, nor any single set of answers to life's major questions. As such, these "teachings" gave the religion common to all the Greeks a totally undogmatic character. The gods of course aided men and they must be worshipped, flattered and obeyed. The welfare of the state could depend on this. To deny the gods was dangerous, even unpatriotic. But there was no creed or sets of tenets to which a man must subscribe. Although the Greeks often quarreled over the physical control of their shrines, they never fought a religious war over faith. Ironically, the adherents of the later higher religions have suffered the embarrassment of bloodshed in the name of sacred books. Homer's writings actually united the Greeks by reconciling them to the common dilemma of human existence.

Courage and honor were the unquestioned standards by which a warrior lived. The intransigence of Achilles about an offence to his honor followed from the kind of man he was. Agamemnon was a warrior too. The quarrel between them which brought grief to themselves and others was rooted in their pride. Yet Homer was concerned with more than a particular incident between these two men. He recognized the inevitability of human differences and therefore the inevitability of conflict and sorrow. Tragedy has to do with conditions which men cannot change. No matter how much individuals may alter their course, a diversity of personality and temperament persists. In short, parts of the human complexion may shift places, but the total complexion remains the same. There will always be conflicts in which both the innocent and the guilty suffer. Here is the essence of tragedy. Long afterwards the poet Aeschylus gave this message a dramatic setting. It has been expressed many times since. In the literature of the Western world, Homer said it first, beautifully, once and for all.

Suggestions for Further Reading

CHADWICK, JOHN, *The Decipherment of Linear B*. Cambridge: Cambridge University Press, 1958.

FINLEY, M. I., *The World of Odysseus*. New York: The Viking Press, 1954.

PAGE, DENYS, *History and the Homeric Iliad*. Berkeley: University of California Press, 1963.

PALMER, LEONARD R., *Mycenaeans and Minoans*, rev. ed. New York: Alfred A. Knopf, 1965.

SAMUEL, ALAN E., *The Mycenaeans in History*. Englewood Cliffs, N.J.: Prentice-Hall, 1966.

STARR, CHESTER G., *The Origins of Greek Civilization*. New York: Alfred A. Knopf, 1961.

VENTRIS, MICHAEL and JOHN CHADWICK, *Documents in Mycenaean Greek, with Commentary and Vocabulary*. Cambridge: Cambridge University Press, 1956.

VERMEULE, EMILY, *Greece in the Bronze Age*. Chicago: University of Chicago Press, 1964.

The Greek City-State

The material, organized, and literate circumstances of life that together provide the foundations of civilization appeared in Mesopotamia and Egypt shortly before 3000 B.C. But these societies never passed beyond the stage of vast despotisms that enslaved the masses and supported themselves with the aid of religious sanctions in order to maintain the labor force for irrigation and construction projects. This kind of society was to become characteristic of Oriental civilizations; indeed, even in modern times it could be found in Africa and Asia. No one will deny that the distinctive qualities of Western civilization go beyond these congealed despotisms of the East. We look for the rule of law, the participation of citizens in a self-governing community, the recognition of the dignity of the individual, the vision of the high potentiality of human reason, and the development of scientific and philosophical systems that aim to explain and ultimately to control the forces of nature. Thus, whatever might be said about the economic prosperity and technological ingenuity of the Middle Eastern despotisms, it is to the Greek city-states of the fifth century B.C., particularly to Athens, that we have to turn if we are to see the emergence and definition of the distinctive qualities of Western civilization.

Greece was not much more fruitful and prosperous in the fifth century B.C. than it is today, and although the Greeks

FROM M. I. Finley, *The Ancient Greeks* (New York: Viking Press, 1963), pp. 37–73.

were good farmers and assiduous merchants, their contribution to economic and technological change was negli-
gible. But there never has been another society which has
exhibited such astonishing political and intellectual creativity as Athens in the late fifth and early fourth centuries B.C.
When we read Thucydides' account of Athenian government and politics, the teachings of Plato and Aristotle on
the nature of man and the universe, and the moral issues
presented in the dramas of Sophocles and Euripides, we are
constantly shocked by the recognition that their problems
and values are still our own. There has been some mysterious and unprecedented cultural and social breakthrough.
Orientalism has been overcome, and we have entered the
political and moral context of Western society. "Athens is
the school of Hellas," said the Athenian leader Pericles, as
reported by Thucydides; Athens was also the school of the
West. This fact was readily admitted by the Roman conquerors of Greece, and it was a cardinal belief of all the
important thinkers in Europe from the twelfth to the end of
the nineteenth century. They all saw themselves as students
in the school of Hellas, as the perpetuators and cultivators
down the long centuries of European history of the humanist tradition that had sprung full-blown from the Greek
mind, as intellectual dwarfs standing on the shoulders of
the Athenian giants.

What exactly was the Hellenic achievement? The Greeks
were the first people to create a genuine political community to which men belonged by free choice as equal citizens
and in which they shared a common life and a communal
responsibility. This is the form of political life diametrically
opposite to the Oriental despotism into which men are born
as slaves, from which they cannot withdraw, in whose destiny they have no decision, and in whose achievements they
can have no pride. Man, said Aristotle, is a "*polis*-being";
he is a man of the *polis*, of the political community, the
city-state. The Greeks believed passionately—there was
more unanimity on this point than anything else—that no
man is an island and that the fulfillment of the potential
of human nature can take place only in the context of
political action and group life.

The second Greek achievement was the exaltation of the critical intellect. They assumed that there were forces greater than man in the universe, but they also believed in the individual's rational faculty to discover what the good life is and then to apply his rational knowledge to the attainment of justice, truth, and beauty. "The unexamined life is not worth living," said Socrates. What separates man from animals is the use of his critical intellect. He knows himself by the exercise of reason and he is able to make the choice between good and evil. Among the Greek peoples, the Athenians in particular believed in the morality of rational choice. Self-realization of the individual, the dignity of human nature, requires the freedom to choose between alternative courses of action. The good life is not subservience to a religious hierarchy or automatic obedience of the command of the state. It is the rational choice of a free man.

There is very little to say about moral philosophy after the Greeks. The main theme of Greek drama was the difficult choices that men have to make, the burdens and responsibilities of freedom, in other words, the realities of the human condition. It is for this reason that the tragedies of Sophocles and Euripides still have great relevance and meaning for us.

The third area of achievement of fifth-century Greece was in philosophy and science. It is a simple fact that the two intellectual systems that dominated Western thought, and even molded the course of Christian theology until the seventeenth century, were fully developed by two Athenians, Plato and Aristotle. The whole of Western thought, said Alfred North Whitehead, is a series of footnotes to Plato—a plausible thesis. It is from Plato that the Western world derives the view that beyond the ephemeral and the particular there lie universal and eternal forms or patterns, and that the creative power of ideas makes a viable and comprehensible world out of formless matter. It is from Aristotle that the Western world derives its conviction that general laws about the workings of nature can be extrapolated from the empirical data of sense experience and that the most fundamental of these laws is the process of cause and effect.

It is the task of modern scholarship to account for the phenomenal creativity of Athens and the emergence of Western civilization at this distant time and this rather improbable place. By and large it must be said that historians as yet have not succeeded in this immensely important and difficult task. They are frustrated by the fragmentary and usually mythical nature of the sources before the fifth century B.C. It is as if the Greeks, having broken through the barrier separating our civilization from orientalism, intentionally enshrouded this breakthrough in obscurity and preferred to forget about it. However, with help from new archaeological evidence, a minute examination of the Homeric materials, and a great deal of a priori reasoning, some suggestive speculation has been accomplished.

Recent archaeological work has provided evidence that Greek society arose sometime before 1400 B.C. as the result of the meeting of Minoan culture, Oriental culture, and Greek-speaking peoples descending from the north. This meeting of East and West resulted in the Mycenaean Age, which was the model for the heroic society described in Homeric poetry. What was most important in this heroic society was the ideal of honor cultivated by a warrior elite. Aristocratic honor was a self-realizing, self-enhancing ethic, and we can see it as the beginnings of the Greek view of life that developed fully in the fifth century.

During the half-millennium after 1200 B.C., two other factors molded Greek culture and society. One was the geographical and economic environment—the development of social life in narrowly circumscribed valleys amid formidable mountains inculcated a strong sense of community and self-reliance and the need for planning and organization of the city-state. In addition, on the economic side, was the powerful impact of the sea, its impetus to enterprise and its provision of ready lines of communication with other parts of the Mediterranean. The other conditioning factor in Greek history was the prevalence of slavery, in Athens taking in at least a quarter of the population, which allowed for the wealth and leisure of an aristocratic elite who cultivated the life of the mind.

These are the factors that, according to modern scholarship, lie behind the culture and society of the fifth century

and shaped its ideas and institutions. They are too meagre
to be quite satisfactory as explanations. Far more successful
in recent scholarship has been the portrayal of the life of
the *polis* in the fifth century, the political and social context
of intellectual and literary creativity. In the older historical
accounts fifth-century Athens resembled a Victorian gentleman's club, all serene, convivial, and restrained. Recent
scholarship has given us a markedly different view—of a
society constantly undergoing great stress and strain, severely conditioned by class conflict, and trying desperately
and ultimately unsuccessfully to maintain the precarious,
short-lived balance that made possible the glories of Periclean Athens. The most perceptive and careful of these
accounts is the following study of the *polis*, published in
1963, by M. I. Finley, an American-born and -educated
scholar, and for the past twenty years a professor of ancient
history at Cambridge University. The book from which this
essay is taken, *The Ancient Greeks*, is distinguished by its
wide learning and balanced appraisal of the realities of
Greek life and is the best general introduction to the history
of classical Greece.

The Greek word *polis* (from which we derive such words as
"political") in its classical sense meant "a self-governing state." However, because the *polis* was always small in area and population, the
long-standing convention has been to render it "city-state," a practice
not without misleading implications. The biggest of the *poleis*, Athens,
was a very small state indeed by modern standards—about 1000 square
miles, roughly equivalent to the Duchy of Luxemburg or the state of
Rhode Island—but to call it a *city*-state gives a doubly wrong stress: it
overlooks the rural population, who were the majority of the citizen
body, and it suggests that the city ruled the country, which is inaccu-
rate. And Athens, in the extent and quality of its urbanization, stood at
one end of the Greek spectrum, together with a relatively small number
of other states. At the other end were many which were not cities at
all, though they all possessed civic centres. When Sparta, for example,
in 385 defeated Mantinea, then the leading *polis* in Arcadia, her terms
were that the "city" be razed and the people return to the villages in

which they had once lived. It is clear from Xenophon's account that the hardship caused was only political and psychological: the inhabitants of the "city" of Mantinea were the owners of landed estates, who preferred to live together in the centre, away from their farms, in a style visible as far back as the Homeric poems and which had nothing else to do with city life.

How small the scale really was can best be indicated by a few numbers, all of them estimates since no exact figures are available. When the Athenian population was at its peak, at the outbreak of the Peloponnesian War in 431, the total, including men, women and children, free and slave, was about 250,000 or perhaps 275,000. With the possible exception of Syracuse, which is not properly comparable for various reasons, no other Greek *polis* ever approached that figure until the Roman period with its altogether changed conditions. Corinth may have counted 90,000, Thebes, Argos, Corcyra and Acragas 40,000 to 60,000 each, and the rest tailed off, many to 5000 and even fewer. Space was equally compact, again with the few exceptions that spoil most generalizations—Sparta, which occupied Messenia, or Syracuse and Acragas, which swallowed neighbouring territories in Sicily.

The Greeks themselves had no hesitation, however, in calling Sparta or Syracuse a *polis*, the latter even though it was ruled by tyrants during much of the classical period, when "tyrant" and *polis* had come to have virtually contradictory connotations. Nor did they deny the term to those backward regions in which political organization and the civilization itself were still so rudimentary that they were admittedly more like that of the *Iliad* than like their contemporaries. In the old days, wrote Thucydides (I 5), piracy by land and sea was an honourable occupation among the Greeks as among the barbarians, and "even today much of Hellas lives in the ancient manner: the Ozolian Locrians and the Aetolians and the Acarnanians and others in that part of the mainland." And of course the word *polis* did not distinguish the structure of government; it implied nothing about democracy or oligarchy or even tyranny, any more than does "state."

Loose as the usage may have been at times, it never passed beyond certain limits. Its furthest extension was to equate *polis* with any independent Greek community (or one which had temporarily lost its independence). *Polis* was not applied to a league of states, no matter how voluntary the alliance; nor to a district such as Arcadia, which had a sort of autonomous (if abstract) existence, held together by common myths, dialect and cult, but which was not a political organism; nor, under any circumstances, to barbarian states. All these, in Greek eyes, were, each in its own way, something essentially different from the true political community, and size was no unimportant part of the difference. They looked upon their compactness in territory and numbers not as a mere accident of history or geography but as a virtue. In Aristotle's words (*Politics* VII 1326b), "A state composed of too many . . . will not be a true *polis* because it can hardly have a true constitution. Who can be the general of a mass so excessively large? And who can be herald, except Stentor?" The *polis* was not a place, though it occupied a defined territory; it was people acting in concert, and therefore they must be able to assemble and deal with problems face to face. That was a necessary condition, though not the only one, of self-government.

Ideally, self-sufficiency was another condition of genuine independence. It was admitted that this could rarely be achieved, if ever, because material resources were not evenly distributed (it is enough to mention iron), but, within the limits imposed by nature, much could be accomplished towards that objective. How much depended partly on size again—the *polis* must not be so small that it lacked the manpower to carry on the various activities of a civilized existence, including the requirements of defence. Given adequate numbers, the problem was one of proper rules of conduct and proper organization of social life. And there agreement stopped. The Athenian answer and the Spartan answer were radically different. Within Athens—using that city-state only as an example—there was no single answer either, hence the long, complicated political debate which went on there.

That debate was conducted within a small closed circle inside the total population, for the *polis* was an exclusive community. In the middle of the fifth century the Athenians adopted a law restricting citizenship to the legitimate children of marriages in which both parents were themselves of citizen stock. This was an extreme measure, probably neither rigidly enforced for very long nor frequently repeated in other states, but the thinking behind it was fairly typical. There had been a time, only two or three generations earlier, when Greek aristocrats often arranged marriages for their children outside the community, sometimes even with barbarians (but then only on the level of chieftains). Pericles was a descendant in the fourth generation of an external alliance, his great-grandmother having been the daughter of the then tyrant of Sicyon; while his political opponent Cimon was the grandson on his mother's side of a Thracian king named Olorus. Now, under

Pericles, Athens declared all such marriages illegal, their offspring bas-
tards.

In a sense, the word "citizen" is too weak, though technically correct;
it does not—at least in our day—carry the full weight implicit in being
a member of a *polis* community. And if one were not born into the community, it was nearly impossible to get in at all. There was no routine
naturalization procedure, not even in a state like Athens which welcomed immigrants from other Greek cities, gave them considerable freedom and opportunity, and accepted them socially. Only by formal action of the sovereign assembly could an outsider become a citizen of
Athens, and the evidence is that very special considerations were necessary before the assembly could be persuaded. It was not enough, for
example, to have been born in Athens, to serve in her armies, and to
behave decently and loyally, if one's parents were not citizens. Needless
to say, more xenophobic states were, if anything, even more closed in.
To open the doors wide was a sign of some deficiency, and it is more
than coincidental that by the end of the fourth century some city-states
were driven to sell citizenship in order to raise funds, precisely in the
period when the classical *polis* was a declining, not to say dying, organism.

In the more urban and more cosmopolitan city-states in particular,
therefore, a minority constituted the community proper. The majority
included the non-citizens (the word "foreigners" is best avoided since
most of them were Greeks), of whom the permanent residents were
called "metics" in Athens and some other places; the slaves, a still more
numerous class; and, in a fundamental sense, all the women. Whatever
their rights—and that was entirely in the power of the state—they suffered various disabilities as compared with the citizens, and at the same
time they were fully subject to the authority of the state in which they
resided. In that respect their position was no different from that of the
citizens, for in principle the power of the Greek *polis* was total: it was
the source of all rights and obligations and its authority reached into
every sphere of human behaviour without exception. There were things
a Greek state customarily did not do, such as provide higher education
or control interest rates, but even then its *right* to interfere was not in
question. It merely chose not to. The *polis* was inescapable.

The question then arises, if the *polis* had such limitless authority, in
what sense were the Greeks free men, as they believed themselves to be?
Up to a point their answer was given in the epigram, "The law is king."

Freedom was not equated with anarchy but with an ordered existence within a community which was governed by an established code respected by all. That was what had been fought for through much of the archaic period, first against the traditional privilege and monopoly of power possessed by the nobility, then against the unchecked power of the tyrants. The fact that the community was the sole source of law was a guarantee of freedom. On that all could agree, but the translation of the principle into practice was another matter; it brought the classical Greeks up against a difficulty which has persisted in political theory without firm resolution ever since. How free was the community to alter its established laws? If the laws could be changed at will, and that means by whichever faction or group held a commanding position in the state at any given moment, did that not amount to anarchy, to undermining the very stability and certainty which were implicit in the doctrine that the law was king?

So put, the problem is too abstract. In real life the answer normally depended on the interests of the respective protagonists. The sixth century saw the emergence in many communities of the common people as a political force, and against their demand for a full share in government there was promptly raised the defence of the sanctity of the law, of a code which, though it now recognized every citizen's right to a fair trial, to a minor share in government perhaps, even to the ballot, and to other undeniably new and important features of social organization, nevertheless restricted high civil and military office, and therefore policy-making, to men of birth and wealth. *Eunomia*, the well-ordered state ruled by law, had once been a revolutionary slogan; now it stood for the status quo. The people replied with *isonomia*, equality of political rights, and since the people were numerically in the majority, *isonomia* led to *demokratia*. Whose law, in other words, was to be king?

The underlying trouble, of course, was that the sense of community, strong as it was, clashed with the gross inequality which prevailed among the members. Poverty was widespread, the material standard of life was low, and there was a deep cleavage between the poor and the rich, as every Greek writer concerned with politics knew and said. This has been common enough in all history; what gave it an uncommon twist in Greece was the city-state, with its intimacy, its stress on the community and on the freedom and dignity of the individual which went with membership. The citizen felt he had claims on the community, not merely obligations to it, and if the regime did not satisfy him he was not loath to do something about it—to get rid of it if he could. In consequence, the dividing line between politics and sedition (*stasis* the Greeks called it) was a thin one in classical Greece, and often enough *stasis* grew into ruthless civil war.

The classic description of extreme *stasis* is Thucydides' account of the singularly brutal outbreak in Corcyra in 427, treated by the historian explicitly as a model of this chronic evil in Greek society. Nothing reveals the depths of the bitterness better than the fact that both sides appealed to the slaves for support. Thucydides explained the phenomenon psychologically, as having its roots in human nature. It was Aristotle who tied it more closely, and very simply, to the nature and idea of the *polis*. "Speaking generally," he said in the *Politics* (V 1301b), "men turn to *stasis* out of a desire for equality." By its nature the *polis* awoke this desire, which men then had difficulty in achieving. Hence the bitterness of factional strife, the comparative frequency and virulence of civil war. There were exceptions, important ones—notably Athens and to a degree Sparta—but the rough generalization may be made that in the Greek *polis* it was not so much policy which caused the most serious divisions, but the question of who should rule, "the few" or "the many." And always the question was complicated by external affairs, by war and imperial ambitions.

WAR AND EMPIRE

Because of their geographical situation the mainland Greeks were for a long time free from direct foreign pressure or attack. Not so, however, the settlements to the east and west. Apart from frequent troubles with more primitive peoples, such as the Scythians to the north or the Thracians to the west of the Black Sea, there was the more serious matter of the powerful civilized empires. In Asia Minor the Greek cities came under the suzerainty of the Lydians in the sixth century, and then under the Persians. In Sicily they were repeatedly invaded by Carthage, which maintained a toe-hold on the western end of the island but never succeeded in conquering the rest.[1]

Persian rule meant annual payment of tribute, which was sizable but in no sense crushing, passivity in foreign affairs and economic and cultural freedom. Where Persia impinged most on the internal life of the Greek states was in her backing of tyrants, and this ultimately led to revolt, which broke out in 500 or 499, under circumstances which are

[1] Rome did not become a factor until about 300 B.C.

far from clear. The Ionians immediately asked the mainland Greeks for help and received none, except for twenty ships from the recently established Athenian democracy and five more from Eretria in Euboea. Even so it took Persia the better part of a decade to regain complete control, and she followed up her success with two massive invasions of Greece itself, the first in 490 sent by King Darius, the second in 480 under his successor, Xerxes.

Many communities followed their refusal to help the Ionian revolt by surrendering in fright to the invaders—"Medizers" they were contemptuously called thereafter—and even the Delphic oracle played an equivocal role, at best. The Spartans, backed by the Peloponnesian League, had the only powerful army on the Greek side, but partly because of difficulties at home, partly because of a false strategic conception, they were dilatory in defence, though they proved what they could do, when tested, at Thermopylae and later at Plataea. It remained for Athens to deliver the most significant blows, at Marathon in 490 and off Salamis in 480. The latter was a most remarkable affair: persuaded by Themistocles, the Athenians hurriedly enlarged their fleet, withdrew from the city when the Persians came and allowed it to be destroyed, and then with their allies smashed the invaders in a great sea battle. The power of Athens, and therefore the history of classical Greece, henceforth rested on control of the sea.

The Persians were badly beaten; they were far from crushed. It was generally assumed that they would return for a third attempt (that in the end they did not was largely the result of troubles within their empire, which could not safely be forecast). Ordinary prudence therefore required combined anticipatory measures, and since they had to be taken in the Aegean and on the Asia Minor coast, rather than on the Greek mainland, it was natural that the leadership should be given to Athens. A league was organized under Athenian hegemony, with its administrative centre on the island of Delos (therefore historians call it the Delian League). Planned by the Athenian Aristeides on a system of contributions either in ships and sailors or money, the League within a decade or so cleared the Persian fleet from the Aegean. As the danger lifted, the old desire for complete autonomy began to reassert itself, but Athens would not allow withdrawal from the League and forcibly put down any "revolt." So the League became an empire, and the symbol of the change was the transfer of its headquarters and treasury in 454 from Delos to Athens. All but three of the member states now contributed money and not ships, which meant that Athens provided, manned and controlled virtually the whole fleet herself. An indication of the magnitude of the annual tribute is that it approximately equalled the Athenian public revenue from internal sources.

For the next quarter-century the Athenian Empire was the most important single fact in Greek affairs, and Pericles was the dominant figure in Athenian affairs. His policy was expansionist, though highly controlled and disciplined. He greatly strengthened Athenian connexions in Thrace and southern Russia, which had strategic significance but were above all important as the main source of Athens' vital corn imports; he made alliances with Sicilian cities; he tried, unsuccessfully, to attack Egypt; he came to terms with Persia. But Athenian relations with Sparta were increasingly difficult. Friendly at least in a formal way in the years following the Persian Wars, the two power blocks came into open conflict in the 450s, with some actual fighting, and then returned to a state of uneasy peace which lasted another two decades. Two major incidents involving Corinthian spheres of influence, at Corcyra and Potidaea, then precipitated the Peloponnesian War, which lasted with interruptions from 431 to 404, ending in the total defeat of Athens and the dissolution of her empire. Corinth may have been the chief advocate of war on the Spartan side, but, as the war's historian Thucydides wrote (I 23,6), "The growth of the power of Athens, and the alarm which this inspired in Sparta, made war inevitable." Pericles probably thought so too, for he had been accumulating a large cash reserve, a most uncommon practice among Greek states, which customarily spent all their income quickly.

It seems to have taken Thucydides a long time to make up his mind about the underlying cause of the Peloponnesian War; more precisely, that there was a deep cause, as distinct from one or more triggering incidents. This was one of his boldest and most original conceptions. War, everyone recognized, was part of life. Plato opened his last and longest work, the *Laws*, with praise of the ancient "lawgiver" of Crete for the way in which he prepared the community for war, "since throughout life all must forever sustain a war against all other *poleis*." This may be rhetorical exaggeration; it is not Platonic irony. War was a normal instrument of policy which the Greeks used fully and frequently. They did not particularly seek war—the heroic ideals of the Homeric poems had been thoroughly damped down—but neither did they go to lengths to avoid it. In the fourth century, to be sure, there were signs of war weariness and even talk of a "common peace" within Hellas. Nothing came of this, however, and the individual states went

right on quarrelling, blaming others when war came and justifying
their own actions simply in terms of political necessity. The interests of
the state were always justification enough, whether of war or of diplomacy and negotiation or of capitulation (if necessary, even to the Persians). The choice of instruments in any given situation was arguable
only on the question of tactics, pragmatically but not morally.

The immediate causes of war were therefore as varied as the policies
and interests of the different states, as the objectives they were pursuing at any given time. The desire for power and aggrandizement,
border incidents, material enrichment through booty (with human chat-
tels high on the list), protection of corn supply and transport, the search
for outside support for internal faction—these all came into play, intensified by the fragmentation of Hellas, which had the effect of multi-
plying the number of independent, or would-be independent, states rub-
bing against one another. What was rare as a motive, however, was
either trade, in the sense of a struggle over sea lanes and markets, as in
the Anglo-Dutch wars, for example; or territorial expansion, the direct
incorporation of conquered land or its economic exploitation (other than
by the collection of tribute).

Both the casualness of armed hostility and the way in which typical
motives could be combined and at the same time create a conflict of
interests are nicely illustrated in one particular situation in the Peloponnesian War. In 426 the Spartans settled a colony, for a number of reasons connected with the war, at Heraclea in Trachis, near the sea, a few
miles from the pass of Thermopylae. The colony was in trouble at once
because, Thucydides says (III 93, 2), "the Thessalians, who were in control of that area, . . . feared that it would be a very powerful neighbour
and they continually harassed and made war upon the new settlers."
The Thessalians, a loose federation of tribes, were in fact allied with
Athens, yet Thucydides fails to give that as the ground for their hostility to Heraclea. His reasons do not emerge for some pages, until he
comes to the year 424 and the campaigns of the Spartan general Brasidas, who set out for the north with 1700 hoplites to carry the war into
Thrace. Arriving in Heraclea, Brasidas "sent a messenger to his friends
in Pharsalus [a Thessalian town] asking them to conduct him and his
army through the territory." His "friends" included a number of the
leading oligarchs and they did as he requested. "The majority of Thessalian citizens," Thucydides then explains (IV 78), "had always been
favourable to the Athenians. Had there been genuine constitutional
government in Thessaly rather than the customary rule by a narrow

clique, Brasidas would never have been able to proceed." As it was, he rushed through just in time, before the opposition was sufficiently mobilized to stop him. Thus it was the interests of internal faction which decided policy, rather than the obligations of a formal external alliance. And there is no reason not to believe Thucydides that the Thessalians made war against Heraclea simply because a strong neighbour was someone to fear.

On the other hand, since war was a means and not an end, peaceful alternatives were also tried, and they did not always fail. It was power, in the end, which was the strongest force for peace—earlier the power of the tyrants, now the power of a few great city-states. Their superior ability to wage war was reinforced by a general realization that they would do so promptly if required. By itself no Greek state could generate that much power, but if one were big enough to begin with, persistent enough, sufficiently unified and under competent leadership, it could create and wield a power block. Alliances were valuable above all because they provided the leading states with auxiliary manpower. And in the pregunpowder world, it was usually the weight of properly trained and equipped men which decided battles; among the Greeks, the heavy-armed hoplite infantry. Partly, therefore, peace was the result of simple arithmetic. Towards the end of the sixth century, for example, Sparta succeeded in bringing under alliance most of the free states of the Peloponnese. Some needed pressure, others did not, but who could say that the latter were more willing rather than just more cautiously calculating? Thereafter war among the Peloponnesian states was very rare indeed, until Thebes smashed Spartan power in 371. That blow at once proved to be a mixed blessing even to those who detested Sparta: it brought about the emancipation of the Messenian helots, but it also led to a holocaust of *stasis* and petty warfare all over the peninsula. The sums had been changed, so to speak, and war therefore returned, occupying the newly created power vacuum.

What modern historians call the Peloponnesian League was known to contemporaries by the more awkward, but revealing, name of "Sparta and her allies." The point is that there was a network of treaties tying each of the "member states" to Sparta, and only the loosest sort of league organization under the hegemony of Sparta. This was a significant distinction, preserving the individual state's image of its autonomy. In an alliance it could pretend to be an equal, still a fully independent entity retaining its sovereign freedom of action; in a league it could be outvoted and lose control over its own actions. The reality did not coincide with the image, of course: states were rarely equals and bargaining between them was rarely free, and on the other hand even Sparta could not effectively mobilize the support of her allies without consulting them and obtaining their approval of the proposed course of action. Nevertheless, the myth of independence was so compelling that genuine leagues in Greek history were restricted either to the amphictyonies, which organized and shared control of certain pan-Hellenic shrines such as Delphi; or to the most backward areas, where the *polis* never came to life; or to the isolated and complicated instance of the Boeotian League, in which one powerful member, Thebes, sought domination in her own interest, and paid for her insistence by having to fight her neighbours over and over again.

The Boeotian League exposed the thinness of the line that separated allies from subjects, but it was the Athenian Empire, with an effective membership of more than 150 states in Asia Minor, the Hellespontine region, Thrace and the Aegean islands, which brought that issue to a head in classical Greece. After 454 there was no pretence about it: membership was compulsory and secession prohibited; members paid an annual cash tribute which was fixed, collected and spent by Athens at her sole discretion; these imperial resources enabled Athens to conduct a complicated foreign policy, which she alone determined; and there was a growing tendency for the Athenians to interfere in the internal affairs of the member states, in particular to support and strengthen democratic elements against their oligarchic opponents. Some contemporaries began to refer to the "tyrant city," a reproach which is readily repeated by historians today, chiefly on the authority of Thucydides. Yet that is far too one-sided a judgment; it looks only at the question of *polis* autonomy and ignores other, by no means meaningless, desires and values. Thucydides himself noted the friendliness to Athens among the majority of citizens in Thessaly, and the evidence suggests that the same was widely true among communities in the Empire. In the unending struggle between the few and the many, Athens usually came down on the side of the many, who often needed such aid to maintain their position, and who therefore felt that tribute and some loss of autonomy were a price well worth paying in return for democratic government at home and peace abroad.

The decisive test came in the Peloponnesian War, in which few Greek states escaped some involvement except those in the outermost fringes of Hellas. This was a war quite without precedent in every respect, in the number of participants (both numbers of states and numbers of men), in its duration and therefore in the expenditure of resources and

in the pressure on morale, in the crucial importance of sea power, and
in the way in which the scene of actual fighting moved all over the place,
from Asia Minor to Sicily, often in several widely dispersed areas simultaneously. It was a war which had therefore to be played by ear, as
neither statesmen nor commanders had adequate precedents from which
to learn. Ever since the invention of the massed hoplite formation,
Greek wars were customarily short-lived affairs in the summer months,
culminating in a single infantry engagement between the heavy armour
on both sides, numbering in the hundreds or thousands. Eventually one
side or the other broke and fled, and the battle—and usually the war—
was over. The enemy was also harassed by raiding of crops, occasionally
by a siege, usually unsuccessful unless treason took over, or by cavalry
movements—but the encounter of the hoplites was normally the one
decisive action. Hence there was no occasion for deep strategy, little
need for financial preparations, nothing that one could seriously call
logistics.

But these were wars between single states, with or without the support of a handful of allies, having an obvious battle terrain in which to
contend. The Peloponnesian War involved great blocks of states and a
wide choice of battle areas with little chance for a decision so long as
the two centres, Sparta and Athens, remained intact. It was Pericles'
idea not to risk a decision on the hoplite engagement, even at the expense of allowing the Spartans to raid Attica repeatedly without resis-
tance. He counted on Athenian financial resources, on her peerless navy,
and on her intangible psychological superiority. In a word, he had a
strategic idea, if not a plan, of considerable complexity, and its foundation was the solidity of the Empire. He was not wrong. Whatever the
explanation for the ultimate defeat of Athens, it was not eagerness in
the Empire to be released from the Athenian yoke. Naturally enough,
both sides found in the course of twenty-seven years a very considerable unevenness in the reliability of their allies, and both sides did what
they could to unhinge the alliances, using force, cajolement and, most
effective of all, support for *stasis*. Brasidas was not alone in having
"friends" in the allied states of the other camp. The important thing
about the Athenian Empire is not that there were defections but that so
much support continued to come to the "tyrant city," even in the final
decade when all seemed lost and one might have expected elementary
raison d'état to drive her subjects to a quick bargain with the enemy.

In truth there is no simple and obvious explanation why Athens lost,
and it is necessary to remember that she almost escaped. The peace of
421 was a victory in the restricted sense that not one of the main

Spartan objectives was achieved. Then came the renewal of the war, and in 415 the Athenians decided on a major stroke, the invasion of Sicily. It ended in a complete disaster, and though the war dragged on for another nine years, that defeat was clearly the turning point. Yet it was a defeat by a hair's breadth; more competent leadership would almost certainly have turned the invasion into a success, with consequences that cannot be realistically guessed at, though they surely should not be underestimated. This failure of leadership, it is widely held on the inevitable authority of Thucydides, was symptomatic of a very deep and general decline in Athenian political behaviour after the death of Pericles in the second year of the war, and that is probably the commonest explanation of Athens' defeat. Perhaps, but it is at least arguable that this was a war Athens could lose but could not really win, simply because—given its size, its resources in men and materials, the incapacity of its rudimentary economy and technology to expand, and the incapacity of the Greeks either to transcend the *polis* or, in most instances, to live at peace with themselves within it—final victory would have come to Athens only if she succeeded in bringing all Hellas within her Empire, and that was apparently beyond reach.

The war ended in 404 and the most important condition laid down by the victorious Spartans was the dissolution of the Empire. The war was therefore a disaster not only for Athens but for all Greece: it disrupted the one possible road towards some kind of political unification, though admittedly a unity imposed on others by an ambitious city. Sparta fought the war under the slogan of restoring to the Greek cities their freedom and autonomy, and she honoured that aim first by effectively returning the Asia Minor Greeks to Persian suzerainty (in payment for Persian gold, without which she was unable to bring the war to a close); then by attempting to establish a tribute-paying empire of her own, with military governors and garrisons, on the corpse of the Athenian Empire. That incompetent effort did not last a decade. In the fourth century the power vacuum in Greece became a permanent condition, despite the efforts of Sparta, Thebes and Athens in turn to assert some sort of hegemony. The final answer was given by no Greek state but by Macedon under Philip II and his son Alexander.

ATHENS

It has been estimated that one-third or slightly more of the citizens of Athens lived in the urban districts at the outbreak of the Pelopon-

nesian War in 431, a proportion which a century later had risen to perhaps one-half. The free non-citizens, barred by law from owning land,
were concentrated in the city and the harbour town. So were many of
the slaves. The purely demographic consequence was that Athens and
the Piraeus were each more populous than a majority of Greek states
taken whole. This urban quality of Athenian life was of the greatest
importance, a necessary condition for the power and much of the glory
of the state. Nevertheless, the tenacity of the attachment to the soil
must not be overlooked. The urban dwellers included no small number
whose economic interest, in whole or in part, remained in the land.
There is evidence that even at the end of the fifth century three-fourths
of the citizen families owned some landed property, though not always
enough for a livelihood. Of these it would be the wealthier, in particular,
who resided in the city. As for the countrymen proper, when they were
all brought behind the walls in the summer of 431, in anticipation of the
first of the Spartan incursions, "they were depressed," Thucydides reports (II 16, 2), "and they bore with bitterness having to leave their
homes and hereditary shrines."

In the city were some hundreds of families of outstanding wealth:
citizens living on the income from their estates and, occasionally, on
investment in slaves; non-citizens whose economic base was trade or
manufacture or money-lending. Among both groups there were men
who were very rich indeed. Pericles' chief political opponent in his
earlier years was Cimon, a member of one of the greatest of the old
aristocratic families, and he, according to Aristotle (*Constitution of
Athens* XXVII 3), "possessed the fortune of a tyrant, . . . supported
many of his fellow demesmen, every one of whom was free to come
daily and receive from him enough for his sustenance. Besides, none
of his estates was enclosed, so that anyone who wished could take from
its fruits." Or there was Nicias, commander of the army destroyed in
Sicily, who is reported to have owned a thousand slaves; or the man,
whose very name is unknown, who itemized in court his personal contributions to the navy and to the cost of public festivals in the final
seven years of the Peloponnesian War, totalling nearly eleven talents,
the equivalent of a year's wages for well over two hundred skilled
workmen.

Such men were essentially *rentiers*, free to devote themselves to
politics or learning or plain idling. This was as true of Nicias as of the
absentee landlords, for Nicias did not employ his slaves directly but
hired them out on a per-diem rental to entrepreneurs holding conces-

sions in the silver mines at Laurium. Even those who, like Cleon, made use of their slaves in their own industrial establishments and therefore cannot be called *rentiers* in a strict sense were (or at least could be if they wished) no less men of leisure; their businesses were managed in the same fashion as were large landed estates, by slave bailiffs or foremen. The exact number of slaves in Athens is in dispute; it may be doubted if any contemporary could have given the figure, in the absence of either a register or a periodic census. Probably 60,000 to 80,000 is a fair estimate, which is about the same proportion of the total population of the state as prevailed in the American South before the Civil War. The heaviest concentrations were in the mines and in domestic service, the latter a broad category including thousands of unproductive men and women retained by men of means because it was the thing to do. Plato, for example, mentioned five domestics in his will, Aristotle more than fourteen, his successor, Theophrastus, seven. In agriculture and manufacture the slaves were fewer in number, and they were outnumbered in these branches of the economy by the free peasants and probably also by the free, independent craftsmen. Nevertheless it was in these productive areas that the significance of slaves was perhaps the greatest, because they released from any economic concern, or even activity, the men who gave political leadership to the state, and in large measure the intellectual leadership as well.

The overwhelming mass of the Athenians, whether they owned a slave or two apiece or not, found themselves largely occupied with procuring a livelihood, and many never rose above the minimum standard. There were many poor families in the countryside, and there were probably even more in the town. Nevertheless, in the classical period Athens remained free from the chronic Greek troubles arising out of a depressed and often dispossessed peasantry. Furthermore, even the poor often found both time and the opportunity to participate in the public life of the community, both in government (broadly defined) and in the rich festival activity associated with the cults of the state. How these exceptional patterns of behaviour came into being is one of the central questions in Athenian history.

Part of the answer can be found in the distribution of the military burdens and obligations. When the war with Sparta became a fact, Pericles personally led a great invasion—more properly it can be called a demonstration or parade—into the territory of Megara with 13,000 hoplites, 10,000 of them citizens, the rest metics. Another 3000 were at that moment engaged in the siege of Potidaea, and the evidence suggests that the two groups together made up the full hoplite force in 431, or very nearly so. (Army figures cited by a writer such as Thucydides, unlike general population figures, are apt to be accurate: Greek states conducted no censuses, but for obvious reasons they kept reliable registers of their armed forces, and these could be consulted by any citizen in a state such as Athens.) The total number of adult male citizens at that time was of the order of 40,000 to 45,000; therefore about one-third of the citizens (ignoring the metics in this calculation) had sufficient means to be classed as hoplites. Granted that those just above the minimum qualification may have found this a hardship, as those just below might well have thanked their good fortune for their narrow escape, the proportion still offers a useful indication of the spread of wealth in the state.

Every citizen and metic was liable for military service, the size of any given levy being determined by the Assembly. Most commonly, however, only the hoplites and cavalry, that is, the two wealthier sectors, were called out. They were required to provide and maintain their own equipment, and they received from the state nothing more than a per-diem allowance while on duty (in the fourth century, when the treasury could not stand the strain, often not even that). Although the so-called light-armed levies were occasionally summoned to duty, it remains accurate to say that in Athens the army, conscript and not professional in any modern sense, was strictly an upper- and middle-class institution. The navy, in contrast, was altogether different, and differently organized. Command of the vessels was distributed among the richer citizens, who were also responsible for a considerable share of the operating costs, while the crews were paid professionals. Much of the detail remains very obscure, but it seems probable that some 12,000 men were so engaged normally up to eight months in the year. Although the citizen-body could not have supplied anything like that number, there were enough citizens to constitute a very significant element. For the urban poor the navy was a most important source of livelihood, at least while the Athenian Empire existed, a fact which was perfectly visible to every contemporary, as were its political implications. "It is the *demos*," wrote an anonymous fifth-century pamphleteer commonly and too amiably referred to as the Old Oligarch, "which drives the boats and gives the state its strength."

Now *demos* was a word with a complicated history. The Old Oligarch used it in its sense of the "common people," the "lower classes," with the pejorative overtones proper to all right-thinking men as far back as the *Iliad*. But *demos* also meant the "people as a whole"; in a democracy, the citizen-body who acted through its assembly. Hence decrees of the Athenian Assembly were passed, in the official language of the documents, "by the *demos*" rather than "by the *ecclesia*" (the Greek word for "assembly"). The Assembly met frequently—at least four times in every thirty-six-day period in the fourth century and perhaps as often in the fifth—and every male citizen who had reached his eighteenth birthday was eligible to attend whenever he chose, barring a few who had lost their civic rights for one offence or another. Obviously a mere fraction of the forty thousand came, but those who were present at any single meeting were the *demos* on that occasion, and their acts were recognized, in law, as the actions of the whole people. Then, by a curious extension of this principle, it was held that the jury-courts, selected by lot from a panel of six thousand men, volunteers from among all the citizens, were also equal to the whole *demos* in matters which fell within their competence.

Direct participation was the key to Athenian democracy: there was neither representation nor a civil service or bureaucracy in any significant sense. In the sovereign Assembly, whose authority was essentially total, every citizen not only was entitled to attend as often as he pleased, but also had the right to enter the debate, offer amendments and vote on the proposals, on war and peace, taxation, cult regulation, army levies, war finance, public works, treaties and diplomatic negotiations, and anything else, major or minor, which required governmental decision. Much of the preparatory work for these meetings was done by the *boule*, a Council of five hundred chosen by lot for one year—and again everyone was eligible, save that no man could be a member more than twice in his lifetime. Then there were a large number of officials, of varying importance, most of them also designated by lot for one year: the few exceptions included the ten generals (*strategoi*) who were elected and could be re-elected without limit, and temporary *ad hoc* commissions for diplomatic negotiation and the like. There was no hierarchy among the offices; regardless of the significance or insignificance of any post, every holder was responsible directly and solely to the *demos* itself, in the Council or the Assembly or the courts, and not to a superior officeholder.

This system was of course the product of a considerable evolution, completed in its essentials by the third quarter of the fifth century but subject to further modification as long as Athens remained a democracy. The Athenians sometimes called Solon the father of their democracy, but that was an anachronistic myth. Although both Solon and Peisistratus in different ways laid some of the groundwork by weakening the archaic system, especially the political monopoly of the aristocratic families, neither man, it need hardly be said, had democracy in view. The change, when it came, was sharp and sudden, following the overthrow of the tyranny in 510 with Spartan help, and a two-year civil war which ensued; and the architect of the new type of government was Cleisthenes, a member of the noble family of the Alcmaeonids. Cleisthenes was no theorist and he seems to have become a democrat virtually by accident, turning to the common people when he urgently needed their support in the confused struggle to fill the vacuum left by the deposed tyrant, Hippias, the son of Peisistratus. We are too ill informed to say how much of a model for his new set-up Cleisthenes was able to find elsewhere in Greece, in Chios for example, but the final result was in any case original in the best Greek sense. Having committed himself to a major innovation, Cleisthenes with his advisers, whoever they may have been, created the institutions which they thought their new objective required, retaining what they could, but not hesitating to demolish and to invent boldly and radically.

The Cleisthenic structure was not yet the Periclean: two full generations were required to perfect the system, a period which included not only the Persian Wars and the building of the Empire, but also much internal conflict, for the forces opposed to democracy were far from crushed in 508. The details of that struggle can no longer be retraced with any clarity; of all the gaps in our knowledge of classical Greek history this is perhaps the most frustrating. The man who played the decisive role between Cleisthenes and Pericles was Ephialtes, and we know next to nothing about him or his career. He was assassinated in 462 or 461, a political crime which passed almost unnoticed in Greek literature, and that silence is sufficient commentary on the tendentiousness of Greek writers, a one-sidedness with which the modern historian must grapple all the time, and never more than in the study of the history and functioning of the Athenian democracy.

In the end the pivotal mechanisms were election by lot, which translated equality of opportunity from an ideal to a reality; and pay for office, which permitted the poor man to sit on the Council and jury-courts or to hold office when the lot fell to him. It was not without reason that Pericles could boast, according to Thucydides, that it was one of the positive peculiarities of Athens that poverty was no bar to public service. When one adds up the Assembly, the Council, the courts and the large number of rotating offices, the total—several thousands —indicates a direct participation in the work of government widely shared among the citizen-body, an uncommon degree of political experience cutting right across the class structure. The distribution was, of course, not an even one: that would have been too utopian. In particular, the rural population was probably under-represented in ordinary circumstances, and at the top, among the men who gave the leadership and formulated policy, very few are known (and they not before the fourth century) to have come from the lower classes.

In a sense, amateurism was implicit in the Athenian "definition" of a direct democracy. Every citizen was held to be qualified to share in government by the mere fact of his citizenship, and his chances to play a part were much intensified not only by the wide use of the lot but also by the compulsory rotation in the Council and most offices. Though the pay was sufficient to compensate a man for the wages he might have lost as a craftsman or labourer, it was no higher than that. Hence no man could count on officeholding as a regular livelihood, or even as a better one for some periods of his life. At the same time, a large state like Athens, with its Empire and its (by Greek standards) complex fiscal, naval and diplomatic affairs, absolutely needed full-time politicians to guide and coordinate the work of the more or less temporary amateur participants. And it found them among the men of wealth, the *rentiers* who were free to devote themselves wholly to public affairs. Down to the Peloponnesian War these men were apparently drawn entirely from the old landed families. Then new men broke their monopoly—Cleon, Cleophon, Anytus—whose leisure was provided by slave craftsmen, and for the remaining century of democratic government in Athens the balance of leadership perhaps leaned more on that side, punctuated occasionally by really poor men who worked their way to the top, not without incurring suspicion that monetary corruption played some part in their rise.

It became increasingly common to refer to these men as "orators," almost as a technical term and not just as a description of their particular abilities in that direction. Because the Assembly alone made policy and held control, in conjunction with the courts, not only over the affairs of state but also over all officials, military or civil, leadership of the state lay in the Assembly. It met in the open, on a hill near the Acropolis called the Pnyx, where thousands gathered (just how many thousands is another frustrating unknown) to debate and decide. The Assembly, in a word, was a mass meeting, and to address it required,

in the strictest sense, the power of oratory. Because it had no fixed composition, because no one was chosen to attend, it had no political parties
or "government," nor any other principle of organization. The president
for the day was chosen by lot from the members of the Council on the
usual scheme of rotation, motions were made, argued and amended, and
the vote was taken, all in a single sitting, except in rare circumstances.
Anyone who sought to guide it in its policy-making had to appear on
the Pnyx and present his reasons. Neither the holding of office nor a
seat on the Council was a substitute. A man was a leader so long, and
only so long, as the Assembly accepted his programme in preference
to those of his opponents.

Ancient critics and their modern followers have not been sparing in
their condemnation: after Pericles, they say, the new type of leader was
a demagogue, pandering to the *demos* in the Assembly and the courts,
at the expense of the higher interests of the state. No doubt not all the
men who achieved political eminence in Athens were selfless altruists,
and mass meetings on the scale of those on the Pnyx obviously invited
emotional and even inflammatory speech-making. It would be odd,
however, if dishonest politicians and excessive rhetoric were wholly
unknown in the earlier years of the democracy, then to come on with
a rush when Pericles died. Besides, there is enough evidence to suggest
that the over-all record and achievement of the Assembly remained
credible to the end. It is a fact that the state often followed a consistent
line for rather long periods, in each instance identified with one individual or a small group. For all their experience, most citizens were unable
to cope with the intricacies of finance or foreign affairs and tended, quite
rightly, to give their support to those full-time politicians whom they
trusted (and whom they could always check). Hence not only Pericles in
the fifth century and Demosthenes late in the fourth were permitted to
develop long-term policies, but also less famous though far from un-
talented men such as Thrasybulus or Eubulus in the intervening years.

It is also a fact that Athens never ran short of men of the highest
ability who were willing to devote themselves to politics, though the
rewards were largely honorific and the personal risks considerable.
Conflict was often sharp, and the issues were serious, and not just
shadow-boxing for prestige or personal status. The long struggle to
anchor the democracy itself, the growth of the Empire, the Peloponnesian War and its strategy, public finance, and finally the question of
Philip and Alexander—these were matters worthy of passion. And they
were fought with passion. Whoever aspired to leadership could not do

otherwise, and in a system lacking the buttressing and mediating institutions of party and bureaucracy, such men lived under constant tension. It is not surprising that they sometimes reacted violently, that they seized the occasion to crush an opponent; or that the *demos* was sometimes impatient with failure, real or imaginary. There was no immunity from the risks: even Pericles suffered temporary eclipse and a heavy fine early in the Peloponnesian War. Others were ostracized, sent into a kind of honorary exile for ten years, but without loss of property and without social disgrace. When ostracism was dropped as a practice near the end of the fifth century, ordinary exile on "criminal charges" remained as a possibility. And a very few met death, legally or by assassination.

One could easily compile a catalogue of the cases of repression, sycophancy, irrational behaviour and outright brutality in the nearly two centuries that Athens was governed as a democracy. Yet they remain no more than so many single incidents in this long stretch of time when Athens was remarkably free from the universal Greek malady of sedition and civil war. Twice there were oligarchic coups, in 411 and 404, but they were short-lived, came under the severe stress of a war that was being lost, and the second time succeeded for a few months only because of the intervention of the victorious Spartan army. Thereafter no more is heard of oligarchy in Athens (outside the writings of some philosophers) until another invader, the Macedonians, closed this chapter of Greek history completely in 322. Not a few of the supporters of the 404 coup—known thereafter by the deservedly malodorous name of the Thirty Tyrants—had been active in the oligarchy of 411. That they lived to play their seditious role twice in a decade is not unworthy of note. Indeed, even so staunch a libertarian as John Stuart Mill thought this was perhaps too much. "The Athenian Many," he wrote, "of whose democratic irritability and suspicion we hear so much, are rather to be accused of too easy and good-natured a confidence, when we reflect that they had living in the midst of them the very men who, on the first show of an opportunity, were ready to compass the subversion of the democracy."

By the middle of the fifth century the "few" and the "many" among the Athenian citizens had established a satisfactory working balance, which is but another way of saying that they had achieved a system which was virtually *stasis*-proof. For the "many" the state provided both significant material benefits and a very considerable share in government, for the "few"—and they were a fairly numerous class—the honours and satisfactions that went with political and military leadership. Political success and economic prosperity served as unifying factors, making it possible to meet the enormous costs of office and the fleet, without which the participation, and even the loyalty, of thousands of the poorest citizens would have been uncertain at best; and providing powerful psychological stimuli to civic pride and close personal identification with the *polis*. Without the Empire it is hard to imagine the initial triumph of the system Ephialtes and Pericles forged. Then the system generated its own momentum, sustained by an active sense of civic responsibility—so that the wealthy, for example, carried a heavy burden of financial charges and the main military burden, while the *demos* accepted leadership from their ranks—and not even the disasters of the Peloponnesian War or the loss of the Empire seriously threatened the structure of government. Fourth-century Athens found resources within herself to maintain the political and civic organization which the Empire had helped erect in the previous century.

Athens prospered as did no other classical Greek state. The greatest of her boasts, attributed to Pericles, was that she was the "school of Hellas." In two centuries she produced an incredible succession of superb writers and artists, scientists and philosophers. Many who were not native, furthermore, were powerfully attracted to the city, and some of them settled there more or less permanently. There were not many important figures in Greek cultural life between the years 500 and 300 who were not associated with Athens for at least part of their careers, including some of the bitterest critics of her system. None was more severe than Plato, a native Athenian who found much to admire in the state often held up as her ideal opposite, namely, Sparta. He and those who thought like him conveniently forgot that in Sparta they would never even have begun to think, let alone been permitted to teach freely as they did.

SPARTA

It has been said that Sparta had two separate histories, its own and that of its image abroad (or "mirage" as one French scholar calls it). Considering how much was written about Sparta in antiquity, it is remarkable how confused, contradictory and incomplete the picture is. Partly this is because the mirage is constantly cutting across the reality, distorting it and often concealing it altogether; and partly because the Spartans themselves were so completely silent. There was a time, in the

archaic period, when Sparta played a leading part in the development
of the main lines of Greek civilization: in poetry, as we know from the
bits that still exist; in music, according to reliable ancient traditions;
even, it seems, in seafaring and in creating some of the germinal institutions of the city-state. After about 600, however, there was an apparently abrupt break. From then on not a single Spartan citizen is
remembered for any cultural activity. Their famed "laconic speech"
was a mark that they had nothing to say, the final consequence of the
peculiar way of life they had brought to completion by this time.

In population Sparta did not rank with the bigger states. The largest
number of Spartans ever to engage in battle, so far as we know, were
the 5000 at Plataea in 479. Thereafter they declined steadily, until in
the mid-fourth century they could not muster 1000 men. That figure is
cited by Aristotle as a symptom of the defectiveness of their system,
for, he argued, the territory under their control could support 1500 cavalry and 10,000 infantry. By conquest Sparta held the districts of Laconia and Messenia, quite fertile by Greek standards, giving her access
to the sea and supplying that rare and invaluable natural resource, iron
(a fitting counterpart to the Athenian silver). What this territory supported was not a free population but subject peoples of two kinds. The
helots were in outright servitude, a compulsory labour force working
the land for the Spartans. Their number cannot even be guessed, but it
was certainly many times that of the Spartans themselves. The others,
known as *perioeci*, retained their personal freedom and their own community organization in return for surrendering all right of action to
Sparta in the military and foreign fields.

Thus restricted, the communities of the *perioeci* were, strictly speaking, incomplete *poleis;* yet there is no sign that they struggled to free
themselves from Spartan authority in the way the smaller Boeotian
states persistently battled Theban efforts to establish an overlordship.
No doubt resignation was the only prudent course, but other considerations were also present: peace, protection and economic advantage. It
was the *perioeci* who managed the trade and industrial production for
Spartan needs, and it was they who maintained Laconian ware on a
respectable, and sometimes high, level of craftsmanship and artistry.
The helots were an altogether different matter. The usual practice
throughout most of antiquity, when a city or district was enslaved, was
to sell off the inhabitants and disperse them. The Spartans, however,
had adopted the dangerous alternative of keeping them in subjugation
at home, in their native territory—and they paid the price. Whereas

Greek history was astonishingly free from slave revolts, even where there were large concentrations as in the Attic silver mines, helot revolts were always smouldering and occasionally burst out in full flaming force.

What kept the helots enslaved and prevented still more frequent rebellion was the emergence of Sparta as an armed camp, a development to which the key lay in Messenia, conquered later than Laconia and much more thoroughly reduced (so much so that this district remained virtually empty of the great architectural works which everywhere else were the visible marks of Hellenism). Soon after the middle of the seventh century the Messenian helots revolted: tradition calls that conflict the Second Messenian War and gives it a duration of no less than seventeen years. The Messenians were finally crushed, and the lesson they taught was translated into a thorough social and constitutional reform, the establishment in its final form of the Spartan system, and ultimately of the Spartan mirage. Henceforth the Spartan citizen-body was a professional soldiery, bred from childhood for two qualities, military skill and absolute obedience, free from (indeed, barred from) all other vocational interests and activities, living a barrack life, always ready to take the field in strength against any foe, whether helot or outsider. Its needs were met by the helots and the *perioeci*; its training was provided by the state; its obedience was secured by education and by a set of laws which tried to prevent economic inequality and any form of gainful pursuit. The whole system was closed in against outside influence, against outsiders in person and even against imported goods. No state could match Sparta in its exclusiveness or its xenophobia.

The governmental structure was often praised in antiquity for its "mixed" character, supposedly providing a balance between monarchical, aristocratic and democratic elements. The two hereditary kings commanded the armies in the field and were members of the Council of Elders, the others, twenty-eight in number, being elected for life from among the citizens over sixty years of age. The Assembly included everyone, but its role seems to have been a rather passive one: it could neither initiate action nor amend proposals submitted to it; it could only approve or vote them down; and one may wonder how much independence of judgment was exercised by a body of men for whom strict military obedience was the paramount virtue. Most powerful of all were the five ephors, elected annually from all the citizens. They had a general supervisory position over the affairs of the state, as well as important judicial functions.

Spartan discipline and Spartan military prowess—the Spartans were a professional army in a world of citizen militias and mercenary bands—elevated Sparta into a major power, far beyond what her size would otherwise have warranted. Her first and only unwavering concern was peace at home in the Peloponnese. This she never fully achieved, but she came near enough through the instrumentality of the Peloponnesian League. The League gave Sparta military assistance, and it was this help, together with armies from among the *perioeci*, which built her strength, in numerical terms, to major proportions. In the sixth century Sparta became beyond question the greatest Greek military force on land, and her allies provided adequate naval support too, until that arm was surpassed by the creation of the all-powerful Athenian fleet.

Yet the fact remains that, from the Persian Wars on, Spartan history is one of decline, despite her coalition victory (aided by Persian gold) over Athens in 404. Her xenophobic society was marked by a steadily decreasing population, for she stubbornly refused to recruit new citizens even when the need for manpower became desperate, preferring to arm freed helots, all sorts of social outcasts and even mercenaries. The Peloponnesian War put unbearable pressure not only on manpower but also on leadership: continuous campaigning by numbers of armies had not been provided for in the system, and some of the new commanders, most notably Lysander, who achieved the final victory, revealed no virtues other than ruthless military competence tied to ugly personal ambition. Lack of vision and mental inflexibility, whether in politics or social matters, proved most ruinous in times of success. Even Sparta's famed egalitarianism turned out to be incomplete and finally unworkable. Kings and commanders quarrelled frequently, among themselves or with the ephors, and the suspicion seems justified that the disagreements were not merely over tactics or policy. Abroad Spartans were quickly corrupted and unmanageable. The property system broke down, though we do not quite know how: an increasing number of Spartans lost their land allotments, held by them from the state and worked for them by helots, and with their land they automatically lost their status as full Spartiates. Others accumulated wealth, though that could be done only illegally. Herodotus suggests the widespread accessibility of Spartans to bribery as early as the beginning of the fifth century, with their kings commanding the highest price.

The Sparta which won the Peloponnesian War proved to be far more hollow than any contemporary could reasonably have guessed. In another decade her balanced constitution and her *eunomia* failed, and *stasis* struck, though only briefly. Then came the defeat by Thebes in 371. Thereafter, though Sparta still played a role in Greek politics, it was as a ghost of past glory. In a real crisis—as Philip of Macedon saw —she was only a minor state, like hundreds of others, no longer a serious force in the real world. And in the third century, finally and ironically, she virtually blew up in one of the most virulent civil wars in all Greek history. But the myth of Sparta was nevertheless strong and tenacious. The brilliance of Athens must not blot out the fact that there were Greeks (and men in all later ages too) for whom Sparta was the ideal. She was the model of the closed society, admired by those who rejected an open society with its factional politics, its acceptance of the *demos* as a political force, its frequent "lack of discipline," its recognition of the dignity and claims of the individual.

THE DECLINE OF THE POLIS

After the battle of Chaeronea in 338, Philip II of Macedon was effectively the master of Greece (excluding the Sicilian and other western Greeks). He then summoned all the states to a congress in Corinth, where a League of the Hellenes was founded, with the king as head and commander-in-chief, and with two objectives explicitly stated. One was an invasion of Persia on the remarkably thin pretext of getting revenge for the Persian desecration of Greek shrines 150 years earlier. The other was to employ the combined strength of the member states to insure, in the words of an anonymous writer later in the century (Pseudo-Demosthenes XVII 15), that in no city-state "shall there be execution or banishment contrary to the established laws of the *poleis*, nor confiscation of property, nor redistribution of land, nor cancellation of debts, nor freeing of slaves for purposes of revolution."

No single action could have summed up more completely the change that had come over Greek politics. *Stasis* had always been a threat, and sometimes a bitter reality, but never before had it been possible, or even thinkable, that the other Greek states, including Athens, should organize to maintain the status quo as a matter of general policy, not to be confused with intervention by one state, usually a more powerful one, in the internal affairs of another to protect its own state interests. Relations with Persia had had a chequered history, but now, as Isocrates, the most persistent and straight-talking propagandist of the war-of-revenge programme, revealed on more than one occasion in his pamphlets, invasion of the Persian Empire was proposed as the only way to save Greece from itself: to provide a cause which would divert the Greeks from fighting one another, to provide booty with which to fill empty public treasuries, and to open up territory for emigration. And the saviour, the man under whose hegemony all these great things were to be accomplished, was a despot and an outsider, at best an "honorary Hellene," whose own motives and interests, it need scarcely be said, were fundamentally not those of the Greeks he was to lead.

The success of Philip, repeated by his son Alexander, illustrated once again, and for the last time, the rule that the political difficulties which were rooted in the fragmentation of Hellas were susceptible only to an imposed solution, whether by a more powerful Greek state or by a powerful outsider. No one, not even the proponents of pan-Hellenic peace and coalition, suggested political integration of the city-states into larger units, for example. And no one was able to suggest, even hypothetically, how to overcome the poverty of natural resources and the low level of technology, except by moving out against Persia. Whenever in Greek history economic difficulties became critical, and that meant agrarian crisis, they were solved either by revolutionary means or by looking abroad, whether by emigration to new lands, as in the long colonization period, or by one or another form of pressure on other Greeks. Now, in the fourth century, the areas open to expansion abroad were severely restricted, and the relative weakness of the once great states gave much scope for intra-Hellenic warfare almost without end. Not even the sanctuaries were immune; in 356 the Phocians seized Delphi and used its treasure to hire a mercenary force of 10,000 and become for a fleeting moment the greatest military power in all Greece.

The available evidence suggests that in the period 399–375 there were never less than 25,000 Greek mercenaries in active service somewhere, and that later the figure rose to 50,000. The significance of these numbers is underscored by matching them against the low population figures as a whole, and by noticing how widely the mercenaries ranged, how indifferent they were to "national" considerations in their search for employment. The century opened with the most famous of all Greek mercenary armies, the "Ten Thousand" of Xenophon's *Anabasis* who marched east on behalf of the younger brother of the Persian king in his unsuccessful attempt to seize the throne. In 343 we find another 10,000 Greeks—1000 from Thebes, 3000 from Argos, and 6000 from Asia Minor—in the army with which the Persians recaptured Egypt for their empire.

Nor were mercenaries the only footloose Greeks at the time. The number of political exiles was very large too, though they cannot be counted: the story is inherently improbable that 20,000 of them assembled at the Olympic Games in 324 to hear read out Alexander's decree ordering the Greek states to accept the return of all exiles, but there is no reason to suspect the figure itself as a clue to how many exiles there were to be dealt with under the decree. Many more exiles, furthermore, were established in new homes and had no wish to return to the old. In the years immediately before Chaeronea, for example, the Corinthian Timoleon, following a spectacular campaign to clear Sicily of tyrants, recolonized a badly depleted Syracuse with volunteers from the Greek mainland and islands and even from Asia Minor. Tens of thousands apparently answered the call, some political exiles but no small number ordinary Greeks hoping to find a better livelihood.

All this movement, like the constant *stasis*, marked a failing of the community, and therefore of the *polis*. The more the *polis* had to hire its armed forces; the more citizens it could no longer satisfy economically, and that meant above all with land, so that they went elsewhere in order to live; the more it failed to maintain some sort of equilibrium between the few and the many; the more the cities were populated by outsiders, whether free migrants from abroad or emancipated slaves (who can be called metaphorically free migrants from within)—the less meaningful, the less real was the community. "Decline" is a tricky and dangerous word to use in this context: it has biological overtones which are inappropriate, and it evokes a continuous downhill movement in all aspects of civilization which is demonstrably false. Yet there is no escaping the evidence: the fourth century was the time when the Greek *polis* declined, unevenly, with bursts of recovery and heroic moments of struggle to save itself, to become, after Alexander, a sham *polis* in which the preservation of many external forms of *polis* life could not conceal that henceforth the Greeks lived, in Clemenceau's words, "in the sweet peace of decadence, accepting all sorts of servitudes as they came."

And again Athens was the exception. Her political system made extraordinary demands on the political skill and stability of her citizens and on their financial resources, which the loss of empire intensified many times over. It was no accident that several of her most important fourth-century leaders were experts in public finance, a theme which recurs persistently in the political speeches of Demosthenes. Or that so much diplomatic activity was concentrated on the Black Sea areas, where Athens was compelled to guarantee and protect her vital corn supplies by skill in diplomacy alone, now that she was no longer mistress of the Aegean in an imperial way. The final test was set by the Macedonians, and after years of understandable hesitation and debate the Athenian *demos* decided to fight for the independence of the *polis* (which is the same thing as saying the survival of the *polis*) and they almost succeeded. They failed, and then the end came rapidly, symbolized in a single action, the handing over in 322 of Demosthenes and a number of his colleagues to the Macedonians for execution.

Yet even fourth-century Athens was not free from signs of the general decline. Contemporary political commentators themselves made much of the fact that whereas right through the fifth century political leaders were, and were expected to be, military leaders at the same time, so that among the ten generals were regularly found the outstanding political figures (elected to the office because of their political importance, not the other way round), in the fourth century the two sides of public activity, the civil and the military, were separated. The generals were now professional soldiers, most of them quite outside politics or political influence, who often served foreign powers as mercenary commanders as well as serving their own *polis*. There are a number of reasons for the shift, among which the inadequate finances of the state rank high, but, whatever the explanation, the break was a bad thing for the *polis*, a cleavage in the responsibility of the members to their community which weakened the sense of community without producing visibly better generalship. In the navy the signs took a different form. A heavy share of the costs still fell on the richest 1200 men and the navy continued to perform well, but there was more evasion of responsibility, more need than before to compel the contributions and to pursue the defaulters at law. The crews themselves were often conscripted; voluntary enlistment could no longer provide the necessary complements. No doubt that was primarily because the treasury was too depleted to provide regular pay for long periods, just as the unwillingness of some to contribute their allotted share of the expenses resulted from an unsatisfactory system of distributing the burden, rather than from lack of patriotism. Wherever the responsibility lay, however, the result was again a partial breakdown in the *polis*.

There is no need to exaggerate: Athens nearly carried it off, and the end came because Macedon, or at least Alexander, was simply too powerful. But Macedon did exist, and so did Persia and Carthage, and later Rome. The *polis* was developed in such a world, not in a vacuum or in Cloud-Cuckoo-Land, and it grew on poor Greek soil. Was it really a viable form of political organization? Were its decline and disappearance the result of factors which could have been remedied, or of an accident—the power of Macedon—or of inherent structural weaknesses? These questions have exercised philosophers and historians ever since the late fifth century (and it is noteworthy how the problem was being posed long before the *polis* could be thought of as on its way out in any literal sense). Plato wished to rescue it by placing all authority in the hands of morally perfect philosophers. Others blame the *demos* and their misleaders, the demagogues, for every ill. Still others, especially in the past century or so, insist on the stupid failure to unite in a national state. For all their disparity, these solutions all have one thing in common: they all propose to rescue the *polis* by destroying it, by replacing it, in its root sense of a community which is at the same time a self-governing state, by something else. The *polis*, one concludes, was a brilliant conception, but one which required so rare a combination of material and institutional circumstances that it could never be realized; that it could be approximated only for a very brief period of time; that it had a past, a fleeting present, and no future. In that fleeting moment its members succeeded in capturing and recording, as man has not often done in his history, the greatness of which the human mind and spirit are capable.

Suggestions for Further Reading

BOWRA, C. M., *The Greek Experience*. London: Weidenfeld and Nicolson, 1957.

DICKINSON, G. LOWES, *The Greek View of Life*. New York: Collier Books, 1965.

DODDS, E. R., *The Greeks and the Irrational*. Berkeley: University of California Press, 1951.

EHRENBERG, VICTOR, *The Greek State*. London: Basil Blackwell, 1960.

FORREST, W. G., *The Emergence of Greek Democracy 800–400 B.C.* New York: McGraw-Hill, 1966.

JAEGER, WERNER, *Paideia: The Ideals of Greek Culture*, 2nd ed., 3 vols. New York: Oxford University Press, 1945.

JONES, A. H. M., *Athenian Democracy*. London: Basil Blackwell, 1957.

KITTO, H. D. F., *The Greeks*. Baltimore, Md.: Penguin Books, 1960.

STARR, CHESTER G., *The Ancient Greeks*. London: Oxford University Press, 1971.

RONALD SYME

The Crisis of the Roman Republic

✦✦✦ From the seventh decade B.C. to the final establishment of the new principate of Augustus Caesar in 23 B.C.,
the Roman Republic was wracked by a series of civil conflicts that ultimately brought about its extinction and the
creation of Caesarian imperial authority. What went wrong
with the Republic? Why did the old republican constitution
no longer resolve the power conflicts in Rome? By what
steps did Rome pass from Republic to Empire? There is no
more important question in the history of the ancient world,
and few subjects that can provide a stage on which is
played out a drama of the highest intensity with a cast of
characters so colossal in personality and so violent in conduct.

The fall of the Roman Empire and the triumph of Caesar-
ism, which inspired powerful rhetoric and great poetry
among Roman writers of the late first century B.C., is indeed
a drama so compelling that Shakespeare employed it for the
plots of two of his best historical dramas. It is a subject to
which superior historical minds have devoted themselves
from the time of Tacitus at the end of the first century A.D.
down through the Italian humanists of the Renaissance and
the scholars of the nineteenth century—especially the enormously learned German, Theodor Mommsen—to writers of
the twentieth century. Yet the definitive history of these
events, which has fundamentally reshaped our understand-

FROM Ronald Syme, *The Roman Revolution* (Oxford:
Clarendon Press, 1939), pp. 1–18, 54–60, 121–122, 512–522.

ing of the political and social framework of the Roman Republic, was not published until 1939. This book was *The Roman Revolution* by the Oxford scholar Ronald Syme. In the quarter of a century since the publication of Syme's work on the transition from Republic to Empire, his book has withstood the test of subsequent research and criticism and he appears to have penetrated into the realities of government and society in a convincing and realistic manner achieved by no previous writer who tried to understand the significance of the great Roman drama of the first century B.C. A young and still relatively little-known scholar when his controversial book appeared, Syme has now received the accolade of a knighthood and holds the eminently distinguished chair of ancient history at Oxford University.

In spite of, or perhaps because of, the deep feelings aroused by the crisis of the Republic, the sources the historian has to analyze in order to understand these events are difficult, fragmentary, and at times obscure. Nearly all the surviving political writings of the period are party propaganda, and very little remains of the writings of disinterested and unbiased observers. All historians dealing with this subject before Syme were led astray by the writers of the first centuries B.C. and A.D. who sought to make either heroes or villains of Julius and Augustus Caesar and who viewed the conflicts of the period 60–23 B.C. as the clash of irreconcilable ideals. Syme's achievement was principally that of penetrating the veil of party propaganda and personal apologetics which flowed freely from the pens of contemporary Roman writers and statesmen, and finding the root of the crisis in a ruthless struggle for power and wealth among competing groups of aristocratic families. His thesis, worked out in great detail with unequaled knowledge of aristocratic Roman family relationships, is that the Roman Republic, after it had conquered much of the Mediterranean world, became a prize too tempting for the noble families that had already enriched themselves with foreign booty. When there was very little in the world left to conquer, the aristocratic factions turned toward the seizure of the Roman state itself and fought each other with terrible ferocity, until in the end only the harsh, but ultimately beneficent,

Augustan peace could preserve order and stability in Italy. Power, wealth, family connections, and party loyalty— these were the mean but intensely compelling motives which inspired the famous leaders of the period and drove them to tear at one another until only Augustus Caesar was left. To the Roman aristocracy of the first century B.C. may be applied Tacitus' aphorism, "They make a desert and call it peace."

The coldly realistic, almost acerbic and bitter portrayal of the transition from Republic to Empire which Syme gives us was certainly influenced by the dismal experiences of Western society in the 1930's. Looking from a world dominated by Hitler, Mussolini, Stalin, and Neville Chamberlain, who could find high ideals and moral conduct in the European past? Although writers before Syme found at least one hero of high ideals and good faith in the assorted conflicts of the first century B.C., Syme's interpretation leaves no important leader with an unblemished reputation. Even the darling of the humanists, Cicero, is found to be a camp follower, and a rather inept one at that. More immediately, Syme's method and assumptions were heavily indebted to the studies of eighteenth-century English government and society published in the 1920's and 30's by L. B. Namier, a professor at the University of Manchester and later at London University. Just as in Namier's work the high idealism of Edmund Burke, the famous eighteenth-century English orator and political theorist, is regarded as very skillful propaganda for one of the aristocratic factions of Georgian England, so in Syme's book Cicero's rhetoric is found to be image-building in the interests of factional intrigue. Just as Namier was able to map out the crossroads of power in aristocratic England, so does Syme draw upon his mastery of family relationships in republican Rome to remove the surface gloss and show us the underlying structure of politics in the last decades of the Roman Republic, and it is not a pretty picture.

The magnitude of Syme's achievement and his fundamental revision of the historical understanding of a whole critical era in European history, following on Namier's contributions to English history, point to a necessary method for the political and social historian of the aristocratic, pre-

industrial era of European history. The public declarations
of statesmen and the eloquent doctrines of theorists must
continually be evaluated in the context of the ever-recurring
struggle for wealth and power among dominant, wide-
ranging, aristocratic connections.

◆§§◆

The greatest of the Roman historians [Tacitus] began his *Annals*
with the accession to the Principate of Tiberius, stepson and son by
adoption of Augustus, consort in his powers. Not until that day was
the funeral of the Free State consummated in solemn and legal ceremony. The corpse had long been dead. In common usage the reign of
Augustus is regarded as the foundation of the Roman Empire. The era
may be variously computed, from the winning of sole power by the last
of the dynasts through the War of Actium, from the ostensible restoration of the Republic in 27 B.C., or from the new act of settlement four
years later, which was final and permanent.

Outlasting the friends, the enemies and even the memory of his
earlier days, Augustus the Princeps, who was born in the year of
Cicero's consulate, lived to see the grandson of his granddaughter and
to utter a prophecy of empire concerning Galba, to whom the power
passed when the dynasty of the Julii and Claudii had ruled for a century. The ascension of Caesar's heir had been a series of hazards and
miracles: his constitutional reign as acknowledged head of the Roman
State was to baffle by its length and solidity all human and rational
calculation. It lasted for forty years. No astrologer or doctor could have
foretold that the frail youth would outlive, by a quarter of a century,
his ally and contemporary, the robust Agrippa; no schemer could have
counted in advance upon the deaths of his nephew Marcellus, of Drusus
his beloved stepson, of the young princes Gaius and Lucius, grandsons
of Augustus and heirs designate to the imperial succession. Such accidents of duration and fortune the future held. None the less, the main
elements in the party of Augustus and in the political system of the
Principate had already taken shape, firm and manifest, as early as the
year 23 B.C., so that a continuous narrative may run down to that date,
thence to diverge into a description of the character and working of
government.

'Pax et Princeps.' It was the end of a century of anarchy, culminating
in twenty years of civil war and military tyranny. If despotism was the
price, it was not too high: to a patriotic Roman of Republican senti-

ments even submission to absolute rule was a lesser evil than war between citizens. Liberty was gone, but only a minority at Rome had ever enjoyed it. The survivors of the old governing class, shattered in spirit, gave up the contest. Compensated by the solid benefits of peace and by the apparent termination of the revolutionary age, they were willing to acquiesce, if not actively to share, in the shaping of the new government which a united Italy and a stable empire demanded and imposed.

The rule of Augustus brought manifold blessings to Rome, Italy and the provinces. Yet the new dispensation, or 'novus status', was the work of fraud and bloodshed, based upon the seizure of power and redistribution of property by a revolutionary leader. The happy outcome of the Principate might be held to justify, or at least to palliate, the horrors of the Roman Revolution: hence the danger of an indulgent estimate of the person and acts of Augustus.

It was the avowed purpose of that statesman to suggest and demonstrate a sharp line of division in his career between two periods, the first of deplorable but necessary illegalities, the second of constitutional government. So well did he succeed that in later days, confronted with the separate persons of Octavianus the Triumvir, author of the proscriptions, and Augustus the Princeps, the beneficent magistrate, men have been at a loss to account for the transmutation, and have surrendered their reason to extravagant fancies. Julian the Apostate invoked philosophy to explain it. The problem does not exist: Julian was closer to the point when he classified Augustus as a chameleon. Colour changed, but not substance.

Contemporaries were not deceived. The convenient revival of Republican institutions, the assumption of a specious title, the change in the definition of authority, all that made no difference to the source and facts of power. Domination is never the less effective for being veiled. Augustus applied all the arts of tone and nuance with the sure ease of a master. The letter of the law might circumscribe the prerogative of the First Citizen. No matter: the Princeps stood pre-eminent, in virtue of prestige and authority tremendous and not to be defined. *Auctoritas* is the word—his enemies would have called it *potentia*. They were right. Yet the 'Restoration of the Republic' was not merely a solemn comedy, staged by a hypocrite.

Caesar was a logical man; and the heir of Caesar displayed coherence in thought and act when he inaugurated the proscriptions and when he sanctioned clemency, when he seized power by force, and when he based authority upon law and consent. The Dictatorship of Caesar, revived in the despotic rule of three Caesarian leaders, passed into the predominance of one man, Caesar's grand-nephew: for the security of his own position and the conduct of affairs the ruler had to devise a formula, revealing to the members of the governing class how they could cooperate in maintaining the new order, ostensibly as servants of the Republic and heirs to a great tradition, not as mere lieutenants of a military leader or subservient agents of arbitrary power. For that reason 'Dux' became 'Princeps'. He did not cease to be *Imperator Caesar.*

There is no breach in continuity. Twenty years of crowded history, Caesarian and Triumviral, cannot be annulled. When the individuals and classes that have gained wealth, honours and power through revolution emerge as champions of ordered government, they do not surrender anything. Neglect of the conventions of Roman political terminology and of the realities of Roman political life has sometimes induced historians to fancy that the Principate of Caesar Augustus was genuinely Republican in spirit and in practice—a modern and academic failing. Tacitus and Gibbon knew better. The narrative of Augustus' rise to supreme power, supplemented by a brief analysis of the working of government in the new order, will reinforce their verdict and reveal a certain unity in the character and policy of Triumvir, Dux and Princeps.

Whether the Princeps made atonement for the crime and violence of his earlier career is a question vain and irrelevant, cheerfully to be abandoned to the moralist or the casuist. The present inquiry will attempt to discover the resources and devices by which a revolutionary leader arose in civil strife, usurped power for himself and his faction, transformed a faction into a national party, and a torn and distracted land into a nation, with a stable and enduring government.

The tale has often been told, with an inevitability of events and culmination, either melancholy or exultant. The conviction that it all had to happen is indeed difficult to discard. Yet that conviction ruins the living interest of history and precludes a fair judgement upon the agents. They did not know the future.

Heaven and the verdict of history conspire to load the scales against the vanquished. Brutus and Cassius lie damned to this day by the futility of their noble deed and by the failure of their armies at Philippi; and the memory of Antonius is overwhelmed by the oratory of Cicero, by fraud and fiction, and by the catastrophe at Actium.

To this partisan and pragmatic interpretation of the Roman Revolution there stands a notable exception. To one of the unsuccessful champions of political liberty sympathy has seldom been denied. Cicero was a humane and cultivated man, an enduring influence upon the course of all European civilization: he perished a victim of violence and despotism. The fame and fate of Cicero, however, are one thing: quite different is the estimate of his political activity when he raised up Caesar's heir against Antonius. The last year of Cicero's life, full of glory and eloquence no doubt, was ruinous to the Roman People.

Posterity, generous in oblivion, regards with indulgence both the political orator who fomented civil war to save the Republic and the military adventurer who betrayed and proscribed his ally. The reason for such exceptional favour may be largely assigned to one thing—the influence of literature when studied in isolation from history. The writings of Cicero survive in bulk, and Augustus is glorified in the poetry of his age. Apart from flagrant scandal and gossip, there is a singular lack of adverse testimony from contemporary sources.

Yet for all that, the history of the whole revolutionary period could be written without being an apologia for Cicero or for Octavianus—or for both at once. A section of it was so written by C. Asinius Pollio, in a Roman and Republican spirit. That was tradition, inescapable. The Roman and the senator could never surrender his prerogative of liberty or frankly acknowledge the drab merits of absolute rule: writing of the transition from Republic to Monarchy, he was always of the opposition, whether passionate or fatalistic.

The art and practice of history demanded of its exponents, and commonly reveals in their works, a conformity to certain habits of thought and expression. The debt of Tacitus to Sallustius in style and colouring is evident enough: their affinity goes much deeper than words. Nor would it be rash to assert that Pollio was closely akin both to Sallustius and to Tacitus. All three sat in the Senate of Rome and governed provinces; new-comers to the senatorial aristocracy, they all became deeply imbued with the traditional spirit of that order; and all were preoccupied with the fall of *Libertas* and the defeat of the governing class. Though symbolized for all time in the Battle of Philippi, it was a long process, not a single act. Sallustius began his annalistic record with Sulla's death and the rise to power of Pompeius the Great. Pollio, however, chose the consulate of Metellus and Afranius, in which year the domination of that dynast was established (60 B.C.). Tacitus in his *Histories* told of a great civil war, the foundation of a new dynasty, and its degeneration into despotism; in his *Annals* he sought to demonstrate that the Principate of the Julii and Claudii was a tyranny, tracing year by year from Tiberius down to Nero the merciless extinction of the old aristocracy.

Pollio was a contemporary, in fact no small part of the transactions which he narrated—a commander of armies and an arbiter of high diplomacy; and he lived to within a decade of the death of Augustus. His character and tastes disposed him to be neutral in the struggle between Caesar and Pompeius—had neutrality been possible. Pollio had powerful enemies on either side. Compelled for safety to a decision, he chose Caesar, his personal friend; and with Caesar he went through the wars from the passage of the Rubicon to the last battle in Spain. Then he followed Antonius for five years. Loyal to Caesar, and proud of his loyalty, Pollio at the same time professed his attachment to free institutions, an assertion which his ferocious and proverbial independence of speech and habit renders entirely credible.

Pollio, the partisan of Caesar and of Antonius, was a pessimistic Republican and an honest man. Of tough Italic stock, hating pomp and pretence, he wrote of the Revolution as that bitter theme demanded, in a plain, hard style. It is much to be regretted that he did not carry his *History of the Civil Wars* through the period of the Triumvirate to the War of Actium and the Principate of Augustus: the work appears to have ended when the Republic went down at Philippi. That Pollio chose to write no further will readily be understood. As it was, his path was hazardous. The lava was still molten underneath. An enemy of Octavianus, Pollio had withdrawn from political life soon after 40 B.C., and he jealously maintained his independence. To tell the truth would have been inexpedient; and adulation was repugnant to his character. Another eminent historian was also constrained to omit the period of the Triumvirate when he observed that he could not treat his subject with freedom and with veracity. It was no other than Claudius, a pupil of Livy. His master had less exacting standards.

The great work of Pollio has perished, save for inconsiderable fragments or supposed borrowings in subsequent historians. None the less, the example of Pollio and the abundance of historical material (contemporary or going back to contemporary sources, often biased, it is true, but admitting criticism, interpretation, or disbelief) may encourage the attempt to record the story of the Roman Revolution and its sequel, the Principate of Caesar Augustus, in a fashion that has now become unconventional, from the Republican and Antonian side. The adulatory or the uncritical may discover in this design a depreciation of Augustus: his ability and greatness will all the more sharply be revealed by unfriendly presentation.

But it is not enough to redeem Augustus from panegyric and revive the testimony of the vanquished cause. That would merely substitute one form of biography for another. At its worst, biography is flat and schematic; at the best, it is often baffled by the hidden discords of human nature. Moreover, undue insistence upon the character and exploits of a single person invests history with dramatic unity at the expense of truth. However talented and powerful in himself, the Roman statesman cannot stand alone, without allies, without a following. That axiom holds both for the political dynasts of the closing age of the Republic and for their last sole heir—the rule of Augustus was the rule of a party, and in certain aspects his Principate was a syndicate. In truth, the one term presupposes the other. The career of the revolutionary leader is fantastic and unreal if told without some indication of the composition of the faction he led, of the personality, actions and influence of the principal among his partisans. In all ages, whatever the form and name of government, be it monarchy, republic or democracy, an oligarchy lurks behind the facade; and Roman history, Republican or Imperial, is the history of the governing class. The marshals, diplomats and financiers of the Revolution may be discerned again in the Republic of Augustus as the ministers and agents of power, the same men but in different garb. They are the government of the New State.

. . . . After Sulla's ordinances, a restored oligarchy of the *nobiles* held office at Rome. Pompeius fought against it; but Pompeius, for all his power, had to come to terms. Nor could Caesar have ruled without it. Coerced by Pompeius and sharply repressed by Caesar, the aristocracy was broken at Philippi. The parties of Pompeius and of Caesar had hardly been strong or coherent enough to seize control of the whole State and form a government. That was left to Caesar's heir, at the head of a new coalition, built up from the wreckage of other groups and superseding them all.

The policy and acts of the Roman People were guided by an oligarchy, its annals were written in an oligarchic spirit. History arose from the inscribed record of consulates and triumphs of the *nobiles,* from the transmitted memory of the origins, alliances and feuds of their families; and history never belied its beginnings. Of necessity the conception was narrow—only the ruling order could have any history at all and only the ruling city; only Rome, not Italy. In the Revolution the power of the old governing class was broken, its composition transformed. Italy and the non-political orders in society triumphed over Rome and the Roman aristocracy. Yet the old framework and categories subsist: a monarchy rules through an oligarchy.

Subject and treatment indicated, it remains to choose a date for the beginning. The breach between Pompeius and Caesar and the outbreak of war in 49 B.C. might appear to open the final act in the fall of the Roman Republic. That was not the opinion of their enemy Cato: he blamed the original alliance of Pompeius and Caesar. When Pollio set out to narrate the history of the Roman Revolution he began, not with the crossing of the Rubicon, but with the compact of 60 B.C., devised by the political dynasts Pompeius, Crassus and Caesar to control the State and secure the domination of the most powerful of their number.

. . . . The menace of despotic power hung over Rome like a heavy cloud for thirty years from the Dictatorship of Sulla to the Dictatorship of Caesar. It was the age of Pompeius the Great. Stricken by the ambitions, the alliances and the feuds of the dynasts, monarchic faction-leaders as they were called, the Free State perished in their open strife. Augustus is the heir of Caesar or of Pompeius, as you will. Caesar the Dictator bears the heavier blame for civil war. In truth, Pompeius was no better—'occultior non melior'. And Pompeius is in the direct line of Marius, Cinna and Sulla. It all seems inevitable, as though destiny ordained the succession of military tyrants.

In these last and fatal convulsions, disaster came upon disaster, ever more rapid. Three of the monarchic *principes* fell by the sword. Five civil wars and more in twenty years drained the life-blood of Rome and involved the whole world in strife and anarchy. Gaul and the West stood firm; but the horsemen of the Parthians were seen in Syria and on the western shore of Asia. The Empire of the Roman People, perishing of its own greatness, threatened to break and dissolve into separate kingdoms—or else a renegade, coming like a monarch out of the East, would subjugate Rome to an alien rule. Italy suffered devastation and sacking of cities, with proscription and murder of the best men; for the ambitions of the dynasts provoked war between class and class. Naked power prevailed.

The anger of Heaven against the Roman People was revealed in signal and continuous calamities: the gods had no care for virtue or justice, but intervened only to punish. Against the blind impersonal forces that drove the world to its doom, human forethought or human act was powerless. Men believed only in destiny and the inexorable stars.

In the beginning kings ruled at Rome, and in the end, as was fated, it came round to monarchy again. Monarchy brought concord. During the Civil Wars every party and every leader professed to be defending the cause of liberty and of peace. Those ideals were incompatible. When peace came, it was the peace of despotism. . . .

When the patricians expelled the kings from Rome, they were careful to retain the kingly power, vested in a pair of annual magistrates; and though compelled in time to admit the plebeians to political equality, certain of the great patrician houses, Valerii, Fabii and Cornelii, none the less held in turn a dynastic and almost regal position. The Senate again, being a permanent body, arrogated to itself power, and after conceding sovranty to the assembly of the People was able to frustrate its exercise. The two consuls remained at the head of the government, but policy was largely directed by ex-consuls. These men ruled, as did the Senate, not in virtue of written law, but through *auctoritas;* and the name of *principes civitatis* came suitably to be applied to the more prominent of the consulars.

The consulate did not merely confer power upon its holder and dignity for life: it ennobled a family for ever. Within the Senate, itself an oligarchy, a narrow ring, namely the *nobiles,* or descendants of consular houses, whether patrician or plebeian in origin, regarded the supreme magistracy as the prerogative of birth and the prize of ambition.

The patricians continued to wield an influence beyond all relation to their number; and the *nobiles,* though a wider class, formed yet a distinct minority in the Senate. The *nobiles* are predominant: yet in the last generation of the Free State, after the ordinances of Sulla the Dictator, there were many senators whose fathers had held only the lower magistracies or even new-comers, sons of Roman knights. Of the latter, in the main deriving from the local aristocracies, the holders of property, power and office in the towns of Italy, the proportion was clearly much higher than has sometimes been imagined. Of a total of six hundred senators the names of some four hundred can be identified, many of them obscure or casually known. The remainder have left no record of activity or fame in a singularly well-documented epoch of history.

Not mere admission to the Senate but access to the consulate was jealously guarded by the *nobiles.* It was a scandal and a pollution if a man without ancestors aspired to the highest magistracy of the Roman Republic—he might rise to the praetorship but no higher, save by a rare combination of merit, industry and protection. The *nobilitas* did not, it is true, stand like a solid rampart to bar all intruders. No need for that—the conservative Roman voter could seldom be induced to elect a man whose name had not been known for centuries as a part of the history of the Republic. Hence the *novus homo* (in the strict sense of the term the first member of a family to secure the consulate and consequent ennoblement) was a rare phenomenon at Rome. Before the sovran people he might boast how he had led them to victory in a mighty contest and had broken into the citadel of the nobility: he was less assertive in the Senate, more candid to his intimate friends. There was no breach in the walls—a faction among the *nobiles* had opened the gates. Cicero would have preserved both dignity and peace of mind had not ambition and vanity blinded him to the true causes of his own elevation.

The political life of the Roman Republic was stamped and swayed, not by parties and programmes of a modern and parliamentary character, not by the ostensible opposition between Senate and People, *Optimates* and *Populares, nobiles* and *novi homines,* but by the strife for power, wealth and glory. The contestants were the *nobiles* among themselves, as individuals or in groups, open in the elections and in the courts of law, or masked by secret intrigue. As in its beginning, so in its last generation, the Roman Commonwealth, 'res publica populi Romani', was a name; a feudal order of society still survived in a city-state and governed an empire. Noble families determined the history of the Republic, giving their names to its epochs. There was an age of the Scipiones: not less of the Metelli.

. . . Three weapons the *nobiles* held and wielded, the family, money and the political alliance (*amicitia* or *factio,* as it was variously labelled). The wide and remembered ramifications of the Roman noble clan won concentrated support for the rising politician. The *nobiles* were dynasts, their daughters princesses. Marriage with a well-connected heiress therefore became an act of policy and an alliance of powers, more important than a magistracy, more binding than any compact of oath or interest. Not that women were merely the instruments of masculine policy. Far from it: the daughters of the great houses commanded political influence in their own right, exercising a power beyond the reach of many a senator. Of such dominating forces behind the phrases and the façade of constitutional government the most remarkable was Servilia, Cato's half-sister, Brutus' mother—and Caesar's mistress.

The noble was a landed proprietor, great or small. But money was scarce and he did not wish to sell his estates: yet he required ready cash at every turn, to support the dignity of his station, to flatter the populace with magnificence of games and shows, to bribe voters and jurors, to subsidize friends and allies. Hence debts, corruption and venality at Rome, oppression and extortion in the provinces. Crassus was in the habit of observing that nobody should be called rich who was not able to maintain an army on his income. Crassus should have known.

The competition was fierce and incessant. Family influence and wealth did not alone suffice. From ambition or for safety, politicians formed compacts. *Amicitia* was a weapon of politics, not a sentiment based on congeniality. Individuals capture attention and engross history, but the most revolutionary changes in Roman politics were the work of families or of a few men. A small party, zealous for reform—or rather, perhaps, from hostility to Scipio Aemilianus—put up the tribune Ti. Sempronius Gracchus. The Metelli backed Sulla. The last dynastic compact in 60 B.C. heralded the end of the Free State; and a re-alignment of forces precipitated war and revolution ten years later.

Amicitia presupposes *inimicitia*, inherited or acquired: a statesman could not win power and influence without making many enemies. The *novus homo* had to tread warily. Anxious not to offend a great family, he must shun where possible the role of prosecutor in the law-courts and win gratitude by the defence even of notorious malefactors. The *nobilis*, however, would take pride in his feuds. Yet he had ever to be on the alert, jealous to guard his *dignitas*, that is, rank, prestige and honour, against the attacks of his personal enemies. The plea of security and self-defence against aggression was often invoked by a politician when he embarked upon a course of unconstitutional action.

The dynast required allies and supporters, not from his own class only. The sovran people of a free republic conferred its favours on whom it pleased. Popularity with the plebs was therefore essential. It was possessed in abundance both by Caesar and by his bitter enemy, L. Domitius Ahenobarbus. To win a following at elections, to manage bribery, intimidation or rioting, the friendly offices of lowly agents such as influential freedmen were not despised. Above all, it was necessary to conciliate the second order in state and society, the Roman knights, converted into a ruinous political force by the tribune C. Gracchus when he set them in control of the law-courts and in opposition to the Senate. The *Equites* belonged, it is true, to the same social class as the great bulk of the senators: the contrast lay in rank and prestige.

The knights preferred comfort, secret power and solid profit to the burdens, the dangers and the extravagant display of a senator's life. Cicero, a knight's son from a small town, succumbed to his talents and his ambition. Not so T. Pomponius Atticus, the great banker. Had Atticus so chosen, wealth, repute and influence could easily have procured a seat in the Senate. But Atticus did not wish to waste his money on senseless luxury or electoral corruption, to risk station, fortune and life in futile political contests. Averse from ambition and wedded to quiet, the knights could claim no title of civic virtue, no share in the splendour and pride of the governing class. For that surrender they were scorned by senators. They did not mind. Some lived remote and secure in the enjoyment of hereditary estates, content with the petty dignity of municipal office in the towns of Italy. Others, however, grasped at the spoils of empire, as *publicani* in powerful companies farming the taxes of the provinces and as bankers dominating finance, commerce and industry. The *publicani* were the fine flower of the equestrian order, the ornament and bulwark of the Roman State. Cicero never spoke against these 'homines honestissimi' and never let them down: they were in the habit of requiting his services by loans or legacies.

The gains of finance went into land. Men of substance and repute grew yet richer from the spoils of the provinces, bought the farms of small peasants, encroached upon public land, seized through mortgages the ancestral property of senators, and thus built up large estates in Italy. Among senators were great holders of property like Pompeius and Ahenobarbus with whole armies of tenants or slaves, and financial magnates like Crassus. But the wealth of knights often outstripped many an ancient senatorial family, giving them a greater power than the nominal holders of dignity and office.

Equestrian or senatorial, the possessing classes stood for the existing order and were suitably designated as *boni*. The mainstay of this sacred army of the wealthy was clearly the financiers. Many senators were their partners, allies or advocates. Concord and firm alliance between Senate and knights would therefore arrest revolution—or even reform, for these men could not be expected to have a personal interest in redistributing property or changing the value of money. The financiers were strong enough to ruin any politician or general who sought to secure fair treatment for provincials or reform in the Roman State through the re-establishment of the peasant farmer. Among the victims of their enmity will be reckoned Lucullus, Catilina and Gabinius.

It was no accident, no mere manifestation of Roman conservatism or snobbery, that the leaders of revolution in Rome were usually impoverished or idealistic nobles, that they found support in the higher ranks of the aristocracy rather than in the lower. It is all too easy to tax the Roman nobility in the last epoch of its rule with vice and corruption, obscurantism and oppression. The knights must not be left out of the indictment. Among the old nobility persisted a tradition of service to the State that could transcend material interests and combine class-loyalty with a high ideal of Roman patriotism and imperial responsibility. Not so among the financiers.

The Roman constitution was a screen and a sham. Of the forces that lay behind or beyond it, next to the noble families the knights were the most important. Through alliance with groups of financiers, through patronage exercised in the law-courts and ties of personal allegiance contracted in every walk of life, the political dynast might win influence not merely in Rome but in the country-towns of Italy and in regions not directly concerned with Roman political life. Whether he held authority from the State or not, he could thus raise an army on his own initiative and resources.

The soldiers, now recruited from the poorest classes in Italy, were ceasing to feel allegiance to the State; military service was for livelihood, or from constraint, not a natural and normal part of a citizen's duty. The necessities of a world-empire and the ambition of generals led to the creation of extraordinary commands in the provinces. The general had to be a politician, for his legionaries were a host of clients, looking to their leader for spoil in war and estates in Italy when their campaigns were over. But not veterans only were attached to his cause—from his provincial commands the dynast won to his allegiance and personal following (*clientela*) towns and whole regions, provinces and nations, kings and tetrarchs.

Such were the resources which ambition required to win power in Rome and direct the policy of the imperial Republic as consul or as one of the *principes*. Cicero lacked the full equipment. He imagined that oratory and intrigue would suffice. A programme, it is true, he developed, negative but by no means despicable. It was an alliance of interest and sentiment to combat the forces of dissolution represented by the army-commanders and their political agents. . . . But it was an ideal rather than a programme: there was no Ciceronian party. The Roman politician had to be the leader of a faction. Cicero fell short of that eminence both when a consul and when a consular, or senior statesman, through lack of family-connexions and *clientela*.

Within the framework of the Roman constitution, besides the consulate, was another instrument of power, the tribunate, an anomalous historical survival given new life by the party of the Gracchi and converted into a means of direct political action, negative with the veto, positive with the initiation of laws. The use of this weapon in the

interests of reform or of personal ambition became a mark of the politicians who arrogated to themselves the name of *populares*—often sinister and fraudulent, no better than their rivals, the men in power, who
naturally invoked the specious and venerable authority of the Senate.
But there were to be found in their ranks a few sincere reformers,
enemies of misrule and corruption, liberal in outlook and policy. Moreover, the tribunate could be employed for conservative ends by aristocratic demagogues.

With the Gracchi all the consequences of empire—social, economic
and political—broke loose in the Roman State, inaugurating a century
of revolution. The traditional contests of the noble families were complicated, but not abolished, by the strife of parties largely based on
economic interest, of classes even, and of military leaders. Before long
the Italian allies were dragged into Roman dissensions. The tribune
M. Livius Drusus hoped to enlist them on the side of the dominant
oligarchy. He failed, and they rose against Rome in the name of freedom
and justice. On the *Bellum Italicum* supervened civil war. The party led
by Marius, Cinna and Carbo was defeated. L. Cornelius Sulla prevailed
and settled order at Rome again through violence and bloodshed. Sulla
decimated the knights, muzzled the tribunate, and curbed the consuls.
But even Sulla could not abolish his own example and preclude a successor to his domination.

Sulla resigned power after a brief tenure. Another year and he was
dead (78 B.C.). The government which he established lasted for nearly
twenty years. Its rule was threatened at the outset by a turbulent and
ambitious consul, M. Aemilius Lepidus, claiming to restore the rights
of the tribunes and supported by a resurgence of the defeated causes in
Italy. The tribunes were only a pretext, but the Marian party—the
proscribed and the dispossessed—was a permanent menace. The long
and complicated war in Italy had barely ended. The Samnites, Sulla's
enemy and Rome's, had been extirpated; and the other Sabellic peoples
of the Apennine were broken and reduced. But Eturia, despoiled and
resentful, rose again for Lepidus against the Roman oligarchy.

Lepidus was suppressed. But disorders continued, even to a rising of
the slaves in southern Italy. Then a *coup d'état* of two generals (70 B.C.),
restoring the tribunate, destroyed Sulla's system but left the *nobiles*
nominally in power. They were able to repel and crush the attempt of
the patrician demagogue L. Sergius Catilina to raise a revolution in Italy
—for Catilina attacked property as well as privilege. The government
of the *nobiles*, supported by a sacred union of the possessing classes,

by the influence of their *clientela* among the plebs and by due subservience towards the financial interests, might have perpetuated in
Rome and Italy its harsh and hopeless rule. The Empire broke it.

The repercussions of the ten years' war in Italy echoed over all the
world. The Senate was confronted by continuous warfare in the provinces and on the frontiers of its wide and cumbersome dominion—
against Sertorius and the last survivors of the Marian faction in Spain,
against the great Mithridates and against the Pirates. Lack of capacity
among the principal members of the ruling group, or, more properly,
personal ambition and political intrigue, constrained them, in mastering
these manifold dangers, to derogate from oligarchic practice and confer
exorbitant military power on a single general, to the salvation of Rome's
empire and to their own ruin.

As an oligarchy is not a figment of political theory, a specious fraud,
or a mere term of abuse, but very precisely a collection of individuals,
its shape and character, so far from fading away on close scrutiny, at
once stands out, solid and manifest. In any age of the history of Republican Rome about twenty or thirty men, drawn from a dozen dominant families, hold a monopoly of office and power. From time to time,
families rise and fall: as Rome's rule extends in Italy, the circle widens
from which the nobility is recruited and renewed. None the less, though
the composition of the oligarchy is slowly transformed with the transformation of the Roman State, the manner and fashion of dynastic
politics changes but little; and though noble houses suffered defeat in
the struggle for power, and long eclipse, they were saved from extinction by the primitive tenacity of the Roman family and the pride of their
own traditions. They waited in patience to assert their ancient predominance.

*   *   *   *   *

In its treatment of Caesar the inspired literature of the Augustan
Principate is consistent and instructive. Though in different words,
Virgil, Horace and Livy tell the same tale and point the same moral.

Yet speculation cannot be debarred from playing round the high and
momentous theme of the last designs of Caesar the Dictator. It has been
supposed and contended that Caesar either desired to establish or had
actually inaugurated an institution unheard of in Rome and unimagined
there—monarchic rule, despotic and absolute, based upon worship of
the ruler, after the pattern of the monarchies of the Hellenistic East.
Thus may Caesar be represented as the heir in all things of Alexander

the Macedonian and as the anticipator of Caracalla, a king and a god incarnate, levelling class and nation, ruling a subject, united and uniform world by right divine.

This extreme simplification of long and diverse ages of history seems to suggest that Caesar alone of contemporary Roman statesmen possessed either a wide vision of the future or a singular and elementary blindness to the present. But this is only a Caesar of myth or rational construction, a lay-figure set up to point a contrast with Pompeius or Augustus—as though Augustus did not assume a more than human name and found a monarchy, complete with court and hereditary succession; as though Pompeius, the conqueror of the East and of every continent, did not exploit for his own vanity the resemblance to Alexander in warlike fame and even in bodily form. Caesar was a truer Roman than either of them.

The complete synthesis in the person of Caesar of hereditary monarchy and divine worship is difficult to establish on the best of contemporary evidence, the voluminous correspondence of Cicero. Moreover, the whole theme of divine honours is fertile in misunderstandings. After death Caesar was enrolled among the gods of the Roman State by the interested device of the leaders of the Caesarian party. It might appear that subsequent accounts have been guilty of attributing a part at least of the cult of *Divus Julius* to that very different person, Caesar the Dictator.

The rule of Caesar could well be branded as monarchy on a partisan or conventional estimate. The terms 'rex' and 'regnum' belong to the vocabulary of Roman political invective, applicable alike to the domination of Sulla and the arbitrary power exercised by Cicero during his consulate—for the new man from Arpinum was derided as 'the first foreign king at Rome since the Tarquinii'. It was to silence rumour that Caesar made an ostentatious refusal of the diadem at a public ceremony. 'Caesarem se, non regem esse.' Beyond doubt the Dictator's powers were as considerable as those of a monarch. Caesar would have been the first to admit it: he needed neither the name nor the diadem. But monarchy presupposes hereditary succession, for which no provision was made by Caesar. The heir to Caesar's name, his grand-nephew, attracted little attention at the time of his first appearance in Rome. The young man had to build up a faction for himself and make his own way along the road to power, beginning as a military demagogue.

If Caesar must be judged, it is by facts and not by alleged intentions. As his acts and his writings reveal him, Caesar stands out as a realist and an opportunist. In the short time at his disposal he can hardly have made plans for a long future or laid the foundation of a consistent government. Whatever it might be, it would owe more to the needs of the moment than to alien or theoretical models. More important the business in hand: it was expedited in swift and arbitrary fashion. Caesar made plans and decisions in the company of his intimates and secretaries: the Senate voted but did not deliberate. As the Dictator was on the point of departing in the spring of 44 B.C. for several years of campaigning in the Balkans and the East, he tied up magistracies and provincial commands in advance by placing them, according to the traditional Roman way, in the hands of loyal partisans, or of reconciled Pompeians whose good sense should guarantee peace. For that period, at least, a salutary pause from political activity: with the lapse of time the situation might become clearer in one way or another.

At the moment it was intolerable: the autocrat became impatient, annoyed by covert opposition, petty criticism and laudations of dead Cato. That he was unpopular he well knew. 'For all his genius, Caesar could not see a way out', as one of his friends was subsequently to remark. And there was no going back. To Caesar's clear mind and love of rapid decision, this brought a tragic sense of impotence and frustration—he had been all things and it was no good. He had surpassed the good fortune of Sulla Felix and the glory of Pompeius Magnus. In vain —reckless ambition had ruined the Roman State and baffled itself in the end. Of the melancholy that descended upon Caesar there stands the best of testimony—'my life has been long enough, whether reckoned in years or in renown.' The words were remembered. The most eloquent of his contemporaries did not disdain to plagiarize them.

The question of ultimate intentions becomes irrelevant. Caesar was slain for what he was, not for what he might become. The assumption of a Dictatorship for life seemed to mock and dispel all hope of a return to normal and constitutional government. His rule was far worse than the violent and illegal domination of Pompeius. The present was unbearable, the future hopeless. It was necessary to strike at once—absence, the passage of time and the solid benefits of peace and order might abate men's resentment against Caesar, insensibly disposing their minds to servitude and monarchy. A faction recruited from the most diverse elements planned and carried out the assassination of the Dictator.

That his removal would be no remedy but a source of greater ills to the Commonwealth, the Dictator himself observed. His judgement was vindicated in blood and suffering; and posterity has seen fit to condemn the act of the Liberators, for so they were styled, as worse than a crime —a folly. The verdict is hasty and judges by results. It is all too easy to label the assassins as fanatic adepts of Greek theories about the supreme virtue of tyrannicide, blind to the true nature of political catchwords and the urgent needs of the Roman State. The character and pursuits of Marcus Brutus, the representative figure in the conspiracy, might lend plausible colouring to such a theory. Yet it is in no way evident that the nature of Brutus would have been very different had he never opened a book of Stoic or Academic philosophy. Moreover, the originator of the plot, the dour and military Cassius, was of the Epicurean persuasion and by no means a fanatic. As for the tenets of the Stoics, they could support doctrines quite distasteful to Roman Republicans, namely monarchy or the brotherhood of man. The Stoic teaching, indeed, was nothing more than a corroboration and theoretical defence of certain traditional virtues of the governing class in an aristocratic and republican state. Hellenic culture does not explain Cato; and the *virtus* about which Brutus composed a volume was a Roman quality, not an alien importation.

The word means courage, the ultimate virtue of a free man. With *virtus* go *libertas* and *fides*, blending in a proud ideal of character and conduct—constancy in purpose and act, independence of habit, temper and speech, honesty and loyalty. Privilege and station imposed duties, to family, class and equals in the first place, but also towards clients and dependents. No oligarchy could survive if its members refused to abide by the rules, to respect 'liberty and the laws'.

To his contemporaries, Marcus Brutus, firm in spirit, upright and loyal, in manner grave and aloof, seemed to embody that ideal of character, admired by those who did not care to imitate. His was not a simple personality—but passionate, intense and repressed. Nor was his political conduct wholly to be predicted. Brutus might well have been a Caesarian—neither he nor Caesar were predestined partisans of Pompeius. Servilia reared her son to hate Pompeius, schemed for the Caesarian alliance and designed that Brutus should marry Caesar's daughter. Her plan was annulled by the turn of events in the fatal consulate of Metellus. Caesar was captured by Pompeius: Julia, the bride intended for Brutus, pledged the alliance.

After this the paths of Brutus and of Caesar diverged sharply for eleven years. But Brutus, after Pharsalus, at once gave up a lost cause, receiving pardon from Caesar, high favour, a provincial command and finally the praetorship in 44 B.C. Yet Cato, no sooner dead, asserted the old domination over his nephew more powerfully than ever in life. Brutus came to feel shame for his own disloyalty: he composed a pamphlet in honour of the Republican who died true to his principles and to his class. Then he strengthened the family tie and obligation of vengeance yet further by divorcing his Claudia and marrying his cousin Porcia, Bibulus' widow. No mistake about the meaning of that act; and Servilia disapproved. There were deeper causes still in Brutus' resolve to slay the tyrant—envy of Caesar and the memory of Caesar's amours with Servilia, public and notorious. Above all, to Brutus as to Cato, who stood by the ancient ideals, it seemed that Caesar, avid for splendour, glory and power, ready to use his birth and station to subvert his own class, was an ominous type, the monarchic aristocrat, recalling the kings of Rome and fatal to any Republic.

Brutus and his allies might invoke philosophy or an ancestor who had liberated Rome from the Tarquinii, the first consul of the Republic and founder of *Libertas*. Dubious history—and irrelevant. The Liberators knew what they were about. Honourable men grasped the assassin's dagger to slay a Roman aristocrat, a friend and a benefactor, for better reasons than that. They stood, not merely for the traditions and the institutions of the Free State, but very precisely for the dignity and the interests of their own order. Liberty and the laws are high-sounding words. They will often be rendered, on a cool estimate, as privilege and vested interests.

It is not necessary to believe that Caesar planned to establish at Rome a 'Hellenistic Monarchy', whatever meaning may attach to that phrase. The Dictatorship was enough. The rule of the *nobiles*, he could see, was an anachronism in a world-empire; and so was the power of the Roman plebs when all Italy enjoyed the franchise. Caesar in truth was more conservative and Roman than many have fancied; and no Roman conceived of government save through an oligarchy. But Caesar was being forced into an autocratic position. It meant the lasting domination of one man instead of the rule of the law, the constitution and the Senate; it announced the triumph soon or late of new forces and new ideas, the elevation of the army and the provinces, the depression of the traditional governing class. Caesar's autocracy appeared to be much more than a temporary expedient to liquidate the heritage of the Civil War and reinvigorate the organs of the Roman State. It was going to last—and the Roman aristocracy was not to be permitted to govern and exploit the Empire in its own fashion. The tragedies of history do not arise from the conflict of conventional right and wrong. They are more august and more complex. Caesar and Brutus each had right on his side.

The new party of the Liberators was not homogeneous in origin or in motive. The resentment of pardoned Pompeians, thwarted ambition, personal feuds and personal interest masked by the profession of high principle, family tradition and the primacy of civic over private virtue, all these were in the game. Yet in the forefront of this varied company stood trusted officers of the Dictator, the generals of the Gallic and Civil Wars, rewarded already for service or designated to high office. Their coalition with Pompeians and Republicans calls for explanation.

Without a party a statesman is nothing. He sometimes forgets that awkward fact. If the leader or principal agent of a faction goes beyond the wishes of his allies and emancipates himself from control, he may have to be dropped or suppressed. The reformer Ti. Gracchus was put up by a small group of influential consulars. These prudent men soon refused further support to the rash, self-righteous tribune when he plunged into illegal courses. The political dynast Crassus used Catilina as his agent. Catilina could not, or would not, understand that reform or revolution had no place in the designs of his employer. Crassus drew back, and Catilina went on, to his ruin.

When Caesar took the Dictatorship for life and the sworn allegiance of senators, it seemed clear that he had escaped from the shackles of party to supreme and personal rule. For this reason, certain of the most prominent of his adherents combined with Republicans and Pompeians to remove their leader. The Caesarian party thus split by the assassination of the Dictator none the less survived, joined for a few months with Republicans in a new and precarious front of security and vested interests led by the Dictator's political deputy until a new leader, emerging unexpected, at first tore it in pieces again, but ultimately, after conquering the last of his rivals, converted the old Caesarian party into a national government in a transformed State. The composition and vicissitudes of that party, though less dramatic in unity of theme than the careers and exploits of the successive leaders, will yet help to recall the ineffable complexities of authentic history.

*   *   *   *   *

Lessons might indeed be learned, but from men and affairs, from predecessors and rivals, from the immediate and still tangible past. The young Pompeius had grasped at once the technique of raising a private army, securing official recognition—and betraying his allies. Caesar, more consistent in his politics, had to wait longer for distinction and power. The sentiments which the young man entertained towards his adoptive parent were never revealed. The whole career of the Dictator, however, showed the fabulous harvest to be got soon or late from the cultivation of the plebs and the soldiers. Not less the need for faithful friends and a coherent party. For lack of that, the great Pompeius had been forced at the last into a fatal alliance with his enemies the oligarchs. Caesar had been saved because he had a party behind him. It was clear that many a man followed Caesar in an impious war from personal friendship, not political principle. The devotion which Caesar's memory evoked among his friends was attested by impressive examples; and it was not merely from lust of adventure or of gain that certain intimate friends of the dead autocrat at once lent their support and devotion to his son and heir. Loyalty could only be won by loyalty in return. Caesar never let down a friend, whatever his character and station. Antonius imitated his leader—which came easy to his open nature: Octavianus also, though less easily perhaps. Only two of his associates, so it was recorded, were ever thrown over, and that was for treachery.

Next to magnanimity, courage. By nature, the young man was cool and circumspect: he knew that personal courage was often but another name for rashness. But the times called for daring and the example of Caesar taught him to run risks gaily, to insist upon his prestige, his honour, the rights due to his name and station. But not to excess: Octavianus took a firm stand upon *dignitas* without dangerous indulgence in chivalry or clemency; he perfected himself in the study of political cant and the practice of a dissimulation that had been alien to the splendid and patrician nature of Caesar. He soon took the measure of Antonius: the Caesarian soldier was a warning against the more generous virtues and vices. Another eminent Roman could furnish a text in the school of politics. The failure of Cicero as a statesman showed the need for courage and constancy in all the paths of duplicity. A change of front in politics is not disastrous unless caused by delusion or indecision. The treacheries of Octavianus were conscious and consistent.

To assert himself against Antonius, the young revolutionary needed an army in the first place, after that, Republican allies and constitutional backing. He would then have to postpone the avenging of Caesar until he was strong enough, built up by Republican help, to betray the Republicans. The calculation was hazardous but not hopeless—on the other side, certain moderates and Republicans might be lured and captured by the genial idea of employing the name of Caesar and the arms of Octavianus to subvert the domination of Antonius, and so destroy the Caesarian party, first Antonius, then Octavianus. But before such respectable elements could venture openly to advocate sedition, violence and civil war, Octavianus would have to take the lead and act.

*   *   *   *   *

More reputable and more independent characters than Dellius and Plancus were Messalla and Pollio, the consular patrons of Augustan literature, themselves no mean part of it. The Roman patrician and the Italian *novus homo* alike had salvaged honour and fame, yet had done well for themselves and their families. Messalla changed sides, passing to Antonius after Philippi and from Antonius before long to Octavianus. Along with Agrippa, Messalla occupied the house of Antonius on the Palatine. Pollio had been more intractable during the Civil Wars, the only neutral in the campaign of Actium; he retained his 'ferocia' under the New State. Pollio hated Plancus and composed a memoir to be published after Plancus' death; and it was Messalla who coined as a title for Dellius the phrase 'desultor bellorum civilium'. Yet, on a cool estimate, Pollio as well as Messalla will be reckoned among the profiteers of the Revolution. Enriched by both sides, Pollio augmented the dignity as well as the fortunes of his family. Pollio's son Gallus married Vipsania, his daughter the son of a nobleman, almost the last of the Marcelli. He should have had nothing to complain of under the new dispensation. Pollio himself lived on to a decade before the death of Augustus, tough and lively to the end, Messalla with failing powers until A.D. 13.

In his life and in his writings Pollio professed an unswerving devotion to *Libertas*. But *Libertas* was destroyed when *Virtus* was shattered at Philippi. Political liberty, it could be maintained, was doomed if not dead long before that. Pollio knew the bitter truth about the last generation of the Free State. The historian Tacitus, commenting on the stability of the new régime when the power was to pass from Augustus to Tiberius, remarks that few men were still alive that remembered the Republic—'quotus quisque reliquus qui rem publicam vidisset?' His purpose was expressly to deny the Republic of Augustus, not to rehabilitate anarchy, the parent of despotism.

The rule of law had perished long ago, with might substituted for right. The contest for power in the Free State was splendid and terrible. . . . The *nobiles*, by their ambition and their feuds, had not merely destroyed their spurious Republic: they had ruined the Roman People.

There is something more important than political liberty; and political rights are a means, not an end in themselves. That end is security of life and property: it could not be guaranteed by the constitution of Republican Rome. Worn and broken by civil war and disorder, the Roman People was ready to surrender the ruinous privilege of freedom and submit to strict government as in the beginning of time. . . .

So order came to Rome. . . . The New State might be called monarchy, or by any other name. That did not matter. Personal rights and private status need not depend upon the form of government. And even though hereditary succession was sternly banished from the theory of the Principate, every effort was made to apply it in practice, for fear of something worse: sober men might well ponder on the apparent ridicule and solid advantages of hereditary monarchy.

Under the new order, the Commonwealth was no longer to be a playground for politicians, but in truth a *res publica*. Selfish ambition and personal loyalties must give way before civic duty and national patriotism. With the Principate, it was not merely Augustus and his party that prevailed—it meant the victory of the non-political classes. They could be safe and happy at last. . . . No longer was the proletariat of Italy pressed into the legions to shed its blood for ambitious generals or spurious principles, no longer were the peaceful men of property to be driven into taking sides in a quarrel not their own or mulcted of their lands for the benefit of the legions. That was over. The Republic was something that a prudent man might admire but not imitate. . . .

Even among the *nobiles* there can have been few genuine Republicans in the time of Augustus; and many of the *nobiles* were inextricably bound up with the New State, being indebted to it for their preservation and standing. As more and more sons of Roman knights passed by patronage into the ranks of the governing class, the conviction not merely of the inevitability but also of the benefits of the system must have become more widely diffused in the Senate. Yet while this process was going on, the Republic itself became the object of a sentimental cult, most fervently practised among the members of the class that owed everything to the Empire. The senator Helvidius Priscus, the son of a centurion, may have been sincere in his principles: but the Roman knight who filled his house with the statues of Republican heroes was a snob as well as a careerist.

The Republican profession was not so much political as social and moral: it was more often a harmless act of homage to the great past of Rome than a manifestation of active discontent with the present state of affairs. It need not be taken as seriously as it was by suspicious emperors or by artful and unscrupulous prosecutors. While the Republic still maintained for a season its formal and legal existence, there had been deception enough in the assertion of Republicanism. With monarchy now firmly based in habit and theory as well as in fact, the very absence of any alternative form of rule was an encouragement to the more irresponsible type of serious-minded person. No danger that they would be challenged to put their ideals into practice.

The Republic, with its full record of great wars abroad and political dissensions at home, was a splendid subject for history. Well might Tacitus look back with melancholy and complain that his own theme was dull and narrow. But the historian who had experienced one civil war in his own lifetime, and the threat of another, did not allow his judgement entirely to be blinded by literary and sentimental conventions. Like Sallustius and Pollio, he had no illusions about the Republic. The root of the trouble lay in the nature of man, turbid and restless, with noble qualities as well as evil—the strife for liberty, glory or domination. Empire, wealth and individual ambition had ruined the Republic long ago. Marius and Sulla overthrew *libertas* by force of arms and established *dominatio*. Pompeius was no better. After that, only a contest for supreme power. Tacitus does not even admit a restoration of the Free State if Brutus and Cassius had prevailed at Philippi. Such as the conventional and vulgar opinion: Tacitus himself would have thought it impossible after a civil war.

Like the historian, the student of oratory was tempted to regret the grand and untrammelled eloquence of the closing days of the Republic. He might pause when he reflected that great oratory is a symptom of decay and disorder, both social and political. Electoral corruption, extortion in the provinces and the execution of Roman citizens furnished great themes and orators to match. By definition, the best form of state was spared these evils. Well-ordered commonwealths, lacking that 'licence which fools call liberty', left no record in the annals of eloquence. Not so Athens and Rhodes—they were democracies, and deplorably so. Rome too, so long as Rome was on the wrong path, produced vigorous oratory. There were the Gracchi and Cicero—but was it worth it?

The admirer of ancient eloquence could not have the advantage both ways, enjoying both Republican liberty and the benefits of an ordered state. Nor was there need for orators any more, for long speeches in the Senate or before the People, when one man had the supreme decision in the Commonwealth, and he the wisest. . . .

Tacitus is a monarchist, from perspicacious despair of human nature. There was no escape. Despite the nominal sovranty of law, one man ruled. This is his comment on Tiberius. It was no less true of the Principate of Augustus—rather more so. To be sure, the State was organized under a principate—no dictatorship or monarchy. Names did not matter much. Before long the eloquent Seneca, when counselling the young Nero to clemency, could employ with indifference the names of 'rex' or 'princeps', the more so because a respectable tradition of philosophic thought held monarchy to be the best form of government. It was also primeval, fated to return again when a state had run through the whole cycle of change.

The Roman, with his native theory of unrestricted *imperium*, was familiar with the notion of absolute power. The Principate, though absolute, was not arbitrary. It derived from consent and delegation; it was founded upon the laws. This was something different from the monarchies of the East. The Romans had not sunk as low as that. Complete freedom might be unworkable, but complete enslavement was intolerable. The Principate provided the middle way between these extremes.

It was not long before the Principate gave birth to its own theory, and so became vulnerable to propaganda. Augustus claimed to have restored *Libertas* and the Republic, a necessary and salutary fraud: his successors paid for it. *Libertas* in Roman thought and usage had never quite meant unrestricted liberty; and the ideal which the word now embodied was the respect for constitutional forms. Indeed, it was inconceivable that a Roman should live under any other dispensation. Hence *Libertas* could be invoked as a catchword against unpopular rulers, to stamp their power as illicit, in a word, as 'dominatio', not 'principatus'.

Libertas, it was widely held in senatorial circles, should be the very spirit of the Principate. All too long, soul and body had been severed. It was claimed that they were united in the Principate of Nerva which succeeded the absolute rule of Domitian. There was another side to this fair show of phrases, namely, the real and imminent menace of a civil war. It was averted by the adoption of Trajan, the governor of the military province of Upper Germany: less was heard about *Libertas* under his firm regiment. Tacitus announced an intention of writing in his old age the history of that happy time, when freedom of thought prevailed and freedom of speech, the Principate of Nerva and the rule of Trajan. He turned instead to the sombre theme of the *Annals*.

As a Roman historian, Tacitus had to be a Republican: in his life and in his politics he was a monarchist. It was the part of prudence to pray for good emperors and put up with what you got. Given the nature of man—'vitia erunt donec homines'—it was folly to be utopian. But the situation was not hopeless. A good emperor would dispense the blessings of his rule over the whole world, while the harm done by a bad emperor was not boundless: it fell mostly upon his immediate entourage.

The Roman had once boasted that he alone enjoyed *libertas* while ruling others. It was now evident that obedience was the condition of empire—'idemque huic urbi dominandi finis erit qui parendi fuerit'. This is a far cry from Marcus Brutus. A new conception of civic virtue, derived from the non-political classes of the Republic and inherent in the New State from the beginning, was soon formulated, with its own exemplars and its own phraseology. *Quies* was a virtue for knights, scorned by senators; and neutrality had seldom been possible in the political dissensions of the last age of the Republic. Few were the *nobiles* who passed unscathed through these trials. . . .

With the Principate comes a change. For the senator, as for the State, there must surely be a middle path between the extremes of ruinous liberty and degrading servility. A sensible man could find it. And such there were. M. Aemilius Lepidus enjoyed the friendship of Tiberius; he supported the government without dishonour, his own dignity without danger. Likewise the excellent P. Memmius Regulus, a pillar of the Roman State and secure himself, though married for a time to Lollia Paullina, and the venerable L. Volusius Saturninus who survived all the perils of the Julio-Claudian age and died at the age of ninety-three. As for the family of the Cocceii, they had a genius for safety.

There could be great men still, even under bad emperors, if they abated their ambition, remembered their duty as Romans to the Roman People and quietly practised the higher patriotism. It was not glorious: but glory was ruinous. A surer fame was theirs than the futile and ostentatious opposition of certain candidates for martyrdom, who might be admired for Republican independence of spirit but not for political wisdom. Neither Tacitus nor Trajan had been a party to this folly; the brief unhappy Principate of Nerva was a cogent argument for firm control of the State. Like the vain pomp of eastern kings, the fanaticism of the doctrinaire was distasteful to the Romans. . . .

Tacitus, his father-in-law and his emperor join hands with the time-servers and careerists a century earlier in the founding of the New State. Politics were abolished, or at least sterilized. As a result, history and oratory suffered, but order and concord were safeguarded. . . . The two were now to be reconciled, with constitutional monarchy as a guarantee of freedom such as no Republic could provide. . . .

Such was the 'felicissimus status', as Augustus and Velleius Paterculus termed the Principate, the 'optimus status' which Augustus aspired to create and which Seneca knew as monarchy. Concord and monarchy, *Pax* and *Princeps,* were inseparable in fact as in hope and prayer. . . . The old constitution had been corrupt, unrepresentative and ruinous. Caesar's heir passed beyond it. What was a special plea and political propaganda in the military plebiscite of 32 B.C. became a reality under the Principate—Augustus represented the Populus Romanus: under his trusteeship the State could in truth be called the Commonwealth, 'res publica'. The last of the dynasts prevailed in violence and bloodshed. But his *potentia* was transmuted into *auctoritas,* and 'dux' became beneficent, 'dux bonus'. Ovid perhaps went too far when he spoke of 'dux sacratus'. But Dux was not enough. Augustus assumed the irreproachable garb of Princeps, beyond contest the greatest of the *principes* and better than all of them. They had been selfish dynasts, but he was 'salubris princeps'. He might easily have adopted the title of 'optimus princeps': that was left for Trajan. At the very beginning of Augustus Principate the ideas, later to crystallize into titles official or conventional, were already there. It was not until 2 B.C. that Augustus was acclaimed *pater patriae.* Horace hints at it long before:

> hic ames dici pater atque princeps.

The notion of parent brings with it that of protector:

> optime Romulae
> custos gentis.

And so Augustus is 'custos rerum'; he is the peculiar warden of Rome and Italy, ever ready to succour and to guard:

> o tutela praesens
> Italiae dominaeque Romae!

Greeks in the cities of the East hailed Augustus as the Saviour of the World, the Benefactor of the Human Race, as a God, God's son manifest, Lord of Earth and Sea. Sailors from Alexandria paid public observance to him who was the author of their lives, liberty and prosperity. The loyal town-council of the colony of Pisa showed more restraint, but meant the same thing, when they celebrated the 'Guardian of the Roman Empire and Governor of the Whole World'.

That the power of Caesar Augustus was absolute, no contemporary could doubt. But his rule was justified by merit, founded upon consent and tempered by duty. Augustus stood like a soldier, 'in statione'—for the metaphor, though it may have parallels in the language of the Stoics, is Roman and military. He would not desert his post until a higher command relieved him, his duty done and a successor left on guard. Augustus used the word 'statio': so did contemporaries.

Augustus' rule was dominion over all the world. To the Roman People his relationship was that of Father, Founder and Guardian. Sulla had striven to repair the shattered Republic; and Cicero, for saving Rome in his consulate, had been hailed as *pater patriae*. But Sulla, with well-grounded hate, was styled 'the sinister Romulus'; Cicero, in derision of his pretensions, the 'Romulus from Arpinum'. Augustus, however, had a real claim to be known and honoured as the Founder, 'augusto augurio', in the phrase of Ennius. The Roman could feel it in his blood and in his traditions. . . .

Augustus' relations to the Roman Commonwealth might also be described as organic rather than arbitrary or formal. It was said that he arrogated to himself all the functions of Senate, magistrates and laws. Truly—but more penetrating the remark that he entwined himself about the body of the Commonwealth. The new member reinvigorated the whole and could not have been severed without damage.

His rule was personal, if ever rule was, and his position became ever more monarchic. Yet with all this, Augustus was not indispensable— that was the greatest triumph of all. Had he died in the early years of the Principate, his party would have survived, led by Agrippa, or by a group of the marshals. But Augustus lived on, a progressive miracle of duration. As the years passed, he emancipated himself more and more from the control of his earlier partisans; the *nobiles* returned to prominence and the Caesarian party itself was transformed and transcended. A government was created.

'Legiones classes provincias, cuncta inter se conexa.' So Tacitus described the Empire and its armed forces. The phrase might fittingly be applied to the whole fabric of the Roman State. It was firm, well-articulated and flexible. By appeal to the old, Augustus justified the new; by emphasizing continuity with the past, he encouraged the hope of development in the future. The New State established as the consolidation of the Revolution was neither exclusive nor immobile. While each class in society had its peculiar functions, there was no sharp division between classes. Service to Rome won recognition and promotion for senator, for knight or for soldier, for Roman or for provincial. The rewards were not so splendid as in the wars of the Revolution; but the rhythm, though abated, was steady and continuous.

It had been Augustus' most fervent prayer that he might lay the foundations of the new order deep and secure. He had done more than that. The Roman State, based firmly on a united Italy and a coherent Empire, was completely renovated, with new institutions, new ideas and even a new literature that was already classical. The doom of Empire had borne heavily on Rome, with threatened ruin. But now the reinvigorated Roman People, robust and cheerful, could bear the burden with pride as well as with security.

Augustus had also prayed for a successor in the post of honour and duty. His dearest hopes, his most pertinacious designs, had been thwarted. But peace and the Principate endured. A successor had been found, trained in his own school, a Roman aristocrat from among the *principes*, by general consent capable of Empire. It might have been better for Tiberius and for Rome if Augustus had died earlier: the duration of his life, by accustoming men's minds to the Principate as something permanent and enhancing his own prestige beyond that of a mortal man, while it consolidated his own régime and the new system of government, none the less made the task of his successor more delicate and more arduous.

The last decade of Augustus' life was clouded by domestic scandals and by disasters on the frontiers of empire. Yet for all that, when the end came it found him serene and cheerful. On his death-bed he was not plagued by remorse for his sins or by anxiety for the Empire. He quietly asked his friends whether he had played well his part in the comedy of life. There could be one answer or none.

Suggestions for Further Reading

BARROW, R. H., *The Romans.* Harmondsworth, Middlesex: Penguin Books, Ltd., 1949.

GELZER, M., *Caesar: Politician and Statesman*, translated by P. Needham and E. Badian, 6th ed. Cambridge, Mass.: Harvard University Press, 1968.

GELZER, M., *Roman Nobility*, translated by Robin Seager. New York: Barnes and Noble, 1969.

GRANT, MICHAEL, *The World of Rome.* New York: Praeger Books, Inc., 1970.

HOMO, LÉON, *Roman Political Institutions from City to State.* London: Kegan Paul, Trench, Trubner & Co., Ltd.; New York: Alfred A. Knopf, Inc., 1929.

MARROU, H. I., *A History of Education in Antiquity.* New York: Sheed and Ward, 1956.

MOMMSEN, THEODOR, *History of Rome,* 5 vols. New York: Charles Scribner's Sons, 1911.

RUDOLF BULTMANN

The Foundations of Christianity

ᴥᔓᔓᴥ From the fourth to the eighteenth century, Christian religious doctrine was the foundation of all European thought and culture, and Christian churches and sects played a central and at times dominant role in European society. Not even in our contemporary secular and industrial society is Christianity by any means a spent force, as the revitalization of Protestantism beginning in the 1920's and the reform of Catholicism in the 1950's and 1960's clearly indicate. Those writers who have suggested that since the middle of the nineteenth century European history has entered a post-Christian era probably spoke too soon; it is a reasonable expectation that in the later twentieth century, forms and varieties of Christianity will again have a tremendous impact on the course of Western thought and culture.

It is, therefore, at least plausible to interpret the development of Western civilization in terms of the rise and destiny of the Christian faith. This has not been a fashionable view of European history among academic historians in the twentieth century, nearly all of whom have been secular liberals. But to view the course of European history as the consequence of the interaction between the Christian religion and the world is certainly as valid a theme as the

FROM Rudolf Bultmann, *Primitive Christianity in Its Contemporary Setting,* translated by Reverend R. H. Fuller (Cleveland: World Publishing Company, Meridian Books, 1963), pp. 175–208.

political and economic approaches which have found such favor among twentieth-century academic historians.

If the history of the Christian Church is a central theme in European history, then the origins of Christianity and the life and teachings of Jesus are a subject of the greatest importance for the history of Western civilization. But it is a subject of enormous difficulty and complexity. The sources are fragmentary and obscure, and the historiography of the subject has naturally been heavily conditioned by the partisan feelings of all writers on the subject, whether Protestant, Catholic, Jewish, or liberal humanist in their commitments. It is indicative of the continuing vitality of Christianity in Western civilization that no one can write on the life and teachings of Jesus without being conscious of the relevance of his subject to the experience of humanity in his own time.

The literature on the origins of Christianity and the growth of the Christian Church is a vast one, but in this field Protestant scholars have been preeminent and only in recent years has a valuable body of Catholic scholarship appeared. In the Protestant literature of the past hundred years, there are two distinct phases and fundamental interpretations. In the six decades preceding the First World War, German liberal Protestantism employed the tools of historical scholarship to carry out "the higher criticism" of the New Testament and to establish Jesus and his first disciples as real personalities in the context of their social and cultural environment. While there was strong disagreement on many important points, this German liberal Protestant scholarship had by 1914 attained a substantial degree of consensus in its quest for the historical Jesus. The so-called synoptic Gospels of *Matthew, Mark,* and *Luke* were separated from the fourth Gospel of *John.* The former were held to be difficult but nevertheless circumstantial historical accounts, whereas *John* was viewed as the work of a writer of a later generation whose view of Jesus was conditioned by Greek philosophy. It was widely held that the career and doctrine of Jesus could be understood only in the context of post-Exilic Judaism and the apocalyptic and messianic yearnings of large numbers of Jews who bitterly opposed and even physically resisted Roman rule. But as to the exact connection between Jesus and this febrile Jewish milieu there was wide disparity in interpretation. It was felt, however, whatever the precise content of Jesus' teaching, it was not the sacramental theology of the fourth-century Christian Church, which was a later development under the impress of Platonic and Neo-Platonic philosophy and Oriental mystery religions. The more doctrinaire liberal Protestant scholars believed that Jesus preached an ethical humanism and social gospel which was far removed not only from Catholic dogma but also from predestinarian Lutheran theology.

The holocaust of the First World War and the postwar malaise of Western and particularly German society seemed to a new generation of Protestant theologians, particularly in Germany and Switzerland, to prove the emptiness and falsity of liberal Protestantism and its optimistic belief in man's potentialities to create a good society. Humanist ethics became unfashionable among Protestant scholars, and Lutheran theology with its dichotomy between the Church and the world and its emphasis on God's omnipotence and man's weakness was revivified. The leading spokesman for neo-Lutheran doctrine was the German-Swiss theologian Karl Barth. His claim that Protestantism was primarily an eschatological faith and not a liberal humanist hope, his God-centered religion and pessimistic view of human potentiality was confirmed for many Protestant thinkers by the Nazi triumph and the terror and butchery that followed. This pessimistic tendency in German Protestant thought culminated in the gloomy existentialist philosophy expounded by Martin Heidegger. In a chaotic, absurd, meaningless, and inhuman world the only religious and moral affirmation possible is the day-to-day decision to act in such a way as to affirm human existence and God's power and goodness.

In the last forty years the most learned, influential, and widely esteemed authority on earliest Christianity has been Rudolf Bultmann, born in 1884 and a professor at the University of Marburg. His works have been translated into every Western language and they are constantly studied and debated in all schools of Protestant theology in the Western world. He has also received very respectful consideration, although by no means enthusiastic assent, among the new school of Catholic biblical scholars.

Bultmann's historiographical position is neatly trisected by early twentieth-century liberal Protestant higher criticism, Barth's neo-Lutheranism, and Heidegger's existentialism. It draws upon the learning and methods of the old higher critics to develop a view of Jesus which accords with what might be called Lutheran existentialism. Bultmann agrees with the liberal Protestant scholars that *Matthew*, *Mark*, and *Luke* must be distinguished from *John*. The synoptic Gospels are a distant approximation of historical accounts, but *John* does not have this quality at all. (There are Anglican and Roman Catholic scholars who disagree with this long-held assumption and claim to find evidence that *John* is an early and historically reliable account. This is, however, still very much a minority view among New Testament scholars.) Bultmann also agrees with the view developed by the pre-1914 generation of scholars that Jesus lived in an intensely apocalyptic and messianic environment, and he suggests that Jesus began his teaching as a disciple of John the Baptist. But Bultmann radically dissents from the liberal higher critics' faith that they could extrapolate a picture of Jesus' personality from the Gospels and could find evidence to support their view of Jesus as the teacher of a liberal humanistic ethic.

Bultmann believes that the details of Jesus' life and personality in the Gospels are mere "legendary coloring," the manifestations of contemporary mythology about the conduct and personality of great religious teachers and prophets. In many books and studies, aided by an extremely impressive mastery of Jewish rabbinical and apocalyptic texts as well as a profound New Testament learning, Bultmann has undertaken "the demythologizing" of Jesus and the explication of his original teaching before it was overlaid and mythologized by Jewish and Hellenistic traditions. The result of this investigation is to provide the biblical foundation for the teachings of Barth and Heidegger—and Martin Luther. Jesus, according to Bultmann, pro-

claimed God's absolute power, the imminence of the kingdom of God, man's emptiness on his own, and humanity's
lack of an intrinsic worth. But man has been given a will
and freedom of choice and he is capable of making the existential decision to act in accordance with the imminence of
the kingdom of God. This kingdom of God is not a group of
earthly moral values; it is not the happy fellowship of the
liberal humanists, it is not the good society. "It is supernatural, superhistoric."

Bultmann's interpretation of Jesus and his delineation of
original Christianity were first presented in 1926. In a
formidable array of succeeding works Bultmann revised
and expanded his original thesis, examining all aspects of
the Apostolic Church in its cultural setting. The following
selection, written in the mid-50's, presents Bultmann's own
summary of his life's work.

PRIMITIVE CHRISTIANITY AS A SYNCRETISTIC PHENOMENON

Primitive Christianity arose from the band of Jesus' disciples, who,
after their Master had been put to death by Pontius Pilate on the
Cross, had seen him as one risen from the dead. Their belief that God
had raised him from the dead gave them at the same time the assurance that Jesus had been exalted to heavenly glory and raised to the
dignity of the 'Man' who would very shortly come on the clouds of
heaven to set up the Reign of God. The growing company of those
who awaited his coming was conscious of itself as the Church of the
last age, as the community of the 'saints' and 'elect', as the true people of God, for whom the promises were now being fulfilled, as the
goal and end of the redemptive history of Israel.

The eschatological community did not split off from Judaism as
though it were conscious of itself as a new religious society. In the
eyes of their contemporaries they must have looked like a Jewish
sect, and for the historian they appear in that light too. For the resources they possessed—their traditions about Jesus, which were carefully preserved, and the latent resources of their own faith, led only

gradually to a new form of organization and new philosophy of hu
life, the world and history.

The decisive step was taken when the good news of Jesus, cruc
and risen, the coming Judge and agent of redemption, was carried
yond the confines of Palestinian Judaism, and Christian congrega
sprang up in the Graeco-Roman world. These congregations cons
partly of Hellenistic Jewish Christians, partly of Gentiles, whe
the Christian mission sought its point of contact in the Helle
synagogues. For here, without going farther afield, it was po
to reach many of the Gentiles, who had joined the Jewish comm
sometimes closely, sometimes more loosely. On other occasior
Christian missionaries went direct to the Gentile population, anc
in the first instance, to the lower classes in the cities. There were
ably churches of Gentiles only, but few, if any, of the churches
have been purely Jewish. In any case Christianity found itself in
spiritual environment: The Gospel had to be preached in terms
gible to Hellenistic audiences and their mental outlook, while
same time the audience themselves were bound to interpret the
message in their own way, in the light of their own spiritual
Hence the growth of divers types of Christianity.

By and large, the chief difference between Hellenistic Chr
and the original Palestinian version was that the former ceas
dominated by the eschatological expectation and the philosoph
which that implied. Instead, there was developed a new pa
piety centred in the cultus. The Hellenistic Christians, it is t
tinued to expect an imminent end of the world, the coming of f
and Saviour from heaven and the resurrection of the dead an
judgement. But there were also Christians who became scepti
primitive Jewish Christian eschatology and rejected it. Inde
tried to get rid of it altogether. Above all, the Gentile Christi
the idea of a redemptive history foreign to them, and as a r
lost the sense of belonging to the community of the last d
could no longer feel that they were standing at the culmina
demptive history directed by the providence of God. This w
wherever the tradition of the Synagogue and Christian cate
struction had failed to implant the idea of redemptive hi
speedy disappearance of the apocalyptic title 'Man' is sy
even Paul himself refrains from using it. It was no longer
that 'Christos' was a translation of 'Messiah', and meant tha

the Lord of the age of redemption: the title simply became a proper name. Other titles took its place, such as 'Son of God' and 'Saviour', titles which were already current in the Gentile world to designate agents of redemption. It was however the title 'Kyrios' which became the most popular designation of Jesus. It characterizes him as the cult deity who works supernaturally in the worship of the Church as a cultic body. Hellenistic pneumatology, with ecstasy and speaking with tongues, find their way into the churches. The Kyrios Jesus Christos is conceived as a mystery deity, in whose death and Resurrection the faithful participate through the sacraments. Parallel with this sacramental cultus piety we very soon find Gnostic ideas of wisdom affecting the churches. Ideas originating from the Gnostic redemption myths are used to describe the person and work of Jesus Christ and the nature of the Church, and, accompanying these, ascetic and even libertinist tendencies.

At the same time, however, the Hellenistic Christians received the gospel tradition of the Palestinian churches. Admittedly, the importance attached to this tradition varied from place to place. Paul himself seldom refers to it. Yet almost everywhere the Old Testament asserts itself, being accepted as canonical scripture by all except extreme gnosticizing circles. This adoption of the Old Testament followed as a matter of course in those congregations which grew out of the Synagogue. The latter was also the medium by which Hellenistic Christianity adopted conceptions emanating from philosophical enlightenment, conceptions which the Synagogue itself had assimilated at an earlier stage. Christian missionary preaching was not only the proclamation of Christ, but, when addressed to a Gentile audience, a preaching of monotheism as well. For this, not only arguments derived from the Old Testament, but the natural theology of Stoicism was pressed into service. Quite early on the Christian churches adopted a system of morality, with its pattern of catechetical instruction derived in equal proportions from the Old Testament Jewish tradition and from the ethics of popular philosophical pedagogic, shortly to be enriched by the moral ideals of the Hellenistic bourgeoisie.

Thus Hellenistic Christianity is no unitary phenomenon, but, taken by and large, a remarkable product of syncretism. It is full of tendencies and contradictions, some of which were to be condemned later on by orthodox Christianity as heretical. Hence also the struggles between the various tendencies, of which the Pauline Epistles give such a vivid impression.

Yes, at first sight we are bound to agree that Hellenistic Christianity is the outcome of syncretism. The world is the creation of God, who cares for the birds and decks the grass of the field with its beauty (Matt. 6.26, 30). Yet at the same time it is the realm of Satan, the 'god of this world' (II Cor. 4.4), the 'prince of this world' (John 12.31). The earth is the Lord's and all the fulness thereof (I Cor. 10.26). Yet creation is subject to vanity and corruption, yearning for the day of its deliverance (Rom. 8.19–22). The terms in which this deliverance is conceived are derived partly, and indeed mainly, from the Jewish tradition. The old age is already coming to an end, and the new age is about to dawn soon with the coming of the 'Man', the resurrection of the dead and the judgement. But side by side with these conceptions we get the eschatology of the Fourth Gospel, which uses not the Jewish dualism of the two ages but the Gnostic dualism of the two realms of light and darkness, truth and falsehood, above and below, and which asserts that the judgement and resurrection have already been realized, or at least have been inaugurated because 'the light is come into the world' (John 3.19). Now that Jesus has come, those who believe in him have already passed from death unto life (John 5.24f.). The person of Jesus is sometimes defined in terms of Jewish and apocalyptic categories, sometimes as the 'Lord' of the cultus, as a mystery deity, sometimes again as the Gnostic redeemer, the pre-existent being from the heavenly world, whose earthly body is only an outward garb. This explains why the 'rulers of this world' failed to recognize him, as only 'his own' can. The Christian community is sometimes described in Old Testament categories as the people of God, the true seed of Abraham, sometimes in Gnostic categories as the 'body of Christ', in which individuals are incorporated by means of the sacraments of baptism and the Lord's Supper. Of course, some of these concepts are confined to particular writings or groups of writings in the New Testament (which varies a great deal in its language and thought). But they are also to be found side by side or in combination in the same author, especially in Paul and the Epistle to the Hebrews.

Is Christianity then really a syncretistic religion? Or is there a fundamental unity behind all this diversity? A comparison of primitive Christianity with the various traditions and religious movements in which it was cradled and which influenced its growth should help us to answer this question. Does primitive Christianity contain a single, new and unique doctrine of human existence? The comparison may best be conducted by selecting certain main subjects as test cases. In doing this, we shall rely chiefly on the Pauline and Johannine writings, because they provide the clearest evidence for the Christian attitude to existence.

MAN AND HIS RELATION TO TIME

It is clear that the early Christian doctrine of man is diametrically opposed to that which prevailed in the Greek tradition. Man is not regarded as an instance of universal human Being, which in its turn is seen to be an instance of cosmic Being in general. There is no attempt to escape from the questionableness of man's own individuality by concentrating on the universal law or the cosmic harmony. Like Gnosticism, primitive Christianity was totally uninterested in education or training. It had no use for the Greek dualistic anthropology, with its tension between spirit and sensuality, or the view of life which that implied, viz. the realization of the ideal of the 'gentleman' as a 'work of art'. Man's essential Being is not Logos, reason or spirit. If we ask primitive Christianity where the essential Being of man resides, there can only be one answer: in the *will*. To be a man or to live a human life, means to strive for something, to aspire after something, to will.

Of course, the Greeks and the New Testament are equally aware that man's will can lead him into disaster. But in the Greek view this is due to the failure of reason to control the will. All that is necessary is to train the reason, and then the will should automatically obey it. It is assumed that the will itself always wills what is the good, the best for man. Reason perceives what is best, communicates its insight to the will, and the will automatically obeys its promptings. Such was the teaching of the Stoics, loyal as they were to the Socratic and Platonic tradition.

Such reflection is alien to the New Testament. Not that it was ignorant of the Logos or reason as the organ of the knowledge of good and evil. The category of conscience was taken over from Hellenism, and is employed by some of the New Testament writers, especially Paul, who believes that reason enables man to distinguish between good and evil (Rom. 2.14f.; Phil. 4.8). But in saying this, we have by no means indicated how radical is the New Testament doctrine of man, and explicit reflection on the origin of the knowledge of good and evil is far beyond the range of primitive Christianity.

But the chief point is that the New Testament does not regard the will of man in purely formal terms. It does not automatically aspire to the Good. It is not a clean slate, whose character of good or evil is acquired by the ideas which direct it, ideas which may be right or wrong, and just because of that require the direction of the reason. Rather, the will is regarded as good or evil in itself. It is from the 'heart', i.e. the will, that good or evil deeds proceed (Luke 6.43–5, etc.). And here we may for the moment leave open the question whether there can actually be such a thing as a good 'heart'. However that may be, man is not lord of his will in such a way that the Logos or reason enables him to transcend his will and direct it according to rational thinking. No, a man and his will are identical. If his will is in bondage to evil, which is what the New Testament always assumes, the whole man is in bondage to evil. He cannot therefore dissociate himself from his will, or summon it back from evil. In Romans 7.15–25 Paul unfolds the contradiction between what a man wills and what he actually does—'what I would, that I do not; but what I hate, that do I'. Here the will which wills the 'good' is not man's empirical will, but the basic impulse which lies behind all actual acts of will, the desire for life as something that is good. If this basic impulse is incapable of realization, it means that the empirical will cannot will what it really wills. Consequently education or training of the will is useless. What is needed is to bring home to the will its utter impotence; so that it can cry: 'O wretched man that I am! who shall deliver me from the body of this death?'

Apart from this assertion of the utter impotence of the will, the New Testament doctrine of man keeps close to that of the Old Testament. Here too the nature or essence of man is not his reason. There is nothing like the Greek anthropology with its dualism of spirit and sensuality, or its ideas on education. Here again the knowledge of good and evil is not conceived along rationalistic lines. The New Testament follows this tradition. It is also diametrically opposed to the Greek view on a further point. Evil is not a merely negative thing, a defect which will be put right later. It is something positive, disobedience against God, rebellion, 'sin'. This results in a different conception of becoming free from evil. For the Greek mind the way lay in education and instruction. Evil was simply a survival from an earlier stage of development. Teach man about the Good, inculcate the ideal of nobility, and it will mould his character. By striving after the ideal, he approximates ever more closely to what he already is in the light of the ideal. The rule is: 'become what you are.'

Now all this implies a view of man's relation to time which is in striking contrast to that of the Old and New Testaments. The Bible knows nothing of the development of man, in which evil is left behind as a survival from an earlier stage. Rather, it insists that a man is always what his past has made him. He always brings his past along with him into his present. He can never make a fresh start with a clean sheet. He has no real future in the sense of something entirely new. Since evil is sin, it throws man's relation with God entirely out of gear, just as the relations between man and man are thrown out of gear by the wrongs they do to one another. Just as when one man has wronged another the only way out is for him to own up to it and receive forgiveness, so it is with man's relation to God. Only confession and forgiveness can make him a new man and give him a fresh start. This does not mean that he becomes morally better. In the language of the Old and New Testaments he is now 'righteous', 'justified'. That is to say, God has pronounced him free.

Thus far the New Testament agrees with the Jewish tradition. But it goes further in asserting the impotence of the human will. Man is in radical bondage to evil and cannot will the good. This is not just ordinary pessimism about human nature. There are plenty of examples of this in Greek literature, and still more in the Old Testament. Indeed, Judaism can offer parallels to Paul's theory of the fall of Adam as the cause of sin and death entering the world and bringing men into bondage. But Judaism never supposes that man is totally incapable of good works. On the whole, the best he can hope for, it is true, is to hold the balance, to compensate for his transgressions by fulfilling the law. But since no man does only what is good, every man needs God's forgiveness, although to some extent he can make amends for his transgressions by 'good works', which are not demanded by the law and are therefore supererogatory. Paul thinks otherwise. In his very attempt to obtain righteousness from God through his works, the original sin of man is latent. It shows that what man really is after is something to boast about before God. He imagines he can live in his own strength and earn his acceptance with God. This is simply the Jewish form of a tendency inherent in all men. The Greek form of it is boasting of one's wisdom. This hankering after something to boast about is the root of all other evils. It is sin, rebellion against God. Man is simply blind to the fact that he can only live by the grace of God. 'What hast thou that thou didst not receive? now if thou didst receive it, why dost thou glory, as if thou hadst not received it?' (I Cor. 4.7). This is just what man must own up to. He must make an absolute surrender to the grace of God. That is what is meant by 'believing'. And that is the stumbling-block for natural man, with his hankering after recognition.

That is what makes the gospel message for him a scandal and foolishness (I Cor. 1.23). It is a scandal because it is the message of the Cross. For by causing Christ crucified to be proclaimed as Lord, God crushes human pride. That is why Paul refuses to boast any more 'save in the cross of our Lord Jesus Christ, by whom the world is crucified unto me, and I unto the world' (Gal. 6.14).

Here the Old Testament view of man as a being open to the future reaches its logical conclusion. This is achieved by means of a paradox. While humanity is essentially openness for the future, the fact is that man bars his own way to the future by wanting to live unto himself. He boasts in what he has, in what he is, in what he has made out of himself, in what he can control, in what he takes to be a ground for pride, in what he imagines he can offer to God. When he boasts he lays hold upon what he already has and is—upon his past. But to renounce such boasting, to surrender all his gain and count it but loss, indeed as 'dung' (Phil. 3.7f.), to surrender unreservedly to the grace of God, to believe—all this is simply radical openness for the future. It is to realize that we are always in via, that we have never reached the end:

Not as though I had already attained, either were already perfect: but I follow after, if that I may apprehend that for which also I am apprehended of Christ Jesus. . . . I count not myself to have apprehended: but this one thing I do, forgetting those things which are behind, and reaching forth unto those things which are before, I press toward the mark . . . (Phil. 3.12f.).

This radical openness for the future in absolute surrender to the grace of God is prepared to accept all encounters as tokens of his grace. Incidentally, this provides the answer to the problem of suffering. We may, it is true, still find in the New Testament, including the Pauline writings, the Jewish belief in transcendent glory as the compensation for suffering in this world (e.g. Rom. 8.18; II Cor. 4.17f.); but for Paul such a belief has lost its motive power. The real reason why Paul triumphs over suffering is that he who has died with Jesus has the grace of God alive in him as the resurrection life of Christ. 'For though he was crucified in weakness, yet he liveth by the power of God. For we also are weak in him, but we shall live with him by the power of God toward you' (II Cor. 13.4). Thus Paul is constantly offering himself 'for Jesus' sake' to death, that the life of Jesus might be made manifest in his mortal flesh (II Cor. 4.11). 'For which cause we faint not; but though our outward man perish, yet the inward man is renewed day by day' (II Cor. 4.16). Suffering is thus converted into a blessing, and once he realizes this man becomes free from the world, from all that is transitory and belongs to the past, and becomes open to the transcendent future. When Paul prays that God may deliver him from his bodily sufferings, the answer he receives is not the consoling promise of bliss in heaven as a compensation. Instead, he hears the Lord saying to him: 'My grace is sufficient for thee: for my strength is made perfect in weakness', to which he replies: 'Most gladly therefore will I rather glory in my infirmities, that the power of Christ may rest upon me. Therefore I take pleasure in infirmities, in reproaches, in necessities, in persecutions, in distresses, for Christ's sake; for when I am weak, then am I strong' (II Cor. 12.9f.).

This radical openness for the future is the Christian's freedom. Such a conception of freedom seems to bring Paul very close to Stoicism. Indeed, the very fact that he defines genuine human existence in terms of freedom, a concept unknown to the Old Testament and Judaism, is itself sufficient to suggest an affinity between Paul and the Stoics, to say nothing of the actual vocabulary he uses. The Stoic wise man is, like Paul, free from all external necessities and claims from the outside world, its conventions, judgements and values. Epictetus speaks just as triumphantly about his victories over fate, distress and death as Paul himself. And when Paul says, 'All things are lawful to me', the Stoic can heartily agree, even when he adds the reservation: 'but I will not be brought under the power of any' (I Cor. 6.12). And when Paul says, 'Be not ye the servants of men' (I Cor. 7.23)—that is to say, 'Do not make yourselves dependent on the value judgements of men'—that is perfectly good Stoicism. So is the Pauline paradox, that the slave is a free man (for the Stoics, through wisdom, for Paul, through Christ), although when Paul goes on to say that the free man, since he is 'called', i.e. a Christian, is a slave, viz. of Christ, they begin to part company. The Stoic would say that if the free man is a slave he is a fool. Yet even this could be translated into Pauline terms without much difficulty by saying that the free man who is not called is a slave, viz. of sin (I Cor. 7.22f.). Like Paul, the Stoic could say: 'I know both how to be abased, and I know how to abound: every where and in all things I am instructed both to be full and to be hungry, both to abound and to suffer need.' But he would not continue: 'I can do all things through Christ who strengtheneth me' (Phil. 4.12f.). This is just where the difference lies. The Stoic is free because of his reason. He concentrates on reason by turning his back on all encounters and claims from the outside world. This makes him free *from* the future. He is enabled to escape from the toils of life in time. Paul, on the other hand, is free because he has been made free by the grace of God, and has surrendered freely to his grace. He has been freed from all the claims which seek to bind him to all reality, present, transitory and already past. He has become free *for* the future, for encounters in which he will experience God's grace ever anew as a gift from outside. The Stoic shuts the door to all encounters and lives in the timeless Logos. The Christian opens himself to these encounters, and lives from the future.

The understanding of Christian existence as a life in which God is always One who comes, and as a life which is always a future possibility is, of course, not always fully explicit in the New Testament in all its ramifications. In fact, there was at the outset a serious obstacle to its full realization. That obstacle was the eschatology which the early Church took over from Judaism, with its expectation of an imminent end of the world, and the ushering in of ultimate salvation by a cosmic catastrophe. Only the author of the Fourth Gospel has emancipated himself from this eschatology. But when Paul says that faith, hope and love 'abide', even when 'that which is perfect' is come (I Cor. 13:13), he is bringing an important truth to light. This is that if real life means being open to the future, it can never be regarded as a definitive state of bliss. Faith and hope are the dispositions of those who are always looking for the grace of God as a future possibility.

In another respect, however, the early Christians were quite clear about the implications of freedom. With their sense of being the eschatological people of God, of standing at the end of redemptive history, they no longer identified the redemptive history with the empirical history of Israel. It is, of course, true that the New Testament sometimes uses the history of Israel as a type for admonition or exhortation (e.g. I Cor. 10:1–11; Heb. 3.7–19). The saints of the Old Testament may be regarded as pioneers and examples for the Christians, like Abraham and the heroes of faith enumerated in Hebrews 11. But the history of Israel is no longer their own history. They ceased, for instance, to regard the Jewish festivals as re-enactments 'for us' of the events of the past. When he speaks of the foundation of the Church, Paul no longer points to the exodus from Egypt. The event by which the Church is constituted is the death of Christ. But unlike the giving of the law on Mount Sinai, the death of Christ is not an event in the history of the nation. The sacraments of baptism and the Lord's Supper do not cement the Christians into a nation, but into an eschatological community, which, since it is eschatological, transcends the limits of nationality. The wine of the Lord's Supper is the blood of the 'new covenant' promised by the prophet Jeremiah in the age to come. This idea of an eschatological covenant—that is to say, a covenant which is removed from empirical history, and removes men from it—is now treated seriously. Of course the Christian community is the 'people of God', the 'seed of Abraham', but not as the 'children of the flesh', but as the 'children of promise' (Rom. 9.8; Gal. 3.29). The Old Testament is still the word of God, though not because it contains his word spoken to Israel in the past, but because it is directly typological and allegorical. The original meaning and context of the Old Testament sayings are entirely irrelevant. God does not speak to men through history but through Christ, who is the end of history, and through the word which proclaims him. In the light of this the Old Testament begins to speak with a new meaning.

But this means that God's grace is not an historical phenomenon. It is not the possession of an historical nation, membership of which guarantees the security of the individual. If it were that, trust in grace would be trust in the 'flesh'. That is why Paul counted all that had once been his pride to be but loss (Phil. 3.4–8). In the Christian Church there is neither male nor female, for all are 'one in Christ Jesus' (Gal. 4.28; I Cor. 12.13; Col. 3.11). This also means that man becomes absolutely alone before God. Of course, in belonging to Christ he is a member of his body, and is therefore bound to the other members in the unity of the Church. But before God he stands, in the first place at any rate, in utter loneliness, extricated from his natural ties. The fundamental question which is asked of man, 'Are you ready to believe in the word of God's grace?' can only be answered individually. This individualizing of man's relation to God has its roots in the psalms and Wisdom literature, and above all in Jeremiah. But its full implications were never realized until the time of Paul with his radical conception of the grace of God.

THE SITUATION OF MAN IN THE WORLD

Freedom from the past, openness for the future—that is the essence of human existence. But it is the conviction of the New Testament that man needs first to be restored to his true nature through the event of redemption accomplished in Christ. Until this event has taken place, until man has appropriated the grace of God manifested in that event, he is alienated from his own true nature, alienated from life, enslaved under hostile powers and in bondage to death.

The situation of natural man in the world appears to Christian eyes very much as it does to Gnosticism. In fact, Christianity may employ Gnostic ideas and terminology to describe it. Impotence and fear mark the life of pre-Christian man. When he assures the Roman Christians, 'Ye have not received the spirit of bondage again to fear; but ye have received the Spirit of adoption', Paul is taking for granted that the Romans, as Gentiles, had lived in the bondage of fear. The same idea of man's enslavement is presumed by the Jesus of the Fourth Gospel, when he says: 'If ye continue in my word, then are ye disciples indeed; And ye shall know the truth, and the truth shall make you free' (John 8.31f.), though his audience cannot make head or tail of what he is saying, as the ensuing dialogue shows. For this is the worst feature of man's plight. He is totally unconscious of his enslavement. He has not the least notion what he is doing when he strives to attain life by himself, by his own efforts. The Jew imagines he can do this by his observance of the law. But his zeal in the service of God is futile: it only leads him into death (Rom. 7.14–24, 10.2). When the law is read in the synagogue, there is a veil over their hearts. They are hardened in thought and action, just as the 'god of this world' has blinded the thought and action of those who do not believe (II Cor. 3.14,4.4). Thus the constant misunderstandings to which the sayings of Jesus are exposed in the Fourth Gospel show that men are in darkness and love the darkness rather than the light (John 3.19).

The powers under which man is enslaved are, as in Gnosticism, the cosmic powers. They are the elements of the world, the astral spirits (Gal. 4.3, 9), the 'dominions, principalities and powers' (Rom. 8.38; Col. 1.16, etc.). They are the 'rulers of this world' or even the 'god of this world' or the 'prince of this world' (I Cor. 2.6; II Cor. 4.4; John 12.31, etc.). All these terms are mythological, and are derived from Gnosticism. There is no reason to doubt that the early Christians regarded these powers as real demonic beings. Paul is using mythological concepts derived from Gnosticism when he states that the Old Testament law does not come from God, but was given by angelic powers. If the Gentile Christians adopt the Jewish law, they will be turning again to the 'weak and beggarly elements' (Gal. 3.19f., 4.9). He is equally using the language of mythology when he says that the 'rulers', deceived by the secret wisdom of God, crucified Christ, the 'Lord of glory', because they did not know him. This was because he was disguised in the form of a servant (I Cor. 2.9; Phil. 2.6ff.).

Primitive Christianity never adopted the Gnostic doctrine of the pre-existence of the soul. Paul did indeed make use of the Gnostic myth of the archetypal man in order to make man's situation in the world intelligible. The fall of the archetypal man (which Paul naturally identifies with the fall of Adam as related in Genesis 3) has determined the fate of all men since. Adam brought sin and death into the world, and until Christ their sway has been unquestioned (Rom. 5.12ff.). Paul is drawing even more heavily on Gnostic mythology when he attributes the burden of man's sinful past to the nature of Adam:

The first man is of the earth, earthy: the second man is the Lord from heaven. As is the earthy, such are they also that are earthy: and as is the heavenly, such are they also that are heavenly. And as we have borne the image of the earthy, we shall also bear the image of the heavenly (I Cor. 15.47f.).

And in describing the nature of Adam as 'psychic' and that of Christ as 'pneumatic' (I Cor. 15.44–6) he is again using the language of Gnosticism. Neither classical Greek nor the language of the Old Testament furnishes any precedent for the pejorative sense in which the adjective 'psychic' is used here. Like the Gnostics, Paul distinguishes between 'psychic' and 'pneumatic', the latter meaning those who have 'gnosis', which enables them to fathom the 'deep things of God' (I Cor. 2.10–16).

In this conception of man's situation in the world as a bondage to the hostile cosmic powers, as a fate brought upon him by the fall of the archetypal man, there is a close affinity between Christianity and Gnosticism. But there is also a crucial difference. Both systems agree that empirical man is not what he ought to be. He is deprived of authentic life, true existence. Nor can he ever achieve that existence by his own strength. But according to the Gnostics, this is due to fate or destiny, whereas for primitive Christianity it is due not only to fate, but to man's guilt as well. This is at once apparent from the way Christianity dropped the doctrine of the pre-existence of the soul. It is further apparent in the refusal to abandon the Old Testament doctrine of creation (or the identity of the Creator and Redeemer) and of man's responsibility before God. Now it is true that the exact connexion between fate and guilt is never submitted in the New Testament to theological analysis. Man's enslavement to the cosmic powers and his personal responsibility, his impotence and his guilt are allowed to stand side by side without any attempt to reconcile them. In Romans 5.12ff. sin and death are attributed to the fall of Adam. They are a malignant destiny which has come upon man. In Romans 1.18ff., on the other hand, mankind incurred guilt and continues to incur it by its refusal to perceive

God in the works of his creation. Romans 2.1ff. takes it for granted that man is responsible for his plight, for it speaks of judgement hanging as a threat over him—over Gentile as well as Jew. Indeed, Paul feels obliged to give an explicit proof of the responsibility of the Gentiles: although they did not have the Mosaic law, they had the conscience, and the conscience taught them the law of God (Rom. 2.14f.).

The solution of this contradiction is that man's guilt has become his fate. It is essential to see how Paul (and John likewise) conceives the way in which these cosmic powers in actual practice work in the historical existence of man. They make themselves felt in practice as the powers of the flesh, the law, sin and death.

By 'flesh' Paul means in the first instance the whole realm of concrete, tangible reality. It denotes not merely the sphere of the material or sensual, but equally life under the law, with its tangible achievements in keeping the letter of the commandment. This whole realm becomes a demonic power when man makes himself dependent upon it and lives 'after the flesh'. This may take the form of frivolity and licentiousness (Gal. 5.19ff.), which are thought to offer true life. Or it can be quite serious—scrupulous observance of the law (Gal. 3.3; Phil. 3.6), which again is thought to offer true life. In either case the thing man supposes he can control, whether it be pleasure or serious moral effort, becomes a power which controls him and drags him into the clutches of death. For by supposing that he can attain life from transitory things he makes himself dependent upon them, thus becoming himself a victim of transitory reality. Thus sin results in death, for sin is just this attempt of man to attain life through his own efforts. Sin does not, however, become explicit until man is confronted by the law. This awakens man's desire. This may happen either by his transgressing the law through his lustful impulses, or by his misusing the law in order to be able to 'boast' before God—that is to say, in order to attain life by his own strength (Rom. 5.20, 7.7–11). Thus the law, which is intrinsically holy, righteous and good, and comes from God, becomes a lethal power. That is why at times Paul can speak of it in quite a Gnostic way. Thus the rule is: 'The sting of death is sin, and the strength of sin is the law' (I Cor. 15.56). Once man has set out on this road, there is no turning back. He does not know what he is doing. While fondly supposing he is attaining life, he is on the road to death. Flesh, law, sin and death have become ineluctable powers. Man's guilt has become his fate.

The same truth is expressed in the dominant sense in which the term 'world' is used in the New Testament, often in a typically depreciating manner called 'this world'. Of course, the world, as in the Old Testament and in Judaism, is the creation of God. Yet at the same time it is an alien place for man. Only Christians, it is true, know that they are 'strangers and pilgrims' (I Pet. 2.11; cf. 1.1, 17), that their 'citizenship' is in heaven (Phil. 3.20), that here they have 'no continuing city, but seek one to come' (Heb. 13.14). But they are only realizing what is true of all men. That is what the gospel summons men to realize. It bids them awaken out of sleep, to stop being 'drunk' and to become sober, just as in the preaching of the Gnostics. For this world lies under the thrall of the 'rulers'. Its god is Satan. Hence 'the whole world lieth in the evil one' (I John 5.19). Further, hence, 'the world passeth away, and the lust thereof' (I John 2.17; I Cor. 7.31). The world, like the law, drags the man who has surrendered to it into the clutches of death. It, too, is a demonic power, embodied in Satan, who inspires the world with a spirit opposing the Spirit of God (I Cor. 2.12). Yet the world is not a mythical entity; in the last resort it is an historical one. This is shown by the way in which the world is generally an all-inclusive term for the environment in which men live, and is sometimes used in an even more restricted sense, meaning human society, with its aspirations and judgements, its wisdom, its joys and its sufferings. Thus every man makes his contribution to the 'world'. It is the world in just this sense which becomes a power tyrannizing over the individual, the fate he has created for himself. There is therefore no ultimate cosmological dualism such as we find in the Gnostics. This is proved by the way in which, for those who have been freed by Christ, the world recovers its character as creation, although even now it is not their home: 'The earth is the Lord's, and the fulness thereof.' 'Every creature of God is good, and nothing to be refused, if it be received with thanksgiving.' Thus the Christian is lord of the world (I Cor. 10.26; I Tim. 4.4; cf. Tit. 1.15; Rom. 14.14, 20; I Cor. 3.21f.).

Finally both the affinity between Christianity and Gnosticism and the difference between them are illustrated by the Christian conception of God's transcendence. In both systems that transcendence is conceived radically. There is nothing to suggest the classical view that God is immanent in the world, no suggestion that the orderly, law-abiding process of nature and course of history are proofs of the divine immanence. The New Testament knows nothing of the Stoic conception of providence. There is a great gulf between God and the world. The world is the 'lower region'; the place of darkness. God is 'above'. He is the light and the truth. 'No man hath seen God at any time' (John 1.18), He 'dwelleth in the light which no man can approach unto' (I Tim. 6.16).

The admonition 'Love not the world, neither the things that are in the world' is justified by the assertion that 'all that is in the world . . . is not of the Father, but is of the world' (I John 2.15f.). The Christian receives the Spirit of truth, whom the world cannot receive, because it does not see him or know him (John 14.17).

But this transcendence is not conceived ontologically as in Gnosticism. The gulf between God and man is not metaphysical. Light and darkness are not cosmic forces of a material kind. Nor is the transcendence of God confined to the pure negativity of the 'not worldly'. In the first place, it is his glorious sovereignty, which refuses to tolerate the pride of man or his forgetfulness of his creaturely status. 'God resisteth the proud, but giveth grace to the humble' (Jas. 4.6; I Pet. 5.5, after Prov. 3.34). All human planning must be qualified by the proviso, 'If the Lord will, and we live' (Jas. 4.13–15). God treats man as a potter treats his clay: he has mercy on whom he will, and whom he will he hardens (Rom. 9.18, 20f.). It is 'a fearful thing to fall into the hands of the living God' (Heb. 10.31).

Let no man deceive himself. If any man among you seemeth to be wise in this world, let him become a fool, that he may be wise. For the wisdom of this world is foolishness with God. For it is written, He taketh the wise in their own craftiness. And again, The Lord knoweth the thoughts of the wise, that they are vain (I Cor. 3.18–20).

No flesh may glory before God: 'He that glorieth, let him glory in the Lord' (I Cor. 1.29, 31; II Cor. 10.17).

Up to this point we are still moving within the orbit of the Old Testament tradition. But at this point it acquires an entirely new sense through the New Testament recognition that God, precisely by shattering all human boasting, reveals himself as the God of grace. The transcendence of God and his grace are one and the same thing. The Cross of Christ, which is God's judgement over the world and the means by which he makes the wisdom of this world foolishness, is the revelation of his grace. The man who accepts the Cross as God's judgement upon himself is delivered from the world. 'God forbid that I should glory save in the cross of our Lord Jesus Christ by whom the world is crucified unto me, and I unto the world' (Gal. 6.14). As God's judgement is his grace, so is his grace his judgement. For to be judged is simply to shut our hearts to grace (John 3.18).

The grace of God is not visible like worldly entities. His treasures are hidden in earthly vessels (II Cor. 4.7). The resurrection life is manifested in the world in the guise of death (II Cor. 12.9). Only in human

weakness is the power of God made known. Once again, this means
that the grace of God is never an assured possession. It is always ahead
of man, always a future possibility. As grace, the transcendence of God
is always his futurity, his constant being ahead of us, his always being
where we would like to be. He is always there already as the gracious
God for those who are open to the future, but as the judge for those
who shut their hearts against the future.

REDEMPTION

Man is incapable of redeeming himself from the world and the
powers which hold sway in it. Of these powers, the most important are
the flesh, sin, the law and death. Man's redemption—and at this point
Primitive Christianity and Gnosticism are in agreement—can only come
from the divine world as an event. It is something that must happen to
man from outside. Now Christian faith claims that this is precisely what
has happened in Jesus of Nazareth, in his death and resurrection. The
significance of his person may be expressed in terms derived from many
different sources, though it is not long before one particular interpretation of his person and work becomes the accepted norm. For the original
Palestinian Church Jesus is the 'Man' exalted by God, whose impending
advent is the subject of eager expectation. Through his past activity on
earth, Jesus had gathered around him the community of the last times.
Apparently, a redemptive significance was attached to his death. It was
regarded as an atoning sacrifice for sin, perhaps also as the sacrifice by
which God inaugurated the new covenant with his people. In the Hellenistic churches terms derived from the mysteries had to be used to
describe the redemptive significance of Jesus. He is the Lord worshipped
in the cultus. The initiated participate in his death and resurrection
through the sacraments of baptism and the Lord's Supper. The most
important development, however, was the interpretation of the person
of Jesus in terms of the Gnostic redemption myth. He is a divine figure
sent down from the celestial world of light, the Son of the Most High
coming forth from the Father, veiled in earthly form and inaugurating
the redemption through his work.

Even before Paul this interpretation of the person of Jesus had found
its way into the churches. For Paul is quite obviously quoting a traditional Christological hymn in Philippians 2.6–11, when he relates how
Christ, a pre-existent divine being, left the celestial world and appeared
on earth in the form of a servant, and after his death was exalted as

Lord. The same Gnostic myth lies behind the allusions of Paul to the mysterious divine wisdom, which the 'rulers of this world' did not recognize; for had they done so they would not have crucified the Lord of glory. In his earthly disguise he was invisible to them, and as a consequence, by crucifying him they brought about their own destruction (I Cor. 2.8f.). With these Gnostic concepts Paul combines quite naïvely the already traditional interpretation of the death of Jesus as an atoning sacrifice, which came partly from the Jewish cultus, partly from the juridical notions prevalent in Judaism (Rom. 3.25, etc.). He can just as easily interpret the death and Resurrection of Jesus in terms of the mysteries and their sacramentalism (Rom. 6.2ff.). But the dominant interpretation of the death and Resurrection of Jesus is the Gnostic conception of it as a cosmic event through which the 'old things' have been done away and the 'new' inaugurated (II Cor. 5.17). For Paul, Christ has lost his identity as an individual human person. He knows him no longer 'after the flesh' (II Cor. 5.16). Instead, Jesus has become a cosmic figure, a body to which all belong who have been joined to him through faith and baptism (I Cor. 12.12f.; Gal. 3.27f.). For it is 'into him' that men are baptized (Gal. 3.27), and 'in Christ' that the Christian lives henceforth. The Pauline 'in Christ' is often wrongly interpreted in a mystical sense, whereas it is a Gnostic cosmic conception. It may also be called an *ecclesiological* formula, since the 'body' of Christ is the Church, or an *eschatological* formula, since with the establishment of the body of Christ the eschatological event has been inaugurated.

The most thorough-going attempt to restate the redemptive work of Jesus in Gnostic terms is to be found in the Fourth Gospel. Here Jesus is the pre-existent Son of God, the Word who exists with him from all eternity. He is sent from God, sent into the world, as its light, to give sight to the blind, and to blind those who see (John 9.39). He is not only the light, but also the life and the truth. As the agent of revelation, he brings all these blessings and calls to his side his 'own', those who are 'of the truth'. After accomplishing his Father's mission, he is exalted from the earth and returns to heaven to prepare a way for his own, that they may join him in the heavenly mansions. Indeed, he is himself the 'way' (14.6). 'I, if I be lifted up, from the earth, will draw all men unto me' (12.32).

It is easy to see why the Christian Church took over these ideas from the Gnostic redemption myth. That myth offered a terminology in which the redemption wrought in the person and work of Jesus could be made intelligible as a present reality. The eschatological event was

already being realized in the present. This sense of being the eschatological community, of being already raised from this world by the grace
of God, of deliverance from its powers, could not be adequately con-
veyed to the Hellenistic world in terms of the Jewish eschatological
hope, which looked for redemption in the future. Indeed, a thinker of
Paul's calibre was already sensitive to the difficulty. The eschatological
event must be understood as a process already inaugurated with the
coming of Jesus, or with his death and Resurrection, and the Gnostic
redemption myth lay ready to hand as a vehicle for its expression.

In Paul the Gnostic ideas are still combined with the Jewish apocalyptic element. He still uses the apocalyptic conception of the two ages
thus: 'When the fulness of time came, God sent forth his Son' (Gal.
4.4). But the real pcint is that the coming of Christ is thus designated
as the inauguration of the eschatological event. Isaiah's prediction of
the day of redemption is now being fulfilled: 'Behold, now is the accepted time; behold, now is the day of salvation' (II Cor. 6.2).

The man in Christ is already a 'new creature', for 'old things are
passed away; behold, all things are become new' (II Cor. 5.17). Hence
the triumphant cry:

Death is swallowed up in victory.
O death, where is thy sting?
O death, where is thy victory? . . .
Thanks be to God, who giveth us the victory through our Lord
    Jesus Christ (I Cor. 15.54–7).

The cosmic powers have already been dethroned:

When we were in the flesh, the motions of sins, which were by the
law, did work in our members to bring forth fruit unto death. But now
we are delivered from the law, being dead [with Christ] to [the power]
wherein we were held: that we should serve in newness of spirit, and
not in the oldness of the letter (Rom. 7.5f.).

Or:

But before faith came, we were kept under the law, shut up unto the
faith which should afterwards be revealed. . . . But after that faith is
come, we are no longer under a schoolmaster. For ye are all the children
of God by faith in Christ Jesus. For as many of you as have been baptized into Christ have put on Christ . . . for ye are all one in Christ Jesus
(Gal. 3.23–8).

When we were children, [we] were in bondage under the elements
of the world; but when the time was fulfilled, God sent forth his Son

. . . to redeem them that were under the law, that we might receive the adoption of sons (Gal. 4.3ff.).

With all this, Paul still combines the apocalyptic picture of the parousia, the resurrection of the dead and the judgement. But for the Fourth Gospel, the redemption is exclusively a present process.

And this is the condemnation, that light is come into the world. . . . (John 3.19).
Verily, verily, I say unto you, He that heareth my word, and believeth on him that sent me, hath everlasting life, and shall not come into condemnation; but is passed from death unto life. Verily, verily, I say unto you, The hour is coming, and now is, when the dead shall hear the voice of the Son of God: and they that hear shall live (John 5.24f.).
I am the resurrection, and the life: he that believeth in me, though he were dead, yet shall he live: And whosoever liveth and believeth in me shall never die (John 11.25f.).
Now is the judgement of this world: now shall the prince of this world be cast out (John 12.31).

Christianity thus agrees with Gnosticism in placing the eschatological event in the present. It is inaugurated by the appearance of the redeemer on earth. Hence it follows that for Christianity, as well as for Gnosticism, the present salvation is not visible like an event in history. Indeed, some of the sayings which express this have quite a Gnostic ring. 'Ye are dead, and your life is hid with Christ in God' (Col. 3.3). Or: 'Now are we the sons of God, and it doth not yet appear what we shall be' (I John 3.2). The believers are, in principle, no longer 'in the flesh', though, of course, in practice they are still in it (II Cor. 10.3; Gal 2.20). The outward man is decaying while the inner man is being renewed, but this process is no more visible to the outward eye than the glory of Christ which far outshines the glory which once covered Moses' face (II Cor. 3.7ff.), or the transformation of the believers into this same glory as they behold it (II Cor. 3.18). We live by faith, not by sight (II Cor. 5.7), and the knowledge we have at present is as problematical as an image reflected in a mirror. We shall not see face to face until the end (I Cor. 13.12).

Yet as in Gnosticism, the event of redemption is exhibited in certain phenomena, which somehow or other represent it. Indeed, at first sight it would seem that this is truer of Christianity than it is of Gnosticism. For in Gnosticism the mission and advent of the redeemer and the inauguration of the eschatological event were relegated to a mythical age before history began, while in Christianity these things are events of the recent past. It is the appearance of Jesus of Nazareth and his crucifixion, events whose historicity is vouched for by eye witnesses and by the tradition of which they are the source. All the same, it would be wrong to lay too much stress on this. For to begin with the historical person of Jesus was very soon turned into a myth in primitive Christianity. Furthermore, the Gnostics also believed that the advent of the redeemer was a real event, and the source of the tradition enshrined in their worship and doctrine.

The really important point is that for both Christianity and Gnosticism the tradition is itself the presence of the spiritual world in this world. Or, to put it more precisely, the redeemer is present in the word of preaching, the message from above. In the proclamation the eschatological event is bodied forth into the present. According to Paul, when God inaugurated the event of redemption in the death and Resurrection of Christ, he simultaneously established the word of preaching, the ministry of reconciliation. Where this word is heard, the eschatological redemption becomes a present reality (II Cor. 5.18f., 6.2). Similarly, the Fourth Gospel ascribes to Jesus the title of Logos or Word. Originally, this had been a mythological term. According to John Jesus is the Word because he has received from the Father the commission to proclaim the message with which he has been entrusted to the world, and is fulfilling it (8.26, etc). His words are 'spirit and life' (6.63). They bring both purification and judgement.

In conjunction with the word there are also the sacraments, as in the Gnostic systems. Christian sacramental theology differs little from that of Gnosticism, if at all. But its conception of the word is different, and that is decisive. It is true that in both systems the word is a call to awake, a summons to repentance and a challenge to decision. But in Gnosticism this call could only be a summons to become conscious of one's alienation from the world and to detach oneself from it. That it also meant something positive, a real turning to the grace of God, was something that Gnosticism could only make clear by cosmological instruction, by the myth of the archetypal man and the fate of the spark of light, which was man's true Self. Such mystagogic instruction could hardly have the urgency of a call to decision. Primitive Christian preaching had no use for cosmological instruction or for the doctrine of the pre-existence of the soul. And although it presents the Cross and Resurrection of Jesus in mythological terms, the preaching of the Cross is nevertheless a decisive summons to repentance. This is because the redemptive significance of the Cross (and therefore of the Resurrection also) can only become apparent to those who submit to being crucified with Christ, who accept him as Lord in their daily lives. Adherence to the gospel message is called 'faith', and faith involves a new existential understanding of Self. In it man realizes his creatureliness and guilt. It is an act of obedience, in which man surrenders all his 'boasting', all desire to live on his own resources, all adherence to tangible realities, and assents to the scandalous fact of a crucified Lord. Thus he is freed from the world by being freed from himself. It is true that both primitive Christianity and Gnosticism agree in attributing man's liberation to the act of God. But in Gnosticism what was freed was the true self, the spark of light in man, whereas for Christian faith man is freed *for* his authentic self by being freed from himself—from the self which man, qualified as he is by his guilty past, brings along with him into the present. The Gnostic is one 'saved by nature', the Christian through his faith. Hence the typical designation for the Christian religion is not knowledge, but faith.

This shows that the New Testament understands human existence as an historical existence. The Gnostics, on the other hand, attribute everything to fate, and therefore they understand human existence in the categories of natural Being. This is made abundantly clear in the doctrine of the pre-existence of the soul. For an existence which lies behind me, but must nevertheless be accepted as my own, despite the fact that it lies outside the range of my experience, and I can never be responsible for it, belongs not to history, but to nature. The discovery of the absolute distinction between humanity and its objective environment, the discovery made in the experience of the blows of fate, is nullified when that distinction is interpreted in ontological terms, as can be seen by the use of the phrase 'being saved by nature'.

There is a similar difference when we compare the Gnostic conception of the body of the redeemer with the Pauline doctrine of the body of Christ. Paul, of course, makes use of cosmological categories when he expounds the doctrine of the body of Christ. But in practice he always transposes it into an historical key. For although he does not reject the view that the sacraments of baptism and the Lord's Supper are the means by which men are grafted into the body of Christ, the decisive point is that membership of the body of Christ is acquired by faith. And faith after all is genuine historical decision. Hence Paul can use the Gnostic conception of the body of Christ in combination with the metaphor, common in Graeco-Roman literature, of the body as the social organism of the state in order to describe the solidarity of the Christian community (I Cor. 12.14ff.). The body of Christ thus acquires shape in an historical context founded on preaching and faith, in which the individual members belonging to it are bound together in mutual care for one another, sharing each other's sufferings and joys.

Finally, the affinity and difference between Gnosticism and Christianity are illustrated from their conception of the pneuma or Spirit. The Gnostics identified the pneuma with the spark of light which has its abode in the inward man. When the agent of revelation came, he quickened the divine spark to newness of life, or if it was dead, restored it. This is similar to the Christian idea that the Spirit is imparted to the baptized and that it operates in them as a divine vital power. In popular Christianity, the Spirit was naïvely regarded as the source of miraculous phenomena. As in Gnosticism, such phenomena were, in an illogical manner, accepted as visible demonstrations of the supernatural, otherworldly character of the baptized. We are referring, of course, to prophecy, ecstasy and speaking with tongues. But neither for Paul nor for the author of the Fourth Gospel, nor even for the New Testament as a whole is ecstasy the high water mark of the Christian life, or the visible manifestation of the transcendent. This is all the more remarkable in the case of Paul, for he knows all about such things as ecstasy, and if he wanted to could boast about ecstatic experiences of his own. But that is just what he refuses to do. He prefers to glory in his 'infirmities'. It is here that he sees the divine power at work in himself (II Cor. 12.1–10). But while Paul does not reject the popular view, he gives it a new turn. He finds real evidence of the Spirit's working in Christian moral behaviour, in victory over lust and passion, and in simple, everyday acts of love. Here of course the operation of the pneuma loses its evidential value. This is shown by the way the Gnosticizing Corinthians criticize Paul for not displaying visible evidence of his pneumatic endowments. It is against such criticism that Paul is directing his polemic in II Cor. 10–13.

According to Paul, the pneuma—and here he determines the line of all future development—is not a magic power working in the hearts of the believers, but the norm of practical behaviour. Whereas in the past Christians had lived after the flesh—that is to say, they had centred their lives on visible, tangible realities—they must now orientate their lives on the Spirit. But since the Spirit is already enjoyed as a gift, it is in the last resort equivalent to the new possibility of life opened up by the grace of God, the life of freedom. Just because it is a gift, freedom is power. It is man's own capacity freed from the cosmic powers. And this power is at the same time the norm of behaviour, because freedom means openness for the future—openness, that is, for every fresh claim of God both to action and to the acceptance of his fate. To possess the pneuma does not mean therefore that once a man has made the decision of faith and has been baptized he is now perfect, and need make no further decisions. On the contrary, he is now free as never before for each successive genuine decision in life. His life has become historical in the true sense of the word. Hence the Pauline paradox: 'Work out your own salvation with fear and trembling. *For* it is God which worketh in you both to will and to do of his good pleasure' (Phil. 2.12f.).

Every decision in life involves a renewal of the decision of faith. It means a determination to live 'after the Spirit'. To be 'led by the Spirit' is something realized in the accomplishment of such decisions. It is obedience to the imperative, 'walk in the Spirit' (Rom. 8.12–14; Gal. 5.16f.). So far from being abrogated, the divine imperative is now grounded on the indicative of freedom; 'If we live by the Spirit, let us also walk in the Spirit' (Gal. 5.25; cf. Rom. 5.12–23; I Cor. 5.7, 6.11). The fulfillment of the law is now no longer the way to salvation, for salvation has already been granted as a gift. Rather, it is the outcome of that gift. The law as the way to salvation has been abrogated. But in so far as it is an expression of the good and holy will of God (Rom. 7.12), it is fulfilled as never before 'in us, who walk not after the flesh, but after the Spirit' (Rom. 8.4), and that means the commandment of love, which comprehends all the precepts of the law. Paul is, of course, thinking here only of the ethical precepts of the law. 'For all the law is fulfilled in one word, even in this; Thou shalt love thy neighbour as thyself' (Gal. 5.14). 'For he that loveth another hath fulfilled the law. Love worketh no ill to his neighbour, therefore love is the fulfilling of the law' (Rom. 13.8–10). If there is any demonstration of faith to the world, any proof of the new life, it is love. 'By this shall all men know that ye are my disciples, if ye have love one to another' (John 13.35). Love is the only criterion by which the believer can know that he has ceased to belong to the old world. 'We know that we have passed from death unto life, because we love the brethren' (I John 3.14).

It is those who share the Spirit and are bound in mutual love who make up the body of Christ, the Church. Since it is a fellowship of the Spirit, it is essentially invisible to the world. In one sense, of course, it is visible, like the Gnostic communities. It consists of real men and women, who still live 'in the flesh'. But here we are faced with a paradox. This conglomeration of believers is also the eschatological community, the 'body of Christ', whose existence is not subject to objective proof. Those who are united in the Church are not bound together by any worldly interests or motives. They are not joined by a common nationality, or even by an Idea, but by the Spirit which dwells in each of them. And just because of this, just because the Church depends for its existence, not on worldly motives or resources, but on the power available through the grace of God, Paul can describe it as that cosmic entity, the 'body of Christ'.

The practical behaviour of the Church and its members in the world resembles that of the Gnostics in that it rests upon a sense of superiority over the world, in an awareness that 'neither death, nor life, nor angels, nor principalities, nor powers, nor things present, nor things to come . . . shall be able to separate us from the love of God, which is in Christ Jesus' (Rom. 8.38f.). This absolute independence from the world, however, produces a certain detachment from all worldly interests and responsibilities. Primitive Christianity is quite uninterested in making the world a better place, it has no proposals for political or social reform. All must do their duty to the State. But they have no direct political responsibilities. After all, the Christian is a 'citizen of heaven' (Phil. 3.20). The slave who is 'in the Lord' has become free from the world, but he must not therefore suppose that he ought to seek sociological freedom: 'Let every man, wherein he is called, therein abide with God' (I Cor. 7.17–24). Freedom might in itself breed licence, but against that the Old Testament, the Jewish tradition and the words of the Lord are a surety. Where such tendencies appear, they are vigorously resisted (I Cor. 6.12–20). Instead, this negative attitude to the world tends to find its outlet in asceticism. Such tendencies appear very early in Christian history, even in Paul himself, when he allows marriage as a necessary evil, and regards celibacy as a special charisma. Ritualistic asceticism, which appears here and there, he tolerates as an infirmity (Rom. 14; I Cor. 8, 10), but he knows that 'there is nothing unclean of itself: but to him that esteemeth anything to be unclean, to him it is unclean' (Rom. 14.14). 'All things are pure; but it is evil for that man who eateth with offence' (Rom. 14.20). The fundamental principle behind such questions is: 'Whatsoever is not of faith is sin' (Rom. 14.23). Paul's own standpoint is not one of legalistic asceticism, but a dialectic of participation and inward detachment:

It remaineth that both
they that have wives be as though they had none;
And they that weep, as though they wept not;
and they that rejoice, as though they rejoiced not;
And they that use this world, as though they had no dealings with
    it (I Cor. 7.29–31).

This interior detachment is described in that saying of Paul about his
knowing how to be filled and to be hungry, to abound and to be in want
(Phil. 4.11–13). And when he exhorts his readers to 'Rejoice with them
that do rejoice, and weep with them that weep' (Rom. 12.15), he is, of
course, taking it for granted that the faithful share in the ordinary
experiences of life.

Yes, in a certain sense action and experience in this world is not a
matter of indifference, but vital and essential. It is the action and
experience of the free man borne along by love. True, the Spirit is not
a principle which can be applied to the improvement of the world. In
this respect, it is the Christian's duty to be indifferent to the world. But
just because he has no definite programme, the Christian must be always discovering new duties. He is a new man, and by 'the renewing
of his mind' he has been given the capacity to 'prove what is that good,
and acceptable, and perfect, will of God' (Rom. 12.2). Hence it was
possible for the early Church to develop a pattern of catechetical instruction, in which it adopted many ethical concepts of Hellenism (Phil.
4.8), the lists of duties formulated in the 'household codes', and finally,
in the Pastoral Epistles, the ideals of the Hellenistic *petit bourgeoisie*.

It would therefore be true to say—and without questioning its fundamentally dialectic attitude to the world—that Christian detachment
from civic duty and from political and social responsibility is not one
of principle, but only a temporary exigency forced upon the Church
by its historical situation. It was due partly to the expectation of an
imminent end of the world, partly to the social composition of the
earliest Christian communities. It would never have occurred to their
members that they might assume social, still less political responsibilities.

In their experience of the Spirit and their knowledge that the grace
of God makes men free to love, the problem which was so fatal for
Gnosticism, i.e. the problem of the unworldliness of the Self, finds its
solution. In Gnosticism the unworldly self could only be described in
negatives. It could only be a matter of faith. It was a point from which

every possible human action and experience was denied. In primitive Christianity, on the other hand, that same problem found a positive solution. It was still an object of faith, for it always lay in the future. It could never be present as an objective datum. Yet in the moment of action it was a present reality. For in the moment of action man is always grasping at the future, always being translated anew into the future. In the love which is grounded on faith (Gal. 5.6) the unworldly always becomes a present, objective reality, while in hope it is still in the future. Every act of love, though performed in the objective world, is paradoxically an eschatological event.

In the last analysis, however, the future can never, as in Gnosticism, be conceived in fantastic cosmic terms, despite all the apocalyptic imagery which has found its way into the New Testament. It can only be understood in the light of God's grace as the permanent futurity of God which is always there before man arrives, wherever it be, even in the darkness of death. Paul can certainly speak of a glory which is ready to be revealed for us (Rom. 8.18), of the eternal 'weight of glory' which awaits us (II Cor. 4.17). But at the same time he speaks of faith, hope and love as things which will not cease, even when that which is perfect is come (I Cor. 13.13). In other words he can conceive no state of perfection in which the unworldly is a mere possession. The openness of Christian existence is never-ending.

Suggestions for Further Reading

BULTMANN, RUDOLF, *Jesus and the Word.* New York: Charles Scribner's Sons, 1934.

DANIEL-ROPS, H., *Jesus and His Times,* 2 vols., rev. ed. Garden City, N.Y.: Image Books, 1958.

ENSLIN, M. S., *Christian Beginnings.* New York: Harper & Brothers, 1956.

GOODSPEED, EDGAR J., *A Life of Jesus.* New York: Harper & Brothers, 1950.

GRANT, ROBERT M., *Augustus to Constantine.* New York: Harper & Row, 1970.

JAEGER, WERNER, *Early Christianity and the Greek Paideia.* Cambridge, Mass.: Harvard University Press, 1961.

KLAUSNER, JOSEPH, *From Jesus to Paul.* London: Allen and Unwin, 1944.

NEILL, STEPHEN, *The Interpretation of the New Testament 1861–1961.* London and New York: Oxford University Press, 1964.

PELIKAN, JAROSLAV, *The Christian Tradition: A History of the Development of Doctrine*, Vol. I *The History of the Catholic Tradition to* A.D. *600*. Chicago: University of Chicago Press, 1971.

PELIKAN, JAROSLAV, *The Development of Christian Doctrine: Some Historical Prolegomena*. New Haven, Conn.: Yale University Press, 1969.

SCHWEITZER, ALBERT, *The Quest of the Historical Jesus*. New York: The Macmillan Company, 1948.

MICHAEL ROSTOVTZEFF
The Roman Empire—
Greatness and Decline

❧ The greatest historian of the economic and social
life of the Mediterranean world from the third century B.C.
to the fourth century A.D. was the Russian-born historian
Michael Rostovtzeff, who died in 1952. Rostovtzeff belonged to that great generation of Russian intellectuals and
scholars who witnessed, and in many cases took a leading
part in, the revolutions of 1917. At the time of the fall of
tsardom and the triumph of the Bolsheviks, Rostovtzeff,
although still a young man, had achieved an international
reputation as an archaeologist and historian of the ancient
world. He was one of those liberals who wanted political
and social reform in Russia and the emancipation of the
masses, but who found the Communist dictatorship even
less palatable than the tsarist autocracy. Consequently,
Rostovtzeff joined the ranks of liberal emigrés from Russia
after the establishment of the Leninist dictatorship. He
went first to England, where his broad interests in the
course of social and economic change in Hellenistic and
Roman imperial eras were not appreciated by the rather
narrow classical scholarship prevailing at Oxford in the
early 1920's. Therefore, Rostovtzeff came to the United
States and became a professor of ancient history first for

FROM M. Rostovtzeff, *A History of the Ancient World*,
Vol. II, *Rome* (Oxford: Clarendon Press, 1927), pp. 258–265,
286–291, 293–297, 299–304; and M. Rostovtzeff, *The Social and
Economic History of the Roman Empire*, Vol. I (Oxford: Clarendon Press, 1957), 2d ed., pp. 502–507, 509–527, 530–534.

a short time at the University of Wisconsin and then for the last twenty-five years of his life at Yale University.

Rostovtzeff's *A History of the Ancient World*, the first volume of which is devoted to Greece and the second to Rome, was published in 1927. This work was remarkable for its exhaustive learning, including archaeological and artistic material, its clear style, and its easily comprehensible portrayal of social change and political and economic institutions. It immediately established its author as his generation's eminent authority on ancient history. This survey of Greek and Roman history still remains the best introduction to the subject for the undergraduate student and lay reader. But with his indefatigable energy and unflagging dedication, Rostovtzeff published two additional works which are among the great monuments of twentieth-century scholarship: a two-volume *Social and Economic History of the Roman Empire* and a three-volume *Social and Economic History of the Hellenistic World*. These works opened up new horizons for students of ancient history, and all subsequent research on the social and economic history of the Mediterranean world between 300 B.C. and 400 A.D. has taken Rostovtzeff's studies as their starting point. All further interpretations of the subject must be related to Rostovtzeff's theses, either by way of affirming or amending them.

The following selection, taken from *A History of the Ancient World* and *The Social and Economic History of the Roman Empire*, presents Rostovtzeff's general view of the destiny of Mediterranean civilization in the first four centuries of the Christian era. Although a refugee and dissenter from the Bolshevik revolution, Rostovtzeff was deeply influenced by the Marxist theory of the primacy of the dialectical class struggle in history, which was to some degree affirmed for him by the agonies and conflicts within Russian society in the first two decades of the twentieth century. Therefore while he praised the Roman Empire for the effectiveness of its political and legal institutions, he was deeply conscious of the elitist character of ancient civilization. He perceived, as no previous historian of the Roman Empire had clearly seen, a fatal dichotomy between, on the one hand, a narrow elite in whose hands lay all the political and economic power and, on the other, the vast majority of the population, a genuinely disinherited, disenfranchised, alienated, and illiterate proletariat.

With astonishing clarity and persuasive eloquence, Rostovtzeff depicted the process by which the Mediterranean elite, consisting of remnants of the old Roman aristocracy and the newer high bourgeoisie of the Mediterranean cities, lost their control over society. He identified fundamental weaknesses in the governmental and economic institutions of the Empire which even in the second century A.D.—what Edward Gibbon called the golden age of mankind—were producing ever-increasing decentralization, agricultural and industrial decline, and diminution of the power of the imperial elite. Almost inevitably, according to Rostovtzeff, these factors produced the civil wars and social conflicts of the third century and the rise to power, and finally to the imperial throne itself, of proletarian leaders who were able to triumph over the old elite through their position as generals in the proletarian-dominated army. By the end of the third century, therefore, the government of the Roman Empire passed into the hands of men whose provenance was the masses rather than the elite, and these at best half-educated leaders could but dimly if at all comprehend the classical ideals and upper-class culture which had for so long been synonymous with ancient civilization.

Rostovtzeff's study of the development of the Roman Empire consequently ended with a lesson of great relevance to twentieth-century society. He saw in the history of the ancient world a tragic pattern: when an elite group which established a civilization but failed to absorb the masses lost its control, the masses absorbed the civilization but in so doing debased, barbarized, and finally extinguished it. Rostovtzeff seems to have seen a somewhat similar pattern in the history of early twentieth-century Russia, and he posed as a great question for contemporary Western civilization: Could it hope to achieve genuine democracy and at the same time maintain the culture originally developed by an elite? Rostovtzeff was not alone in raising this crucial question—in 1930 the Spanish philosopher of history Ortega y Gassett defined the same crisis for modern man in his book *The Revolt of the Masses*—but Rostovtzeff was able to assess the problem in the context of the history of the ancient world and therefore to present it in a particularly trenchant and convincing way.

In the four decades since the publication of the first edition of the *Social and Economic History of the Roman Empire*, Rostovtzeff's general interpretation of the development of the Roman Empire has been severely criticized by scholars who feel that he superimposed an arbitrary scheme of class conflict on the complex processes of political, social, and economic change in the Mediterranean world of the first four centuries of the Christian era. It is held that his interpretation is too arbitrary and oversimplified. He is criticized for his tendency toward historical determinism, that is, his inclination to believe in the inevitable consequence of long-range social and economic factors. It is claimed that Rostovtzeff did not sufficiently allow for the choices, fortunate or unfortunate, made by individual men. He is also criticized for seeming to assume that in the ancient world men were conscious of their class identification and were motivated by class conflicts. Because an emperor like Diocletian or Constantine came from peasant stock, so the argument runs, it does not mean that his policies were inspired by a proletarian antagonism against the old elite.

The debate on the merit of Rostovtzeff's thesis is not likely to be soon resolved because it raises the most difficult and profound questions on the nature of historical understanding and the validity of historical interpretation. Nevertheless, the view Rostovtzeff gave of the development of Mediterranean society under the Roman Empire is the only fundamental reinterpretation of the era since Edward Gibbon's *Decline and Fall of the Roman Empire,* written in the later eighteenth century. Rostovtzeff's work remains the only thesis providing a general pattern of change for these four critical centuries of European history.

❧ॐॐ❧

The government of the empire, whose main lines were laid down by Augustus during his long principate, was developed by his successors in the direction indicated by him, becoming more and more methodical and systematic. The most successful and most fruitful work in this department was done by Claudius with his private staff, by Vespasian, and by Hadrian. By the second century we find in existence a system of government where the main principles were unalterably fixed and the changes introduced were chiefly alterations and improvements of detail that did not affect the general structure.

All the threads of administration met in the hands of the emperor and the Central Office attached to his person, where the different heads of departments assumed more and more the character of ministers for the whole empire. Here were worked out, in adaptation to particular cases, all the principles of administration, justice, and finance; and from here all the emperor's missives—either direct edicts (*edicta*), or instructions to high officials (*mandata*), or letters (*epistulae*), or replies (*rescripta*) to letters and petitions—streamed out into every part of the empire, where they were either published or preserved in the archives of the recipients. Copies were kept in the imperial archives at Rome and afforded the precedents by which later emperors were guided. Great importance attached also to the decisions of law courts, over which the emperor presided in person, generally sitting as a judge of appeal. Such appeals were put in order by a special department of the imperial offices.

This Central Office was divided into departments for the separate branches of imperial business; and each department was supervised by a single chief, who was originally a freedman, a personal servant, of the emperor; but occasionally from Otho's time, and regularly after Hadrian's accession, he was an official of equestrian rank. The most important department managed the finances and property of the emperor, his *rationes*, or accounts; and the head of this department was styled *a rationibus*; a subdivision of this department dealt with the private property (*patrimonium*) of the ruler. Other important departments were these: the *ab epistulis* and *a libellis*, which dealt with letters and petitions; the judicial department (*a cognitionibus*); the department of records (*a memoria*); and the department for collecting evidence concerning matters of dispute (*a studiis*). All imperial business was recorded in a special journal (*commentarii*) kept by an official styled *a commentariis*.

There is no doubt that, as the principate developed, the administrative activity of the ruler grew more and more comprehensive. But the government of the empire in the first and second centuries was far from being a bureaucracy in the modern sense of the word. The ordinary subject, except the inhabitants of the capital, came much less into contact with the officials of the central government than he does in any modern state except America. The imperial officials or, to put it more generally, the direct instruments of the state in general, including the governors of imperial or senatorial provinces, were a mere superstructure added to self-governing communities throughout the empire. The elective magistrates of these communities were the links that connected the man in the street with the state. They and the municipal councils in Italy and the provinces had entire control over the town and its affairs; they were also judges of first instance, and gave orders to the police of the town and district; they acted as government agents in settling and collecting the direct taxes; and they enforced other obligations on the inhabitants, such as making and maintaining roads, and conveying government officers or stores or the government post. They discharged these duties, not only for the town but also for the district, often very large, which formed the territory belonging to the town. In ordinary cases the agents of the central government merely supervised the municipal authorities and heard complaints brought against them by the local inhabitants.

It is true that the right of interference in municipal affairs, possessed by proconsuls and propraetors, and the imperial legates and procurators, was limited by no law but by tradition only; and a tolerably free use of this right was sometimes made at a crisis, when these great men issued written edicts or verbal proclamations to their military and civilian subordinates. But, as I have said already, the emperor kept a sharp look-out on the doings of provincial governors; and the governor knew that the annual meetings in the provincial capital, where representatives of the towns came to do worship in honour of the emperor and to discuss local business, might at any time complain of illegal or violent action on his part and draw down on him the vengeance of the Senate or the emperor. Nevertheless, as the demands of the state upon the towns, both in the way of taxes and personal obligations laid upon the inhabitants, became more onerous, the interference of the central gov-

ernment in municipal affairs became commoner. Under the pretext that
the towns were sunk in debt and incapable of managing their finances,
special commissions were appointed by the emperor to report on the
facts; and from Trajan's time permanent inspectors (*curatores*) discharged this office, steadily eclipsing the municipal authorities and reducing them to a position in which they were responsible to the state
for the town and its territory, but entirely unable to act freely in town
affairs. The same process is observable in Italy: the magistrates were
overshadowed by the officials who managed the private property of the
emperor in the peninsula and also by the senators who had charge of
the roads; and from the time of Marcus Aurelius special legates with
judicial powers (*legati iuridici*) were the real governors of their different
districts.

The direct control of the emperor, however, extended only to a few
departments of government. He did, indeed, control his own immense
and ever-increasing property; his men of business (*procuratores*) managed his estates, houses, forests, mines, and factories. The number of
these agents, very large in the time of Augustus, grew larger steadily.
A second swarm of procurators, working in the imperial provinces,
collected, chiefly through the agency of the city magistrates, the direct
tax paid by the provincials, and supervised both revenue and expenditure, the latter including pay and maintenance for the armies and the
cost of managing the state domains. Officials of this kind were especially numerous in the rich country of Egypt. In course of time the
emperors thought it necessary to extend their control to the collection
of the so-called 'indirect taxes'—the succession duty, the duty paid on
liberated slaves and on auctions, and the tax on imports and exports.
At first special controllers were appointed to watch the doings of the
different contractors and contracting companies; but later the state took
into its own hands the collection of these imposts, and they were managed by officials nominated by the emperor. The distinction between
state property and imperial property became fainter and fainter, and
the *fiscus,* or treasury of the emperor, became more and more identical
with the public treasury. Thus, for example, even in the senatorial
provinces the management of the emperor's private estates was conducted in the same office as the management of the state domains.

The emperor therefore eventually found himself at the head not only
of an army of soldiers but of another army of officials, who were all
appointed, paid, judged, and punished by himself alone. From a very
early date the highest official posts were given to members of the

equestrian class, while the inferior duties in the innumerable offices were performed by the emperor's freedmen and slaves. Thus a new class in society came into existence, and a new hierarchy, in which the gradations were fixed chiefly by the amount of salary but later by titles of honour as well. Officials of the equestrian rank were styled *vir egregius, vir eminentissimus,* or *vir perfectissimus,* according to the duties they discharged, but the title of *vir clarissimus* was reserved for senators. The chief equestrian officials received a salary ranging from 60,000 to 300,000 sesterces; and such a man might eventually become either commander of the praetorian guard (*praefectus praetorio*), or governor of Egypt, or controller of the Roman corn-supply (*praefectus annonae*); or they might command the city fire brigade or the fleets or serve as procurators in the chief provinces. But the privileged few were sharply distinguished from their subordinates. They belonged to the upper classes and had generally served as officers in the army, while the inferior members were slaves or half-free, with no hope of promotion to the superior class, although there were occasional instances of it, especially under Claudius.

The main business, however, of all these officials was the finance and economic progress of the state. But in matters not financial almost complete freedom was left, as I have said before, to the local self-governing units which composed the state.

As *pontifex maximus* the emperor was the head of the state religion, and worship was paid to him personally throughout the empire. Yet the religious life of his subjects was not affected in its development by any interference on the part of the state: even the worship which he received as chief of the state was managed entirely by the self-governing towns and by voluntary societies of individuals called *Augustales*.

Similarly the emperor had no direct connexion with the administration of justice or with the codification of civil and criminal law. Local courts continued to administer local law in Italy and the provinces. Together with these, Roman citizens, just as in republican times, had access to the tribunals in the capital, which relied upon the services of the *iuris consulti* or specialist interpreters of the law; while the provincials resorted to other judges who formed part of the governor's staff. At Rome, and still more in the provinces, the Roman law and the local codes, especially that of Greece, naturally overlapped and affected one another, so that an imperial system of law grew up. But this was a slow process, and the praetors at Rome and the provincial governors took a share in it as well as the emperors. Nevertheless, the emperors began by degrees to exert a stronger influence in the sphere of law and justice. The highest criminal court for culprits belonging to the senatorial class was now the Senate itself; and its action was governed by the expressed wishes of the emperor. As the ruler of many provinces, the emperor, sitting as a court of appeal, gave sentence in the most important cases that were referred from them. As head of the army, he framed the main rules of martial law; and as head of the financial administration, he employed his procurators and the 'advocates of the *fiscus*' to work out a scheme of legal relations in those cases where, in matters of taxation or in the administration of the imperial *patrimonium*, the rights of the state clashed with the rights of the individual. And lastly, the emperor's decisions, either judicial or administrative, soon acquired the force of law and, as such, became one of the main sources of law. An active part in framing them was taken not only by the imperial officials but also by eminent jurisconsults. Thus by degrees was formed that great structure of Roman law under the empire, which was codified later by two emperors successively, Theodosius and Justinian, and has been preserved to our time in that form.

The protection of the subject and the maintenance of order throughout the empire did not form part of the duties discharged by the central government. The emperor's responsibility was limited to the defence of the frontiers and the policing of the seas. Order within the state was maintained by the municipal bodies by means of the local police. Here, however, we notice again the gradual encroachment of the emperor. The safety and order of the great military roads was not sufficiently assured by the towns through which these roads passed; and for this reason the emperors entrusted the duty to small detachments of soldiers, and stationed military police (*stationes*) at the most dangerous points. Soldiers were also employed to keep an eye on persons suspected of political disaffection, whom the towns could not be trusted to deal with; and this secret police, recruited from the army, increased greatly in numbers from the time of Hadrian.

The means of communication, and the construction and maintenance of the great military roads, had long been among the principal concerns of the central government, and became under the empire indispensable to the safety and prosperity of the state. The emperors recognized this fact and achieved one of their chief public services, when, by using the army and spending immense sums from their own pockets, they created such a network of roads as mankind had never before dreamed of. It was the duty of the local authorities to construct the local and less important roads; but even here the emperors quickened the activity of the communities and kept an eye on what they were doing. The postal service and the conveyance of passengers and goods are matters connected with the making of roads; but these important services the state was never able to perform for the mass of its subjects. A service was organized for officials and official correspondence, and for the conveyance of government stores; but this was maintained with difficulty and by means of requisitions burdensome to the people. The private individual had to arrange these matters for himself.

To provide for the refinement and comfort of life in the capital was a duty which was manfully discharged by the emperors. Rome, the city which we now see in ruins, was their spoilt child. The spacious forums, surrounded by splendid temples and public buildings, were their creation. Following the lead of Pompey, the new lords of Rome converted the Campus Martius from end to end into a range of majestic memorial buildings in a setting of parks. By careful planning, they brought order into the chaotic and haphazard growth of the ancient city, and carried out a series of systematic measures in order to make it, in point of sanitation and police control, reasonably well adapted to its million inhabitants. They controlled and supervised the numerous aqueducts and the drainage; to protect the city from floods, they straightened the banks of the Tiber and built a stone embankment; they provided for the scavenging of the streets and maintained order in the streets and public places; they arranged for the regular and abundant supply of food, and financed and regulated the gratuitous distributions of corn which had become a standing institution. And lastly, the emperors were careful that the people should have a sufficient supply of amusements, and sufficient buildings—bathing establishments which were also clubs—in which to spend their leisure time. All such business the emperors performed through delegates of various ranks—senators, or knights, or freedmen.

The subject in which the imperial government showed least interest was popular education. Just as in America now, the people themselves had to attend to the instruction and education of their children. And it must be admitted that the towns, even more in the East than in the West, did a good deal in this respect. All the towns of the empire possessed gymnasiums and palaestras in which the young received mental and physical training. Public libraries, equipped with a sufficient supply of books, were common. The forums, temples, and other public buildings were museums of sculpture and painting. Games and competitions kept up an interest in athletics, music, and dancing. It is true that all these advantages were confined to the towns and the children of the higher classes; the municipal authorities paid scant attention to the villages and the children of the poor. For the education of youth the emperors did little. At Rome they maintained a number of libraries; they supported the library and museum at Alexandria; and they patronized a few men of eminence in science, literature, or art, who were personally dependent on them. But in general they held aloof from the intellectual life of the state, while keeping up a strict censorship upon all seditious writings. Not until the increasing poverty of the towns endangered the existence of all educational institutions did the emperors step into the breach and undertake to pay a certain number of professors and teachers.

Such was the system of government in the Roman Empire. Its main feature, inherited from the past, is the way in which the utmost possible power of initiative was conceded to the local unit, that is, to the self-governing town. By degrees, however, a tendency develops in the central government to take the local government under its tutelage, and grows steadily, till it threatens to swallow up the independence of the community and to replace the elected representative of the people by the paid official—the agent and servant of the emperor. This process was beginning in the first two centuries and did not reach its height till after the social and political ordeal which Rome underwent in the third century of our era. (In Egypt alone, where urban self-government was unknown, it was different.)

*   *   *   *   *

The Roman Empire of the first and second centuries was beyond all question a brilliant spectacle. It included in one mighty state all that was civilized in the countries fringing the Mediterranean. Nothing was outside it except the savage tribes of Germans, Slavs, and Finns, the nomads of the desert and the negroes of central Africa, and the great Iranian and Mongol population of Asia. Even with these the empire kept up regular and constantly improving relations by commerce and diplomacy, though this connexion was interrupted from time to time by military operations against frontier tribes. Within the empire no pains were spared to secure constant and unhampered communication between its different parts. The population, except the Eastern serfs bound to the soil, could move at will from place to place.

The state did its utmost to make communication safe and easy. The Mediterranean was a Roman lake: from end to end of it, as also on the

Black Sea, the great rivers of Western Europe, and the Nile, ships con-
veyed passengers and goods; and piracy was kept down by fleets at sea
and flotillas on the rivers. Communication by sea with India was fairly
safe from Egyptian and Arabian ports, and the voyage along the north
coast of Europe as far as the Baltic was practicable; but in such enterprises the trader had to rely upon his own resources entirely.

Along the high roads which spread out like a fan from Rome and
Italy it was easy to travel to the Atlantic, or the North Sea, or the Dardanelles and the Black Sea coast. A similar network of roads covered
Asia Minor, Syria, north Africa, and Britain; and every place resembling
a town was linked up with these by branches. Each town kept up the
roads connecting it with the main settlements within its territory. The
general safety was secured by the armed forces controlled by the representatives of central power at home and abroad. The self-governing
communities and the great landlords, each acting within the limits of
their own possessions, organized the local police. The state maintained
special detachments of police in Rome, Lyons, and Carthage; and at
Rome there was a brigade of firemen as well.

Municipal life throughout the empire was almost entirely free from
the irksome control of the central power. The state was satisfied, provided that no clubs or societies of a seditious nature existed within its
boundaries, and that the municipal bodies concerned themselves solely
with local affairs. But indeed no community within the empire was ambitious to stray beyond that limited sphere. We hear nothing of any
political organizations, either at Rome or within the municipalities
abroad, which were regarded as dangerous to the state. The Christian
communities alone were prosecuted; but we do not know whether they
suffered as unlicensed associations (*collegia illicita*), or whether the
Christians individually were held to account for their refusal to take
part in the cult of the emperor which all the empire practised. There
were other societies, some professional and some religious. The latter
included an infinite number of burial clubs (*collegia tenuiorum*, literally,
'associations of the poor'), whose object was to secure to their members
a decent funeral. There were also many other clubs, in which the citizens of the town met according to their ages, and such bodies as philosophic schools, organized like close societies.

Each community lived in accordance with its past traditions, in so far
as these traditions were not offensive to the state. In the Greek East, the
birthplace of the municipal system, the constitutions or charters of the
towns varied greatly both in terms and substance. The Roman government, though indifferent to the details of these charters, supported

aristocratic institutions in the larger communities and looked with dis-
favour on democracy. Hence in most Greek cities the constitution was
oligarchical. Alexandria, the capital of Egypt, was treated exceptionally:
she had very meagre rights and was strictly controlled by the Roman
governor. The cities in the West differed less from one another in their
rights and privileges. A few Italian towns still retained their ancient
charters based upon historic treaties with Rome.

Most communities of Roman citizens in Italy and the provinces possessed charters bestowed on them by the Roman government. In the
provinces a regular colony received its rights from its founder, and
other towns from the particular emperor who conferred on them the
title of *municipium* or *colonia*. All these charters were drawn up on the
same plan. They all provided for the creation of the usual municipal
institutions—magistrates, a council of elders or of *decuriones* (local
senators), and a popular assembly; they all defined the duties and rights
of these bodies, and provided law courts. They contained rules for the
election of magistrates and *decuriones*, rules for the proceedings in the
council, and rules for the management of the popular assembly. In
general they resembled copies of the Roman constitution, in the form
which it had taken during the centuries that urban institutions had
existed at Rome. Most Italian communities in course of time exchanged
their ancient charters for such machine-made constitutions; and it is
very probable that they were encouraged to do so by one of Caesar's
laws, which prescribed that certain rules should be introduced into the
charters of all communities formed of Roman citizens.

Both in the West and in the East the townspeople took a keen interest
in their local affairs. Elections to the magistracy or priesthood or council
were important events, and there was a lively competition for seats. We
see this clearly from the election placards, of which a large number are
still extant at Pompeii; these notices were not pasted up on the walls
but painted in black or red on the plaster which covered the fronts of
the houses. To be elected to the *Augustales*, a corporation consisting
mainly of freedmen, was also an honour for which there was keen
competition; the *Augustales* had to provide the funds for the worship
of the emperor in the country towns. Magistrates and councils were full
of local patriotism. In Asia Minor there was an unceasing struggle for
primacy among the chief cities, and for the honourable titles of *neocori*,
or 'keepers of the emperor's temple'. In return for honours and offices,
for statues in the forum and election to the local priesthood, rich citizens were ready to spend large sums on the adornment of the town or

on the needs and entertainment of the inhabitants. Most of the public buildings in Italian, Greek, and provincial towns were built out of the private subscriptions of well-to-do or wealthy individuals.

Life at Rome was more complicated. The immense population of the capital, reckoned at more than a million, had no political nor even municipal rights: it was absolutely controlled by the emperor with his ministers and by the Senate. On the other hand, the emperors did all that was possible to make life there convenient and agreeable. I have said already that Augustus made Rome the real capital of the world, and that his successors followed in his footsteps. The city became by degrees the most magnificent in the world, and the pleasantest to live in. Order was secured by the imperial police; the emperor maintained seven regiments of firemen, who rendered aid also in case of inundations or earthquakes; special officials attended to the aqueducts, the drainage, the flow of the Tiber, and the upkeep of public buildings, the open spaces, and streets. The public buildings were remarkable for their size, the beauty of their lines, and the elegance of their appointments. Nowhere were there such noble temples, or such richly adorned forums, with triumphal arches, commemorative columns, and a forest of statues; no city in the empire could show such immense theatres, amphitheatres, and circuses; none had so many public libraries and museums, or such a gallery of statues as Augustus erected in his forum in honour of famous Roman commanders. Peculiar to Rome were the vast and luxurious *thermae*—public baths with athletic-grounds, which served also as clubs and restaurants; and also the noble halls, called basilicas, which were used for law courts. No Hellenistic capital could rival the public parks, hygienic markets, and splendid shops of Rome. Apart from all this, the palace of the emperors rose on the Palatine, and their magnificent tombs on the banks of the Tiber. Life was easy and cheerful in this marvellous city. About 200,000 of the poorest class were maintained by the state, and the rest could find work in abundance, if they wanted it. Nor was there any lack of amusements, especially under such rulers as Nero, Domitian, and Commodus; and occasional presents, either in money or in kind, were distributed among the people.

The towns in the provinces, in proportion to their means, kept pace with Rome. And I do not refer to the ancient capitals of the East— Alexandria, Antioch, Pergamum, Ephesus, Athens, Corinth; nor to the later capitals of the West—Lyons, Carthage, Tarragona, which received from the emperors almost as much consideration and as much generosity as Rome herself. The smaller towns, even the new and unimportant colonies and *municipia* in Africa, Gaul, and Britain, were remarkable for careful planning, cleanliness, and good sanitation. The main streets were straight and wide, the side-streets straight and clean, and all were paved; the houses were convenient, with drains and a water-supply, with enclosed gardens and conduits. There were large market-places, temples, basilicas, covered markets, buildings for the council and magistrates to meet in; public latrines built of stone and abundantly supplied with water; fine public baths with central heating; theatres, amphitheatres, circuses; libraries; hotels and inns. And all this could be found —more or less complete, more or less perfect—in almost every provincial town. The dead were cared for as well as the living. No age in the history of the world comes up to the Roman Empire in the number of beautiful and splendid monuments which it erected in memory of the dead. The roads leading to Pompeii give sufficient proof of this: what variety and what beauty is displayed there! What then were the roads like that led to Rome! And the same is true of the provinces. I might point, for example, to the mausoleum of the Julian family at St. Remy in Gaul, to the Igelsaüle near Trèves, or hundreds of other noble monuments still extant in Africa, Greece, Asia Minor, and Syria. Millions were spent upon the dead, tens and hundreds of millions on the comfort of the living. One may say without exaggeration that never in the history of mankind (except during the nineteenth and twentieth centuries in Europe and America) has a larger number of people enjoyed so much comfort; and that never, not even in the nineteenth century, did men live in such a surrounding of beautiful buildings and monuments as in the first two centuries of the Roman Empire.

Thus, the empire was a world-wide state, consisting of a number of urban districts, each of which had for its centre a well-organized town or city. In these towns, and especially in the capital, lived that part of the population which directed the social and economic life of the empire. The chief place among these many millions was held by Italy with a population almost entirely made up of Roman citizens. But the citizen franchise was by no means restricted to Italy. The successors of Augustus grew more and more liberal, and admitted by degrees as citizens the upper class of every city in the empire. The army, which was still recruited, if not in Italy, at least in the Romanized or Hellenized parts of the empire, still represented civilization; and through the ranks many persons of middling or inferior station passed into the class of citizens. So the process went on, by which the body of citizens grew larger and larger, till it included most of the upper and middle classes of the urban population in Italy and the provinces.

Together with this extension there was a radical change in the composition of this body, when compared with the republican age or the reign of Augustus. Above all, the old senatorial nobility had disappeared by the end of the first century, partly in consequence of merciless persecution by the emperors, and partly from natural causes: if they married at all, their marriages were generally childless. Their place was filled by a new imperial nobility, natives either of Italian cities or of the provinces. This change is clearly shown in the case of the emperors themselves: the Julii and Claudii belong to the old patrician aristocracy, the Flavii come from a municipal Italian stock, and most of the Antonines belong to the upper class of the Romanized provinces. The new aristocracy was not much more long-lived than its predecessors: after two or three generations families died out and gave place to others of similar origin. The same indifference to the continuation of the name still led to the same result; and any family which survived for more than two generations was artificially kept alive by the system of adoption.

In the country towns, especially in the upper middle class which aimed at equestrian rank, the same thing is observable—the rapid extinction of families. The equestrian class grows in numbers but is recruited chiefly from without. Here, too, adoption is common, and the adopted son is often a freedman, a former slave of the family. The only class which adds to its numbers is the proletariate in town and country. Of this we have no direct evidence; but it may be inferred from the increasing population of the empire as a whole, which in turn is proved by the steady growth of the cities and increasing area of cultivation in almost all the provinces. It is a marked feature in all the higher classes of the population, that they are unwilling to continue their kind and found a family. Apparently their motive was to secure full enjoyment of their wealth for themselves personally; and they were not willing to hamper their freedom with the cares of a family. Men struggled for wealth in order to secure for themselves a life of peace and comfort, and in order to rise in the social scale. They cared little what became of their riches: they bequeathed them to the emperor, or to their native city, or to some social or religious institution, or to friends and relations, or to flatterers and freedmen.

The senators were still the richest class of the population. But we find in them no desire to increase their wealth by systematic cultivation of their estates. The rich man's object is to receive a safe and steady income with as little personal exertion as possible. Hence money was invested mainly in land. Estates were managed by slaves and freedmen, and were worked by tenants on short or long leases, the latter being preferred. More life and energy was shown by the class of knights and the middle class in the country towns, especially the lower section of it: the higher section, here too, was apt to rest content with what they had got, and preferred spending to acquisition. A stagnation is perceptible throughout the empire, a paralysis even of the desire for gain. Meanwhile, the composition of the highest classes was constantly changing: men of a lower and less refined type replaced the representatives of traditional culture, and then died out themselves before they had time to appropriate entirely the tastes and interests of their predecessors.

How the lower class of the population lived it is difficult to say. In the towns they enjoyed the same advantages of comfort and good order as the rich. At Pompeii or Timgad in Africa there are no houses which one would not care to live in. Things were probably worse in the poor quarters of the capital cities; but their inhabitants could enjoy the splendid squares, gardens, basilicas, and baths. Slaves were, of course, less well off than the free population; but even they, under the empire, attracted more and more the attention and benevolence of the legislator. Of life in the country we unfortunately know nothing. But perhaps this very dumbness is significant. If we hear no paeans of joy, we hear also no complaints. In the troublesome times that followed at the end of the second century and the beginning of the third, the country finds a voice and uses it to complain of its hardships to the emperor. Its silence in the first two centuries is a proof that things were not too bad.

During those centuries the empire was unquestionably rich and, in comparison with other periods, prosperous. What was the source of this wealth? What were the forms assumed by its economic life? These questions are of great importance: in the answer to them lies the explanation of that startling phenomenon in the history of the Roman Empire—the rapid destruction . . . of its prosperity. The material resources of the state were, beyond doubt, immense. She included the richest parts of Europe, Africa, and Asia, on which the prosperity of modern Europe is based. Besides, she developed the resources of Asia and north Africa more thoroughly than is done at present. She commanded fertile districts for cultivation, extensive pastures for stock-raising on the largest scale, virgin forests, mines and quarries almost unworked, rivers and seas abounding with fish. We must admit in fairness that the Romans found out these resources and did their best to make use of them.

Their prosperity was based on agriculture and stock-raising. It is certain that the empire greatly extended the area of cultivation. In modern Africa, for instance, in Algeria and Tunis, immense districts, which were never reached by Carthaginian civilization and contain no traces of Carthaginian cities or farms, and where now, in spite of French colonizing activity, only scanty flocks of sheep and goats wander over the parched plains, were densely populated and thoroughly tilled in the first two centuries, especially in the second. This is abundantly clear from the ruins, which the traveller meets at almost every step, of prosperous towns and productive farms. The origin of that prosperity is revealed by the remains of imposing Roman buildings, intended to make a systematic use of the rain which falls here in abundance during the winter months.

It is certain that Gaul, Britain, and Spain began under the empire to produce for the first time vast quantities of grain for export, after satisfying the local requirements. In the East the area of cultivation did not at least grow smaller, except perhaps in Greece for a reason which will be explained later. The prosperity of the Western provinces is attested by the ruins of many flourishing towns, whose inhabitants were fed by the country and which did not exist before this period. Even stronger evidence is supplied by the ruins of those large and small farms, which have of late years attracted increasing attention from archaeologists. It is surely significant that the soil of Britain is covered in its level parts, with the ruins of large or small 'villas', which were either farms or the central points of large estates. The same is true of France and Belgium and the Rhine country; on the upper Rhine the *decumates agri*, which were included in the province of Upper Germany between the reigns of Domitian and Commodus, were covered with a network of substantial farms. In Egypt the extension of the arable area is proved by documents found there, and by our knowledge of large irrigation schemes undertaken by Augustus.

It is certain that stock-raising also was vigorously developed, and special attention was paid to the cultivation of vines and olive-trees. For this purpose the empire made use of every suitable district within its boundaries. Modern times can boast of few fresh conquests of this kind. Wine, indeed, is now made in Germany; but on the other hand, the southern part of Tunis, which in ancient times was almost completely covered with olive-trees, is now a bare plain. This acclimatization of valuable products is highly characteristic of the empire, and worked remarkable changes in the aspect of the ancient world. The time was past when Greece, and then Italy, supplied the whole world with wine and oil. Under the empire nearly all the provinces grew enough of both commodities to satisfy their own requirements, and even sought to export the excess. This was certainly a serious blow to the agricultural prosperity of Greece and Italy. Having nothing to export in return for the imported grain, they were forced to revert to a more primitive type of agriculture, and once more to grow corn for their own needs.

In spite of the increase in arable area, and the acclimatization of the vine and olive in Western Europe, there was no improvement, but rather a falling off, in agricultural skill. Columella, who wrote a handbook on farming in the first century, complains bitterly of the decay of scientific agriculture in Italy; and we may be sure that the same was true of the Eastern and Western provinces.

The cause of this regression was an extensive development of small farming, which went on together with the growth of great estates. Slave labour applied to the land was no longer of primary importance, even in the East and in Italy. Slaves became dear and free labour cheap, owing to the increasing numbers of the proletariate. The great landlords were glad to give up the plantation system and let their land to smallholders. The emperors were the first to begin this system on their estates. The East followed suit: the owners of large and middling estates lived in towns and had their land cultivated by smallholders who were in many cases bound to the soil they tilled. These conditions were unfavourable to progressive and scientific cultivation. In spite of more land and more workers on the land, the quality of the work steadily deteriorated.

The same fact is observable in a different department—in the exploitation of natural wealth of other kinds. The number of mines and quarries in working increased. The knowledge of their mineral wealth was probably the main reason why some new territories were annexed to the empire. We may suppose that this motive, among others, induced Claudius to conquer Britain, and Domitian to annex part of south-west Germany; and at all events the chief attraction of Dacia was its auriferous sand and wealth in other minerals. Here again, beyond question, the sources of the empire's wealth were added to. But the skill of the workers did not keep up with the development of mines. In mining and metallurgy the Romans did not improve upon the methods of the Hellenistic Age, but even lost ground. The treasury, in other words, the emperor, had worked the mines through substantial contractors employing slaves in great numbers; but now a different method was tried: the work was parcelled out among petty adventurers who had to rely on their own efforts and the help of a few slaves. Under such conditions technical improvements were of course impossible.

Symptoms of this kind are visible in manufacture as well as in agriculture and mining. Districts which had formerly depended upon imports from the large manufacturing centres now began to take a share in production. Hence, the large centres lost their economic position and grew impoverished. The worst plight of all was that of Greece, whose manufactures disappeared almost entirely from the world's market. A few kinds, indeed, of manufactured articles, some of which cannot be called luxuries, were still produced by special districts and exported thence to the ends of the earth, the vast extent of the Roman Empire being a great furtherance to exportation. Some fabrics were still a speciality exported all over the world by Asia Minor, Italy, and Gaul; the copper vessels of Campania still competed successfully against foreign imitations; and Egypt was supreme in the market for linen stuffs and paper. But these special goods, produced for the sake of export only, became more and more exceptional. They were driven out of the provincial markets by similar wares, sometimes not inferior in quality, produced by the local workshops. Thus, for example, the manufacture of earthenware vessels and lamps and of glass was no longer limited to one centre. The first of these products has a history of special interest. Beginning in Greece and Asia Minor the industry passed to Italy: in the second and first centuries B.C. the figured earthenware of north Italy has no rival in the world. In the first century A.D. southern Gaul begins to compete; in the second half of the century the manufacture moves farther north, and reaches the Rhine in the second century. These vessels now conquer not only the northern and northeastern markets but Italy as well; and simultaneously Asia Minor is producing the same article after the same patterns for the southern and south-eastern markets. In the second century A.D. all the provinces, both East and West, are turning out in immense numbers the earthenware lamps which had once been almost a monopoly of the workshops in north Italy. Nothing now, except articles of luxury accessible to few, finds a distant market; and indeed local imitations of the products from great centres of industry crop up everywhere. For instance, the famous purple fabrics of Tyre were imitated in Asia Minor. Thus, in manufacture also production became more and more diffused.

But at the same time the quality grows inferior: there is less both of mechanical skill and beauty. Technique becomes monotonous and somewhat old-fashioned. In jewellery, for instance, it is enough to compare the charming ear-rings and brooches of the Hellenistic Age with the coarse Roman imitations, and the same may be said of the pottery. It is important also to note this: ruins and tombs have yielded up objects of Roman production by the hundred thousand, and these warrant the assertion that practically no new discovery was made in technique: on the contrary, many earlier discoveries fell into disuse. In point of artistic beauty every one knows that the products of the empire are immeasurably inferior to those of the Eastern monarchies, or Greece, or the Hellenistic Age.

We must seek for the cause of this degeneration in the diffusion of production already mentioned. The provinces had started production to satisfy their own needs, and mass-production at low prices. Thus, the finer and dearer article was driven out of the markets; and the factories and workshops of the purely industrial countries, which found a ready sale in earlier times, now stood idle. At the same time the gradual decline, already mentioned, of culture in the middle classes created a demand for a coarser and less artistic product. This failure of skill and artistic feeling was accompanied by a change in methods of production. The system of large factories, which started at Athens and was developed in the chief Hellenistic centres of industry, had reached some cities in Italy by the first century B.C., but declined steadily after the middle of the second century. In the Italian and provincial towns of the second century A.D., the work was chiefly done by workmen in a small way and in small workshops. A rich manufacturer was a man who owned a number of such establishments; and the hands employed were mainly slaves.

Under the empire, especially during the first two centuries, there was a remarkable development of trade, wholesale and retail, both by land and sea. Regular commercial relations were kept up with the most distant markets—China, India, central and southern Africa, Arabia, central Asia, central and southern Russia, Germany, and even Sweden and Norway. These countries imported manufactured articles in exchange for articles of luxury; or, more precisely, they supplied the raw material to be worked up in the shops of the Graeco-Roman world, especially in the East. Africa sent gold, ivory, and precious woods; Arabia sent spices; pearls and precious stones came from India, silk from China, furs from central Asia and Russia, amber from Germany and Scandinavia.

This foreign trade, however, was not really important for the economic development of the empire. The trade carried on within the empire itself, within the different provinces and between them, was of much greater importance. It grew steadily; the class of traders grew larger; and the Semites—Syrians, Jews, and Arameans—became more prominent members of it. Transport between provinces was easy— over the Mediterranean and then along the rivers and highways to the remotest corners. At the end of the third century the Emperor Diocletian published a tariff or list of fixed prices for goods; it was intended for the Eastern provinces, but it includes, together with the manufactures and products of the East, a great number of articles produced by the West, especially by Gaul. Trade was helped also by the moderate amount, varying from 2 to 2½ per cent., of the customs levied at the frontier of each province. This was a great improvement upon the time when each Greek city or petty Hellenistic kingdom extorted duties from every merchant that entered its territory.

It is certain, however, that the same symptoms which we have already noticed in agriculture and industry were present also in trade. As the provinces became more self-sufficient their need of importation decreased, and the market of every town and village was stocked with local products. In the towns most of the workshops were also shops, and most of the eatables on sale were produced within the territory belonging to the town. This state of things was less pronounced wherever traffic was carried on by river, as in Gaul and Britain, on the Rhine and the Danube with its tributaries, and in Egypt; but more pronounced in Italy, Africa, and Asia Minor, where this cheap means of communication does not exist.

The expense and delay of transport by road isolated the markets and made them aim at being self-supporting. The same causes hindered the development of large capitalistic enterprises in the sphere of local trade, except for wares carried by sea, or caravan, or rivers. It is an interesting fact that the Emperor Hadrian, who favoured smallholders in agriculture and petty contractors in the mines, tried to put down the middleman in trade, and to connect the purchaser directly with the producer. In spite of this, capitalistic methods were more successful in trade than in any other department of economic activity during the empire. The merchants, together with the great landowners, were the richest men of the time. They formed important trading companies and associations. The merchants interested in shipping, called *naucleri* or *navicularii*, combined in companies of this kind, and became one of the most powerful economic alliances in the empire.

It appears, therefore, that the empire accomplished a great deal in the sphere of economics. Fresh sources of wealth were discovered. Countries which had previously been content with the most primitive commercial arrangements now became accessible to systematic exploitation. Exchange was facilitated by a better system of roads and protection from pirates at sea. The imposts were not burdensome. In the relation between capital and labour the empire, that is, the government of the empire, remained passive and left the problem to settle itself. Its interposition was rare and governed by no system: at one time it favoured capital and great fortunes, at another it took measures to protect the small proprietor and the working man. The emperors of the second century interfered more than others. I have mentioned already Hadrian's defence of smallholders and tenants. It is right to notice the legislation of all these emperors in order to raise the legal and social level of slaves. It must be remembered, however, that the labour question, as we understand it, was unknown to the ancient world. The existence of slavery and the application of slave labour to industry made it impossible for free labourers to combine and fight the employers. Not only so, but the government frowned on any associations for other than religious purposes and would certainly have suppressed them.

Nevertheless, together with a forward movement we have been forced to notice many disquieting symptoms—the increasing size of landed properties; the change from scientific farming to more primitive methods practised by small tenants on short or long leases; the decline of intensive agriculture in Greece and Italy, and of science applied to agriculture—Columella, mentioned above, is the last original writer who treats the subject; the deterioration of manufactured objects in technical skill and beauty; and the development of small workshops at the expense of large factories and works.

*   *   *   *   *

At the end of the third century, after a bloody and cruel civil and social war which had lasted for scores of years, the general situation was very similar to what it had been at the end of the civil war of the first century B.C. The people, including a large part of the soldiers, were wearied and disgusted and craved for peace and order; the fighting temper of large groups of the population had passed away and everyone was ready to accept, or to submit to, any conditions that should guarantee the security of life and the possibility of resuming daily work without the daily apprehension of a new convulsion, a new wave of war and destruction. But the Roman Empire of the third century A.D. was very different from the Roman Empire of the first century B.C. The civil war of the first century was ultimately a fight against the domination of a small group of families, and an attempt to remodel the structure of the state in accordance with the changed conditions of its life, to adapt the constitution of the city-state of Rome to the needs of the Roman Empire. After a period of transition, inaugurated by the reforms of Augustus—a period when the struggle against the old senatorial class, representing the ancient ruling families of Rome, was brought to a close and the new structure of the state was gradually consolidated and accepted by the population (as was shown in the crisis of 69)—the constitutional Empire of Rome, based on the cities and on the city *bourgeoisie*, enjoyed a period of calm and of peaceful development. The civil war and its sequel, the military tyranny, did not affect the most vital forces of the Empire and of the ancient world in general. It left intact the most important institution of the ancient world, with which ancient civilization stood and fell—the city-state. It seemed as if, after long efforts, a constitutional arrangement had been found by which the city-state was made the basis of a world-empire. That arrangement was the enlightened constitutional monarchy, assisted by an influential and well-trained body of experts, the Roman senate and the Roman knights, and by thousands of similar bodies all over the Empire, the municipal councils.

So long as the Empire was not faced by grave external dangers, so long as the awe which Roman arms, Roman organization, and ancient civilization inspired in the neighbours of the Empire endured, the fabric of the new Roman state remained firm. When, however, the feeling of awe gradually vanished and Rome's neighbours renewed their attacks, the structure of the state began to show dangerous signs of yielding. It became clear that the Empire, based on the propertied classes alone, could not stand the strain of foreign wars, and that an enlargement of the basis was necessary to keep the structure erect and firm. The city *bourgeoisie*, whose economic life had for centuries rested on the work and toil of the lower classes, and especially of the class that tilled the soil, appeared unwilling and unable to shoulder the burden of defending the Empire against foreign enemies. The attempts to revive the *bourgeoisie*, to increase its numbers, and to restore its military spirit, which were made over and over again by all the emperors of the dynasty of the Antonines and of the Severi, proved futile. For the defence of the state the emperors were forced to resort to the tillers of the soil, on whom the economic prosperity of the Empire rested and whose toil and travail never brought them any share either in the civilized life of the cities or in the management of local affairs. The Roman army gradually became an army of peasants, led and commanded by members of the ruling classes, and indeed an army of the poorer peasants, of peasant-proletarians, since they were the only men who would volunteer or would be sent by a village community when a compulsory levy was ordered. As regards its social (though not its racial and political) composition, the army of the second half of the second century was thus no different from the armies of Marius and Sulla, Pompey and Caesar, Antony and Octavian.

It was natural, then, that this army should in the end seek to realize the ambitions of the lower classes of the Empire, just as the armies of the first century B.C. had expressed the desires of the poorer Roman citizens of Italy. The instruments through which it tried to realize them were, of course, its leaders, the emperors, whom it appointed and supported. As its aspirations were never clearly formulated and its programme—if the vague desires of the soldiers can be so described— was more negative than positive, the process assumed very chaotic forms. Moreover, the *bourgeoisie* gradually became aware of the danger which threatened it and strove repeatedly through the same military leaders, the emperors, to save its privileged position and to prevent the overthrow of the structure of the state as it was in the second century. Hence the renewed outbreaks of civil war which raged all over the Empire and brought it to the verge of utter destruction. What the army wanted was an equal share in the management of the Empire, a thorough levelling. As far as this negative side of its programme was concerned, the struggle was crowned with success. The *bourgeoisie* was terrified and decimated; the cities were brought to the verge of ruin; the new rulers, both emperors and officials, sprang mostly from the peasant class.

Gradually, however, as in the first century B.C., it became evident that the civil war was disastrous to the state as a whole, and that its main result was the political and economic ruin of the Empire. On the other hand, as we have said, the masses of the people became weary of the strife and longed for peace at any price. It became evident, too, that the chief task of the moment was the restoration of the fabric of the state, the preservation of the Empire. As soon as this task was achieved by the strenuous efforts of the army itself and of its great leaders, a reorganization of the state in accordance with the changed conditions, stabilizing and systematizing them, became imperative and did not brook delay. It was the same situation as in the time of Augustus. Here again the main lines of reconstruction were dictated by the social and economic conditions, and were laid down by the practice of the leaders in the civil war and the partial reforms which they carried out. To the activity of Marius, Sulla, Pompey, and Caesar corresponded that of Septimius, Gallienus, and Aurelian; and the great work of Augustus, Vespasian, and the Antonines was paralleled by the reorganization of the state effected by Diocletian and Constantine and their successors. The chief reform needed was one which would, above all, stabilize the state and organize it in a manner that would accord with the changed conditions, economic, social, political, and psychological. Levelling and equalization were dictated as the basis of the reform by the imperative desire of the people, and it was evident that in the new state there was no place for the leading role which the cities and the city *bourgeoisie* had played in the state of Augustus and of the Antonines. The state had now to be based on the country and the peasants. On the other hand, a simplification of its structure was a necessary consequence of the changed economic and cultural conditions.

Thus arose the state of Diocletian and Constantine. In organizing it the emperors did not have a free hand. They took over a heavy heritage from the third century, to which they had to conform. In this heritage there was almost nothing positive except the fact of the existence of the Empire with all its natural resources. The men who inhabited it had utterly lost their balance. Hatred and envy reigned everywhere: the peasants hated the landowners and the officials, the city proletariate hated the city *bourgeoisie*, the army was hated by everybody, even by the peasants. The Christians were abhorred and persecuted by the heathens, who regarded them as a gang of criminals bent on undermining the state. Work was disorganized and productivity was declining; commerce was ruined by the insecurity of the sea and the roads; industry could not prosper, since the market for industrial products was steadily contracting and the purchasing power of the population diminishing; agriculture passed through a terrible crisis, for the decay of commerce and industry deprived it of the capital which it needed, and the heavy demands of the state robbed it of labour and of the largest part of its products. Prices constantly rose, and the value of the currency depreciated at an unprecedented rate. The ancient system of taxation had been shattered and no new system was devised. The relations between the state and the taxpayer were based on more or less organized robbery: forced work, forced deliveries, forced loans or gifts were the order of the day. The administration was corrupt and demoralized. A chaotic mass of new government officials was growing up, superimposed on and superseding the former administrative personnel. The old officials still existed but, foreseeing their doom, strove to avail themselves to the full of their last opportunities. The city *bourgeoisie* was tracked out and persecuted, cheated, and maltreated. The municipal aristocracy was decimated by systematic persecution and ruined by repeated confiscations and by the responsibility imposed on it of ensuring the success of the organized raids of the government on the people. The most terrible chaos thus reigned throughout the ruined Empire. In such circumstances the task of any reformer would be to reduce the chaos to some sort of stable order, and the simpler and more primitive the methods, the better. The more refined system of the past was utterly destroyed and beyond restoration. What existed was the brutal practice of the third century, rude and violent as it was. That practice was to a certain extent created by the situation, and the simplest way out of the chaos was to fix and stabilize it, reducing it to a system and making the system as simple and as primitive as possible. The reform of Diocletian and Constantine was the legitimate offspring of the social revolution of the third century, and was bound to follow in the main the same lines. In their task those emperors had as little freedom as Augustus. For both of them the goal was the restoration of the state. By his genius Augustus succeeded in restoring not only the state but also the prosperity of the people. Diocletian and Constantine sacrificed, certainly against their will, the interests of the people to the preservation and the salvation of the state.

The chief object of this volume has been to investigate the social and economic conditions of the early Roman Empire, to trace the evolution which gradually resulted in the suppression of the leading part played by the cities in the history of the ancient world. The new state based on the peasants and the country was a new phenomenon in history, and its progressive development requires as careful an examination as we have endeavoured to make of the history of its genesis. The reader will, therefore, not expect a detailed analysis of its growth in this book. Another volume of the same size, and written from the same point of view, would be necessary for a study of the social and economic conditions of the late Roman Empire. No such book has yet been written. Nevertheless a short sketch of the main lines which the reforms of Diocletian and Constantine followed, as well as a general picture of the social and economic conditions, may be desirable here to convey some idea of the new régime and its relation to the world of the early Roman Empire.

The problems which Diocletian and his successors had to face were manifold. One of the most important was that relating to the central power, the *power of the emperor*. There was no question of eliminating that power. If there was one thing that held together the fabric of the Empire and guaranteed its existence, if there was any institution popular among the masses, it was the imperial power and the personality of the reigning emperor. Everything else was discredited. Despite the convulsions through which the Empire had passed, the idea of the imperial power stood intact. If there was any salvation for the Roman Empire— such was the general belief of the people—it must come from above. There was a deeply rooted feeling among all its inhabitants that without an emperor Rome could not and would not exist. And the bitter facts of the third century showed the truth of this belief. The only question was how to stabilize and organize the supreme power so that the emperor would no longer be a puppet in the hands of the soldiery. The conception of the imperial power formed in the first two centuries was too subtle, too complicated and refined, to be understood by the masses of the peasants on whom it was based. It was a creation of the high culture of the privileged classes. These classes were decimated and demoralized, and even their standard had become degraded and simplified. The idea of the ruler as first magistrate of the Roman citizens, whose authority was based on the conception of duty and on consecration by the great Divine Power ruling the universe, was one which did not reach, and was not comprehensible to, the mass of semi-barbarians and barbarians who now formed the staff of officials, the army, and the class which supplied both—the peasant population of the Empire. A simpler conception was urgently needed, a broader and plainer idea which would be intelligible to every one. Diocletian himself still adhered to the old idea of the ruler as the supreme magistrate, of the imperial power as vested in the best man or the best men, the *princeps* or *principes*. He emphasized, however, the supernatural and sacred character of his power, which was

expressed in the identification of the emperor with God and in the
Oriental ceremonial introduced at court. The cult of the emperor, which
had been impersonal in the second century, became attached to the
person of the emperor. The doctrine thus introduced was not new.
Many attempts had been made to establish it—by Caligula and Nero,
by Domitian and Commodus, by Elagabal and Aurelian. They had failed
because the doctrine had adhered too much to the special religions of
particular sections of the population. Apollo and Hercules were vague
conceptions which made no general appeal; the Syrian Sol, Mithra, the
amalgamation of Jupiter and Donar, appealed to a minority but did not
satisfy the masses. The prominent feature of the spiritual life of the
Empire was the increase of religiosity. Religion was gradually becoming
paramount for almost everybody. The more religious society grew, the
sharper became the divisions between the various groups. A believer in
Mithra would not accept an emperor who was the incarnation of the
German Donar, an adherent of the Egyptian cults would not devote his
soul to the incarnation of such a vague deity as the Stoic Hercules, and
so forth. Moreover, the Christians would resolutely reject them all and
refuse to accept a living incarnation of God in a mortal man. It was
futile to persecute them: every persecution made their cohesion closer
and the organization of the church more solid. In the third century the
Christian church acquired enormous strength. As a state within the
state, its organization steadily improved in proportion as that of the
state deteriorated. Oppression, compulsion, persecution were the mot-
toes of the state; love, compassion, consolation were the maxims of the
church. The church, unique in this respect among the other religious
communities, not only administered spiritual relief but promised and
gave practical help in the miseries of actual life, while the state oppressed and persecuted the helper.

But the Christians, increasing in numbers and in strength, grew tired
of being outcasts and of fighting the state. The time was ripe for a
reconciliation of state and church, each of which needed the other. In
the opinion of some scholars it was a stroke of genius in Constantine to
realize this and act upon it. Others believe this was a major error, to
which he was led by his superstitious tendencies. For my own part, I
believe that both factors combined, and that the final impulse came
from reasons of state. In any case, he offered peace to the church, provided that she would recognize the state and support the imperial power.
The church—to her detriment, as many scholars believe—accepted the
offer. For the first time the imperial power became firmly established on

a solid basis, but it lost almost completely, save for some irrelevant formulae, the last remnants of its constitutional character as the supreme magistrature of the people of the Empire. It now resembled the Persian monarchy of the Sassanidae and its predecessors in the East, the monarchies of Babylonia, Assyria, Egypt, and the rest. It was based at once on force and compulsion and on religion. Individual emperors might fall victims to military conspiracies and court-plots. The imperial power was eternal like the church, which supported it, and it was a world-power as the church was a world-church. The work of simplification was thus accomplished and the new supreme power was acceptable at least to that part of the population which was prepared resolutely to reject any other solution. Gradually the Christian minority became, with the help of the state, a strong majority and imposed itself on those who never were able nor prepared to fight and to make sacrifices for their religious creed. Even to them Christianity brought in the main a satisfactory solution of their religious aspirations.

Second in importance to the question of the imperial power, and intimately connected with it, was the problem of the reorganization of the *imperial army*. Our last chapter showed how critical this problem was for the Empire. In view of the grave foreign wars and the repeated inroads of the tribes bordering on the Empire, the army had to be increased in numbers and its discipline and technique maintained at the level reached under Trajan, Hadrian, and M. Aurelius. On the other hand, an army levied, as the existing army was, by conscription from the ranks of the peasants—a militia composed of the poorer peasants with a long term of service—was an instrument both inefficient and dangerous. The only way out of this difficulty was to return to the more primitive and simpler military system of the Hellenistic and the Oriental monarchies.

The first steps towards a reorganization of the army were taken by Diocletian. Realizing, as no emperor before him had done, the necessity of permanent reserves for the frontier armies of the provinces, he increased the military forces on a large scale; but, while augmenting the number of effectives, he introduced no new methods of recruiting nor did he change the military system. These reforms were reserved for Constantine. The main military force of the Empire, as Constantine saw, could only be an enlarged praetorian guard, a strong army of horse and foot, stationed near the residence of the emperor, or the residences of the co-emperors, and always ready to march against the enemy. This field army, like the armies of the Hellenistic kings (with the exception of the

Antigonids of Macedonia), had to be a mercenary one, consisting mostly of barbarians, recruited among the allied and vassal German and Sarmatian tribes and among those of the same stock who lived within the Empire. It was composed of different corps, some of them strictly belonging to the emperor's bodyguard, but the most important were the *comitatenses*, one part of which was called the *palatini*, and which formed a ready well-trained and well-organized field army. The armies which garrisoned the provinces, and whose duty it was to suppress revolts within their borders and to meet the first onslaughts of external foes, were organized on the pattern of the reserves of the Hellenistic kings. The soldiers of the provincial armies were conscripted from among the men who were settled on the frontiers with the obligation of hereditary military service. These military settlers were largely barbarians, Germans and Sarmatians, while some were descendants of the active soldiers and veterans who had received land from the emperors of the third century in the border districts. If more troops were needed, they were obtained by the enrolment of volunteers and by compulsory enlistment among the population of the Empire, mostly the rural population of the more warlike provinces, Thrace, Syria, Britain, and the two Mauretanias. The emphasis was laid on the *auxilia*, the barbarian units, while the legions, the regiments of Roman citizens, played but a subsidiary part. The leading idea of the Roman Republic and of the early Empire, obligatory military service for all the inhabitants of the Empire, was not dropped. But in practice the obligation of service was transformed into a tax, the *aurum tironicum*, levied from the landowners and expended in meeting part of the cost of the mercenary army and in finding sufficient recruits among men who were not attached to a special profession or to a plot of land within the Empire (*vagi*). In no case was the staff of officers for these types of troops drawn from any special class. The senatorial class was barred from military service, the equestrian class disappeared. Every one who showed military capacity could hope to rise gradually from the position of non-commissioned officer to that of an officer (*tribunus*), commanding a detachment or a legion or an auxiliary regiment, and then to the post of commander of an army (*dux*) or even commander-in-chief of the cavalry or infantry (*magister equitum* or *peditum*). Such at least was the theory and sometimes the practice. Naturally the families of higher officers became in course of time the main source of supply of officers in general, and thus a new military aristocracy was formed, which, however, never became a closed caste.

In remodelling the *administration* of the Empire, the policy of the emperors of the fourth and fifth centuries was to increase the number of officials, to simplify and standardize their duties, and to a certain extent to give the hierarchy a quasi-military character. While the governing bodies of the cities, the municipal councils, lost one after another almost all their rights of self-government, and were reduced to the position of unpaid agents of the state, responsible for the repartition and the collection of taxes, as well as for the apportionment of compulsory work and other burdens lying on the population of the city and the territory attached to the city, the staff of state officials, alike in the capital and in the provinces, grew in numbers and importance. In the early Empire the bureaucratic system was slowly replacing the system of city government in the capital, but was more or less adjusted to, and co-ordinated with, the principle of local self-government in the provinces and in Italy. Now it was systematically developed and extended to every field of administration. We cannot trace here the gradual growth of the organization of the all-powerful bureaucracy of the late Roman Empire, and its successive modifications. It was a sphere in which almost all the emperors endeavoured to introduce some changes and some improvements—a feature which is common to all bureaucratic governments, reforms being here both easy and in appearance efficient. Suffice it to say that from the time of Diocletian and Constantine the aim of the central government was to build up a well-organized bureaucratic machinery which, under central direction, would be equal to the task of managing all the affairs of an immense state. Compared with the delicate and complicated system of the early Empire, in which stress was laid on the self-government of the cities, while the bureaucracy was a subsidiary organ and an organ of control, the system of the late Empire, despite its apparent complexity, was much simpler, much more primitive, and infinitely more brutal. Being supreme and omnipotent, and not subject to any control exercised in one way or another by those who were the life-blood of the state, the bureaucracy gradually became utterly corrupt and dishonest and at the same time comparatively inefficient, in spite of the high professional training of its members. Bribes and illicit gains were the order of the day, and it was idle to seek to put an end to them by means of a vast system of espionage and of mutual control exercised by officials over each other. Every addition to the army of officials, every addition to the host of supervisors, served to increase the number of those who lived on bribery and corruption. The worst were the thousands of secret police agents, the *agentes in rebus*, who were the successors of the *frumentarii* and whose duty it was to keep an eye on the population and on the host of imperial officials. Corruption and inefficiency is the fate of all bureaucracies which are not checked by wide powers of self-government vested in the people, whether they are created in the name of autocracy or of communism. Manifestly a highly elaborate system of bureaucratic government was incompatible with the fusion of military and civil government in the hands of the higher officials; and the two departments, which there had always been a tendency to manage separately, were now sharply divided and highly specialized. Manifestly, also, the host of officials must be recruited not from a special class but from the ranks of those who seemed to be the most suitable. Yet, in view of the privileges attaching to the position of a government officer, official posts naturally tended to become the hereditary privilege of a special caste. The higher posts were distributed among the candidates by the emperors personally, and many new men obtained them in this way. But by force of circumstances a new aristocracy of higher bureaucrats arose, and this aristocracy had practically a monopoly of all the higher offices of the Empire.

It is easy to understand why the emperors replaced the old system of administration by the new. The social revolution of the third century had been directed against the cities and the self-government of the cities, which had practically been concentrated in the hands of the city *bourgeoisie*. It was much easier and much safer for the central government, instead of remodelling municipal self-government on new and more democratic lines—which required a great deal of creative initiative —to accept existing conditions and to kill the whole idea of self-government by making all the members of the city community responsible to the state, and by piling up duties on them without any corresponding rights. The self-government of the cities being thus destroyed, the functions of control had to be performed by somebody else, and supervisors had to be appointed to watch and coerce the municipal councils; the natural candidates for this office were the officials of the central government, who had hitherto played a modest part in the life of the provinces. It is futile to maintain that this reform was gradually and systematically built up by the early Empire because of the bankruptcy of the cities, which had demonstrated their utter incapacity to manage properly municipal affairs. The bureaucracy of the early Empire was different in principle from that of the late Empire. It managed, as was natural, the affairs of the state and interfered very little with the affairs of the cities. If it did interfere, it was to help the cities to develop a more efficient management of their own affairs. The change was brought about by the revolution of the third century. The self-government of the cities was destroyed by the long period of anarchy. Instead of restoring it on new

lines, the late Empire left things as they were, and put the c⸍
under the control, but under the command, of the agents of tⱨ
government, made them the servants and the slaves of the state, aₙ..
reduced their role to that which they had played in the Oriental monarchies, save for their responsibility for the payment of taxes. The
reform was carried out not for the sake of the people but for the sake
of simplifying the government's task. The interests of the people were
sacrificed to what seemed to be the interests of the state. The germs of
self-government, which had developed in the village communities in the
second century and even in the third, were involved in the common ruin
and disappeared.

Closely connected with the reform of the administration was the
momentous and pernicious reform of *taxation*. We have often insisted
on the fact that the taxation of the early Empire, highly differentiated
as it was and based on the traditions prevailing in the various parts of
the Empire, was not very oppressive. The stress was laid on the indirect
taxes and on the income derived by the state and the emperor from the
land and other real estate owned by them. The direct taxes—the land-
tax and the poll-tax—were paid in the various provinces in accordance
with their traditions. Of their amount we have no knowledge except for
the province of Egypt. But we know that many parts of the Empire were
partly or completely (as in the case of Italy) exempt from these taxes,
and that this exemption was rather extended than limited. If the provinces complained of their burdens, it was not because of the taxes. What
bore heavily on them was the extraordinary payments, the provisioning
of the armies and of the officials by means of compulsory deliveries, the
war requisitions, the spasmodic confiscations, and the forced work. The
responsibility for the assessment and the collection of the taxes was not
resented as a very heavy burden by the municipal aristocracy. What
they complained of was the responsibility for the extraordinary burdens
imposed on the population, and compulsory payments like the crown
gold. It was the chaotic manner in which the extraordinary payments
were exacted that ruined the city *bourgeoisie* and the working classes
alike. In the troubled times of the third century these extraordinary payments became the main revenue of the state. The state was living not on
its normal income but on a system of more or less organized robbery.

The Roman state had never had a regular budget, and when it was
faced with financial difficulties, it had no fixed and stable reserve to
draw upon. From time to time thrifty emperors had accumulated some
money, but it was easily squandered by spendthrifts who happened to

occupy the throne, and it never represented capital well managed and invested in good securities. In case of emergency, therefore, the emperors had no reserve to resort to, nor did they ever seek to increase the regular income by a gradual increase in taxation; the usual way of getting the money, according to the principles of the city-state, was to demand it from the population either by means of extraordinary taxation or by means of requisitions and confiscations. It is not surprising that in the difficult times of the third century the ordinary taxes were rather neglected, and that greater store was set by the extraordinary taxes (especially the crown gold) and by extraordinary deliveries of foodstuffs, raw material, and manufactured goods. This and the general insecurity of the times led to the disorganization of trade and industry, and therefore to an enormous decrease in the yield of indirect taxes. The foolish policy of the emperors in systematically depreciating the currency, and the general economic conditions, as well as the system of organized pillage (the liturgies), produced violent and spasmodic fluctuations of prices which did not keep pace with the steady depreciation of the currency. Such were the conditions inherited by the emperors of the fourth century from their predecessors. So long as they lasted, there was no hope of restoring economic stability and of placing the currency on a sound basis. All attempts in this direction failed. The most notorious failure was that of Diocletian, both in respect of the currency and in regard to stabilization of prices. His well-known edict of 301, by which fixed prices were established for the various products, was no novelty. The same expedient had often been tried before him and was often tried after him. As a temporary measure in a critical time, it might be of some use. As a general measure intended to last, it was certain to do great harm and to cause terrible bloodshed, without bringing any relief. Diocletian shared the pernicious belief of the ancient world in the omnipotence of the state, a belief which many modern theorists continue to share with him and with it.

After the civil war had quieted down a little, it became evident to every one that the time had come to settle the mode of taxation. Two courses were open to Diocletian. He might go back to the traditions of the Antonines, cancel the emergency measures which had accumulated like a deposit over the system of the early Empire, and, in doing so, take account of the peculiarities of economic life in the various provinces. This, of course, was the more difficult and the more painful path. To restore the prosperity of the Empire, years of quiet development were required—as many years of peace and of orderly government as were granted to the Roman Empire by Augustus, who had faced almost the same difficulties after the end of the civil wars. Diocletian was unwilling, and probably unable, to wait. Circumstances were not such as to allow him patiently to lead the Empire back to normal conditions. On the frontiers enemies were ready to attack, the internal situation was far from quiet, and the increased and reorganized army absorbed enormous sums of money. Thus, Diocletian and his successors never thought of restoring the ancient complicated and individual system of taxation. They followed the other course which was open to them: to take for granted the practice of the third century, to transform the emergency measures into a system, and to simplify and generalize that system as far as possible by applying it to all the provinces without taking into consideration the peculiarities of their economic life and social structure. As the currency was debased and unstable, the system of taxation could not be a monetary one. In place of money-taxes the emperors of the third century had invented or revived the primitive system of taxes in kind, under the form of repeated emergency collections of foodstuffs for the use of the army, the city of Rome, and the agents of the state; in addition thereto, raw material and manufactured goods were collected in the same way. This was the famous *annona*. What was easier than to transform these emergency deliveries into a regular tax? The needs of the army, the capitals, the court, and the officials would be covered, and the other expenditure of the state might be met as before from the old taxes, which were not abolished, and from the systematized extraordinary payments of the third century. It was not, however, easy to foresee what the needs of the state would be in the future: they might increase or decrease according to circumstances. That was the reason why the *annona* retained its aspect of an emergency delivery. Every year the emperor fixed the amount of payments required for the current year. The *annona* was thus stabilized, but stabilized in the worst possible form. In the third century men still hoped that the day might dawn when taxation would become regular and fixed. By the organization of Diocletian that hope was turned into a dream. Nobody could know in advance what he would have to pay in the next year; no calculations were possible until the state had announced the amount of its demands for that year.

Yet by the establishment of the *annona* as a permanent institution the problem of taxation was far from settled. The most important question was that of a fair and just assessment. In the third century this question had been settled differently for the different provinces. In

Egypt it was based on the elaborate register of cultivated land, in the urbanized provinces on the data of the census and on the paying capacity of the various cities and other large units of taxation (the imperial and senatorial estates, and the land belonging to the temples and to vassal princes). This system was too complicated and elaborate for Diocletian. It depended in most of the provinces on the activity of the cities, and it was not easy to grasp at once in all its details. It was much simpler to leave aside the work of centuries and to introduce the most rough and primitive system of assessment which had ever existed. Every soldier could understand it, although any fool could see that in this case what was simple was not fair and just. The cultivated land, whether arable or planted, was divided into *iuga* or teams of oxen. The size of the *iugum* varied according as the land was situated in a plain or on a mountain slope, and according as it produced grain or wine or olive-oil. No further differentiation was attempted. No local conditions were taken into account. It may be that our idea of the reform of Diocletian, incompletely known as it is, exaggerates its simplicity. Perhaps the system was less rigid than it appears, and varied in different places. However, its main lines are beyond doubt and they show a tendency to simplify the problem of taxation, even if it be to the detriment of the taxpayer. It may be also that the intention was to establish a system adapted to the intelligence of the peasants, on which it depended, and to distribute the burdens equally on the population. The emperors of the period of the military monarchy were anxious to appear just and benevolent to the *humiliores*; this policy was never abandoned, at least in theory, and Diocletian often emphasized it. The *iugum* may have been familiar to Diocletian from his own experience, and may have been used as a unit of taxation among the Illyrians and Thracians who still lived under the conditions of tribal economy.

The division into *iuga*—the *iugatio*—was, however, only one side of Diocletian's system. A plot of land without labour is a lifeless thing: a *iugum* presupposes a *caput*—a head, a man who cultivates it. The question of labour had grown acute in the third century. The population of the Empire became more and more shifting. Oppressed in one place, the tillers of the soil would try another. We have quoted many documents in which the final argument of the peasants is a firm threat to take to flight and seek another home if their desires are not granted. The ancient world grew up in the fixed belief that a man belonged to a particular place, his *origo* or ἰδία. But only the serfs of the old Oriental monarchies were bound to their place of residence. Ever since the Roman Empire had united the civilized world, all others had been free to move as they liked. Such freedom was prejudicial to the success of the primitive *iugatio* of Diocletian. A piece of land might be cultivated one year and left waste the next: the peasant might migrate and settle somewhere else, or he might drop his profession altogether and become a proletarian in one of the cities. The yield of the large estates was proportionate not only to the number of *iuga* which it contained but, above all, to the number of *capita*. The gradual depopulation of the Empire, and especially the decrease in the number of peasant cultivators, made the unit of taxation not so much the *iugum* as the *caput*. Hence the taxable unit after Diocletian was a combination of both. Every one who cultivated a piece of land was supposed to make a declaration of the land which he cultivated and of the number of *capita* employed on it, including the animals. This declaration made the man responsible for his land and his *capita*: wherever he was, he was bound to pay the tax assessed upon it. As he formed with the land a single unit, he lost his liberty of movement, he became bound to his land and to his work, exactly like his predecessors the 'royal peasants' of the Oriental and Hellenistic kings. There was nothing new in this system for Egypt and some parts of Asia Minor, nor perhaps for some Celtic lands; the novelty lay in the revival and general application of a system which in the time of Hadrian seemed to have been doomed to disappear for ever.

The same primitive system of assessment was applied to other taxes, none of which was new. While in respect of foodstuffs and certain raw materials the needs of the state were met by the landowners, the money and manufactured goods required had to be found chiefly by the cities and their inhabitants. The artisans and the shopowners were expected to pay a uniform tax. How it was assessed, we do not know. They were also expected to deliver a certain amount of manufactured goods to the state or to the city at a special price. The large landed proprietors, the senators, paid a special tax in money for their estates (*collatio glebalis*). Finally, the artisans, the cities, and the senators had to pay the traditional crown gold (under different names) once every five years, and additional money when a new emperor came to the throne. The reorganization of taxation brought no improvement in the matter of compulsory exactions in cases of emergency. In time of war, requisitions and robbery reigned as before, and in the long list of the obligations of the people there still figured compulsory work and deliveries of draught cattle for transport (ἀγγαρεῖαι). How heavy the latter burden was, is shown by the 'constitutions' of the Codex Theodosianus and by the

speech of Libanius Περὶ τῶν ἀγγαρειῶν. Everywhere, then, we meet with
the same policy of simplification coupled with a policy of brutal compulsion, to which the ancient world had become accustomed in the dark
days of the third century.

The mode of collecting the taxes has already been spoken of. The
system of the city-state, which used the services of tax-farmers, was to
a large extent gradually superseded under the early Empire, and in those
branches of taxation where it was retained (the customs and the collection of the payments in kind and money-taxes assessed on the imperial
estates) it was very effectively improved. A highly specialized army of
state-officials was created to check the attempts of the tax-farmers to
cheat both the treasury and the taxpayers. Most of the taxes, however,
apart from a few which were managed directly by the state (the inheritance tax, the taxes on manumission and auctions, and the customs-
duties), were collected by the cities and paid by their representatives
into the treasury of a given province. How they were collected inside
the city was a matter of indifference to the state. The co-operation of
the agents of the state—the governors of the provinces and their staffs
and the imperial procurators—with the city magistrates was limited to
a joint settlement of the amount of the taxes to be paid by the city,
which was based on the municipal census and on a similar census carried out for the whole province by the central government. In giving a
free hand to the cities, the emperors insisted upon two main points, that
the assessment must be fair and just, and that the taxes must be paid
in full without arrears. For this the municipal administration was responsible. In actual fact arrears accumulated in difficult times, and the
emperors very often cancelled them completely or partially. To make
the collection of the taxes more methodical and to guarantee themselves
against arrears, the emperors appointed (in addition to the governors
and the procurators) special agents of high standing to assist the cities
in managing their financial affairs. From the time of Hadrian they tried
to check the accumulation of arrears by making the richest members of
the community responsible for them, especially for those connected
with the departments of emergency-deliveries and supplementary taxation. In the third century, when the burdens of collecting the taxes, securing transport for the state, and provisioning the armies became excessively heavy, imperial pressure on the municipal *bourgeoisie* steadily
increased and its responsibility to the state was more and more minutely
regulated. Compulsion was freely used as the *bourgeoisie* became more
impoverished and reduced in numbers, and as the paying capacity of

the taxpayers decreased. Some of the essential rights of free men and citizens of Rome, as the municipal *bourgeois* were from the legal point of view, were curtailed. The government became harsh and sometimes violent. And yet the *bourgeoisie* remained the privileged class of the provincial population and still enjoyed some of its old privileges.

Diocletian made no effort to change the conditions which he inherited from the military anarchy of the third century. He never thought either of reducing the city *bourgeoisie* to the level of the rest of the population of the city territory by making every member of it a mere taxable unit, or of restoring the past glory of the cities. He took over the legislation of his predecessors, which tended to transform the *bourgeoisie* into a group of unpaid hereditary servants of the state, and developed it in the same spirit. The *curiales* (those who were eligible for the municipal council and the magistracies) formed a group of richer citizens responsible to the state through the magistrates and the council both for the welfare, peace, and order of the city and for the fulfilment by the population of all its obligations towards the state. Like the tillers of the soil, each of the *curiales* personally formed a single unit for purposes of taxation, and the whole of the *curiales* formed one large unit, representing the amount of tax and of compulsory work demanded from the population of the city. It was natural that every *curialis* and the group as a whole should be treated in the same way as the individual tillers of the soil. Their responsibility was not only material but personal. Thus they had strictly to observe the rule of *origo*, to remain in their city and not seek to escape to another place of residence, and in dying they had to substitute for themselves another taxable and responsible unit in the person of their children. An army of officials was on the spot to keep close watch on them, and to use compulsion and violence if any of them tried to break away from the iron circle in which he was included. Have we not here the plainest proof of Diocletian's utter incapacity to invent anything new or so to adapt existing institutions to the conditions of his time as to safeguard as far as possible the rights and the prosperity of the people? Like the rest of his reforms, his reorganization of municipal life appears to me to be a striking *testimonium paupertatis*, typical of an age devoid of all creative power and helplessly submitting to current practice, which owed its origin to a period of revolution and anarchy. Augustus had faced the same difficulties, for the time of the civil wars had been a time of oppression and of legalized robbery; but he never dreamt of legalizing robbery and oppression in his turn and making them permanent. In the mind of Diocletian the state meant compulsion, and organization meant organized violence. We cannot say that his hand was forced by the will of the army. Diocletian never thought of eliminating the antagonism between city and country by transferring the responsibility for taxation and compulsory work from the city councils to state officials. He kept the antagonism alive, with the result that in the fourth and fifth centuries the country hated the city as cordially as it had done in the third: witness Salvian and his attacks on the tyrants from the cities. We cannot say, then, that Diocletian had no other course open to him. Many were open to him, but he took the old beaten track which led directly to ruin and slavery.

The return of stable conditions and the restoration of a certain peace and order could not fail to have some effect. The terrors of the second civil war were not followed by an Augustan Golden Age; but it cannot be denied that some improvement in economic conditions occurred after the reforms of Diocletian and Constantine. For example, Egypt enjoyed a certain revival in the fourth century, and the same is true also of various cities of the Roman Empire. It is no less significant that Constantine succeeded in a field where Diocletian had failed: namely in stabilizing the currency and in restoring, to some extent, the prestige of money in public and private life. But this restoration was of brief duration, not because of the external conditions or of the incompetence of the successors of Diocletian and Constantine, but mainly because of the system, which had been responsible for the decay and contained in itself the seeds of a further decline. Oppressive and unjust taxation based on the enslavement alike of the tillers of the soil and of the city-artisans; the immobilization of economic life, which was hampered in its free development by the chains which bound every individual; the cruel annihilation, consciously pursued and gradually effected, of the most active and the most educated class of the Roman Empire, the city *bourgeoisie;* the steady growth of dishonesty and of violence among the members of the imperial administration, both high and low; the impotence of the emperors, despite the best intentions, to check lawlessness and corruption, and their boundless conservatism as regards the fundamental principles of the reforms of Diocletian and Constantine—all these factors did not fail to produce their natural effect. The spirit of the population remained as crushed as it had been in the times of the civil war. The only difference was that a wave of resignation spread over the Roman Empire. It was useless to fight, better to submit and bear silently the burden of life with the hope of finding a better life— after death. The feeling was natural, for the best efforts of honest men were bound to fail, and the more one produced, the more would be taken by the state. If a peasant succeeded in improving his land and adding to it, he knew that his fate was to be promoted to the position of a *curialis*, which meant slavery, oppression, and, in the last resort, ruin. Better to produce enough to support his family and not make useless efforts to better his position. A soldier knew very well that, so long as he was a soldier and so long as he condemned his children to the same life, he might be comparatively prosperous. As soon as he tried to break the spell, he knew that his fate, too, or at least the fate of his children, would be to join the *curia* and exchange bad for worse. The tenant of a large landowner was content to perform his duties and to enjoy the protection, and the oppression, of his master. The fate of his neighbour, the free peasant, was not attractive enough to induce him to strive to become one. The same was true of the artisans of the cities and the unfortunate *curiales*. In moments of despair the individual might try by desperate means to ameliorate his lot: the *colonus* and the peasant might seek to enter the army or to turn to robbery, the soldier to desert the army, the *curialis* to become anything—an official, a soldier, a *colonus*, or a peasant. It was all in vain. If they succeeded, their situation was every whit as bad. Thus the reigning mood was resignation, and resignation never leads to prosperity.

The salient trait of the economic life of the late Roman Empire was gradual impoverishment. The poorer the people became, the more primitive grew the economic life of the Empire. Commerce decayed, not only because of piracy and barbarian inroads, but mainly because customers disappeared. The best clients, the city *bourgeoisie*, decreased constantly in numbers and in purchasing power. The peasants lived in extreme poverty and reverted to an almost pure 'house economy', each home producing for itself what it needed. The only customers left were the members of the privileged classes, the officials, the soldiers, and the large landed proprietors, and they were provided for, as far as the necessities of life were concerned, either by the state (their salary being paid in kind) or by the produce of their own estates. Thus the first branch of commerce to suffer decay was the most important one, commerce in articles of prime necessity within a province and between provinces. Local retail-trade still lingered on, and trade in luxuries even prospered. This accounts, for instance, for the revival of the commerce with the East. The commercial class as such, however, remained unprogressive and despised. There was no chance to develop any large commercial enterprise. As soon as a man tried to do so, as soon as he bought ships or established commercial relations, he was made a member of one of the corporations, the *navicularii* or *mercatores,* and was forced to work for the state, to transport goods on its behalf, and for a miserable remuneration, or to give the state the first offer of what he had to sell. Thus the situation of the merchants and shipowners was as bad as that of the *curiales,* and compulsion was employed to keep the members of these groups bound to their profession and to keep the number of the groups complete by enrolment of fresh members. Like the ownership of land, commerce and transportation became a hereditary burden from which there was no escape. The same held good of industry. Customers were few, the market became more and more restricted, and the state more and more oppressive. Apart from the production of some standardized articles for the masses and some luxuries for the few rich, industry lived on the orders of the state. But the state was a selfish and a brutal customer: it fixed the prices and, if we take into consideration the profits of the officials, fixed them ruinously low for the artisans. Naturally the large industrial concerns gradually disappeared. As the state needed them, especially for the army, for the court, and for the officials, many industrial establishments were transformed into state factories, which were managed on Egyptian and Oriental patterns, with a staff of workmen bound to their profession and bearing a hereditary burden.

. . . We have endeavoured to show that the social crisis of the third century had been, to a large extent, brought about by a revolutionary movement of the masses of the population which aimed at a general levelling. Was this aim achieved by the reforms of Diocletian and Constantine? Can we say that the late Roman Empire was more democratic than the Empire of the Julio-Claudians, the Flavians, and the Antonines? It is true that one privileged class of the past, the equestrian, disappeared. It is true that for a time advancement in the army and in the civil service was open to everybody, especially in the third century. But in actual fact the late Roman Empire, though it was a democracy of slaves, was less democratic than the early Empire. There were no castes in the early Empire. An active and clever man could easily, by increasing his fortune, rise from the position of peasant to that of land-owner, and as such he could join the ranks of the municipal aristocracy, receive the Roman citizenship, become a knight, and finally a member of the senatorial aristocracy. We have seen that such an advance was easily accomplished in two or three generations. Even in the army promotion from the rank of private to the high post of first centurion was normal, although the advance of common soldier to the equestrian or senatorial posts in the army was rare and exceptional. So it was in the civil service. Even slaves were no exception to the general rule. Emancipated slaves had brilliant opportunities of becoming procurators of high standing, and there was nothing to prevent them or their children from entering the ranks of the municipal aristocracy.

The situation was different after the reforms of Diocletian and Constantine. There was no legal way of advancing from the position of a *colonus* even to that of a free peasant or a city proletarian, not to speak of other classes. A *colonus* might exceptionally become a soldier, but it was a very rare exception. The reform of taxation by Diocletian and the edicts of later emperors made the *colonus* a serf, so that, already in fact bound by heredity to his plot of earth, he became bound to his domicile and to his master; he became a member of a close hereditary caste. The same was true of the free small landowner, who was a member of a village community: he was tied to his land, to his village, to his profession. The only possible advance was to the position of a *curialis*, which in fact was a move downwards. Some might serve in the army, particularly if they happened to live in military provinces; but, as the legislation against deserters shows, this was not regarded as an enviable privilege. The municipal landowners, the *curiales*, were in the same position. They were less free than even the small landowners, and they formed a close and very select class, select because everybody dreaded the very idea of entering it. The rest of the city population—the shipowners, the merchants, the artisans, the workmen—were all gradually bound to their profession and to their place of residence. One privileged class was that of the workless proletarians and beggars in the city and in the country, for whom the Christian church was supposed to care. They at least were free—to starve and to riot. Another free and privileged class was the robbers, who steadily increased in numbers on sea and land. The class of officials was not indeed hereditary, at any rate not legally. It was a privilege to be an official, and the emperor was free to recruit his officials from the best men in the country. But his freedom was limited. A *curialis* could not become an official, and if one of them succeeded in evading the rule, he might expect every moment to be sent back to his *curia*. Nor were merchants and shipowners eligible. The peasants and the city proletariate do not come into consideration. The military career was sharply separated from the civil, and a soldier was not eligible for a civil office. Thus by force of circumstances officials were recruited from the families of officials, and the official class became

practically, though not legally, a close caste. The same description applies to the new senatorial aristocracy. It was an aristocracy of service,
admission to which was granted by the emperors to the higher civil and
military officers, and membership was hereditary. Gradually it became
also an aristocracy of birth and education, for the intellectual traditions
of the class were jealously guarded.

From the social point of view, then, there was no levelling and no
equalization. In the late Roman Empire society was subdivided not into
classes, but into real castes, each as close as possible, in some cases because of the privileges connected with the caste, in others because of
the burdens and hardships, which prevented anybody from desiring to
be admitted, and made membership hereditary and compulsory. Nor
was there even equality in the common slavery to the state. There was
indeed equality of a negative kind, for no political freedom was tolerated, no remnant of self-government was left, no freedom of speech,
thought, or conscience was permitted, especially after the victory of
Christianity; but even this equality of slavery was superficial and relative. The great landed proprietors were slaves of the emperor but masters of the tenant-serfs who lived on their estates. The *curiales* were
slaves of the administration and were treated by it as such, but they
were masters not only of the tenants of their estates, but also of the
population of the city and the city territory, inasmuch as they appor-
tioned and collected the taxes and supervised the compulsory work; and
by these they were regarded and hated as masters who were themselves
unfree and could not protect but only cheat their own slaves. Little wonder if these slaves appealed for protection to senators, officials, and
soldiers, and were ready to pay any price for it and to deprive themselves of the little money and the little liberty which they still had.
The working class of the cities stood in the same relation to the members of the various corporations, the owners of ships, shops, and factories. The last were in truth much more like minor supervisors of their
own concerns on behalf of the state than their owners; they were themselves in bondage to the officials of the various departments and of the
commanders of the various military units. Lastly, the officials and the
soldiers of various ranks, though wielding an enormous power over
thousands of men, were subjected to an iron discipline of a servile type
and were practically slaves of each other and of the agents of the secret
police. General servitude was, indeed, the distinctive feature of the age,
but while there were different grades and shades of bondage, there was
no equality. Slavery and equality are incompatible, a fact which should

not be forgotten by the many modern defenders of the principle of equality.

Above all, there was no equality whatsoever in the distribution of property. The senators, the knights, the municipal aristocracy, the petty *bourgeoisie* of the early Empire were, of course, ruined and degraded. Their patient and creative work, by which they had accumulated their fortunes and built up the civilized life of the cities, had disappeared for ever. But the old propertied classes were replaced by new ones, which even from the economic point of view were much worse than their predecessors. The fortunes of the early Empire were the result of the growing prosperity of the Empire in general. They were derived from commerce and industry, and the capital acquired was invested in land, improving its cultivation and the types of crop produced. The wars of the second century undermined these fortunes and retarded or even arrested economic development. Yet they did not work ruin, and a recovery under more normal conditions was possible. The catastrophe of the third century dealt a severe blow to the prosperity of the Empire and weakened the creative energies of the better part of the population. The reforms of Diocletian and Constantine, by giving permanence to the policy of organized robbery on the part of the state, made all productive economic activity impossible. But it did not stop the formation of large fortunes, rather it contributed to their formation, while altering their character. The foundation of the new fortunes was no longer the creative energy of men, nor the discovery and exploitation of new sources of wealth, nor the improvement and development of commercial, industrial, and agricultural enterprises; it was in the main the skilful use of a privileged position in the state to cheat and exploit the state and the people alike. Public officials, both high and low, grew rich on bribery and corruption. The senatorial class, being free from municipal burdens, invested their spoil in land and used their influence, the influence of their caste— which in this respect was more powerful than the emperors and nullified all their good intentions—to divert the burdens of taxation on to the other classes, to cheat the treasury directly, and to enslave ever larger numbers of workmen. We cannot here discuss how and under what title they grabbed large tracts of fertile land, both private and crown property. We have seen them at work in Egypt in the third century. In the fourth they proceeded farther on the same path. Purchase, lease, patronage, lease without term, hereditary lease with the obligation to cultivate (*emphyteusis*) were all used to make the senatorial class the class of large landed proprietors *par excellence*, and to form vast estates scattered all over the provinces and resembling small principalities. Few of the members of the senatorial class lived in the capital or in the cities. The majority of them built large and beautiful fortified villas in the country and dwelt there, surrounded by their family, their slaves, a real retinue of armed clients, and thousands of rural serfs and dependants. We are well acquainted with their mode of life from the descriptions of Ausonius, Paulinus of Pella, Sidonius Apollinaris, and Salvian, from the numerous ruins of their villas, and from some mosaics which portrayed on their floors the beauty of their châteaux in town and country. The class was large and influential. Every successful 'new' man tried hard to become a member of it, and many succeeded. They were good patriots, they possessed a genuine love of Rome and the Empire, they were faithful servants of the emperors, and they appreciated civilization and culture very highly. Their political outlook was narrow, their servility was unbounded. But their external appearance was majestic, and their grand air impressed even the barbarians who gradually became masters of the Empire. For the other classes they had sympathy and understanding in theory only, expressing their commiseration in literature, without practical results. They regarded them as far inferior beings, in this respect resembling the aristocracy of Rome in the first century B.C. and the first century A.D. The senators of the second century were not nearly so exclusive or so self-confident. There were, of course, exceptions, but they were few. Thus, more than ever before, society was divided into two classes: those who became steadily poorer and more destitute, and those who built up their prosperity on the spoils of the ruined Empire —real drones, who never made any contribution to economic life but lived on the toil and travail of other classes.

The social revolution of the third century, which destroyed the foundations of the economic, social, and intellectual life of the ancient world, could not produce any positive achievement. On the ruins of a prosperous and well-organized state, based on the age-old classical civilization and on the self-government of the cities, it built up a state which was based on general ignorance, on compulsion and violence, on slavery and servility, on bribery and dishonesty. Have we the right to accuse the emperors of the fourth century of having deliberately and of their own choice built up such a state, while they might have taken another path and have constructed, not the slave-state of the late Roman Empire, but one free from the mistakes of the early Empire and yet not enshrining the brutal practice of the revolutionary period? It is idle to ask such a question. The emperors of the fourth century, and above all Diocletian, grew up in the atmosphere of violence and compulsion. They never saw anything else, they never came across any other method. Their education was moderate, and their training exclusively military. They took their duties seriously, and they were animated by the sincerest love of their country. Their aim was to save the Roman Empire, and they achieved it. To this end they used, with the best intentions, the means which were familiar to them, violence and compulsion. They never asked whether it was worth while to save the Roman Empire in order to make it a vast prison for scores of millions of men.

Every reader of a volume devoted to the Roman Empire will expect the author to express his opinion on what is generally, since Gibbon, called the decline and fall of the Roman Empire, or rather of ancient civilization in general. I shall therefore briefly state my own view on this problem, after defining what I take the problem to be. The decline and fall of the Roman Empire, that is to say, of ancient civilization as a whole, has two aspects: the political, social, and economic on the one hand, and the intellectual and spiritual on the other. In the sphere of politics we witness a gradual barbarization of the Empire from within, especially in the West. The foreign, German, elements play the leading part both in the government and in the army, and settling in masses displace the Roman population, which disappears from the fields. A related phenomenon, which indeed was a necessary consequence of this barbarization from within, was the gradual disintegration of the Western Roman Empire; the ruling classes in the former Roman provinces were replaced first by Germans and Sarmatians, and later by Germans alone, either through peaceful penetration or by conquest. In the East we observe a gradual orientalization of the Byzantine Empire, which leads ultimately to the establishment, on the ruins of the Roman Empire, of strong half-oriental and purely oriental states, the Caliphate of Arabia, and the Persian and Turkish empires. From the social and economic point of view, we mean by decline the gradual relapse of the ancient world to very primitive forms of economic life, into an almost pure 'house-economy'. The cities, which had created and sustained the higher forms of economic life, gradually decayed, and the majority of them practically disappeared from the face of the earth. A few, especially those that had been great centres of commerce and industry, still lingered on. The complicated and refined social system of the ancient Empire follows the same downward path and becomes reduced to its primitive elements: the king, his court and retinue, the big feudal landowners, the clergy, the mass of rural serfs, and small groups of artisans and merchants. Such is the political, social, and economic aspect of the problem. However, we must not generalize too much. The Byzantine Empire cannot be put on a level with the states of Western Europe or with the new Slavonic formations. But one thing is certain: on the ruins of the uniform economic life of the cities there began everywhere a special, locally differentiated, evolution.

From the intellectual and spiritual point of view the main phenomenon is the decline of ancient civilization, of the city civilization of the Greco-Roman world. The Oriental civilizations were more stable: blended with some elements of the Greek city civilization, they persisted and even witnessed a brilliant revival in the Caliphate of Arabia and in Persia, not to speak of India and China. Here again there are two aspects of the evolution. The first is the exhaustion of the creative forces of Greek civilization in the domains where its great triumphs had been achieved, in the exact sciences, in technique, in literature and art. The decline began as early as the second century B.C. There followed a temporary revival of creative forces in the cities of Italy, and later in those of the Eastern and Western provinces of the Empire. The progressive movement stopped almost completely in the second century A.D. and, after a period of stagnation, a steady and rapid decline set in again. Parallel to it, we notice a progressive weakening of the assimilative forces of Greco-Roman civilization. The cities no longer absorb—that is to say, no longer hellenize or romanize—the masses of the country population. The reverse is the case. The barbarism of the country begins to engulf the city population. Only small islands of civilized life are left, the senatorial aristocracy of the late Empire and the clergy; but both, save for a section of the clergy, are gradually swallowed up by the advancing tide of barbarism.

Another aspect of the same phenomenon is the development of a new mentality among the masses of the population. It was the mentality of the lower classes, based exclusively on religion and not only indifferent but hostile to the intellectual achievements of the higher classes. This new attitude of mind gradually dominated the upper classes, or at least the larger part of them. It is revealed by the spread among them of the various mystic religions, partly Oriental, partly Greek. The climax was reached in the triumph of Christianity. In this field the creative power of the ancient world was still alive, as is shown by such momentous achievements as the creation of the Christian church, the adaptation of Christian theology to the mental level of the higher classes, the creation of a powerful Christian literature and of a new Christian art. The new intellectual efforts aimed chiefly at influencing the mass of the population and therefore represented a lowering of the high standards of city-civilization, at least from the point of view of literary forms.

We may say, then, that there is one prominent feature in the development of the ancient world during the imperial age, alike in the political, social, and economic and in the intellectual field. It is a gradual absorption of the higher classes by the lower, accompanied by a gradual levelling down of standards. This levelling was accomplished in many ways. There was a slow penetration of the lower classes into the higher, which were unable to assimilate the new elements. There were violent outbreaks of civil strife: the lead was taken by the Greek cities, and there followed the civil war of the first century B.C. which involved the whole civilized world. In these struggles the upper classes and the city-civilization remained victorious on the whole. Two centuries later, a new outbreak of civil war ended in the victory of the lower classes and dealt a mortal blow to the Greco-Roman civilization of the cities. Finally, that civilization was completely engulfed by the inflow of barbarous elements from outside, partly by penetration, partly by conquest, and in its dying condition it was unable to assimilate even a small part of them.

Suggestions for Further Reading

AFRICA, THOMAS, *Rome of the Caesars.* New York: John Wiley & Sons, Inc., 1965.

Cambridge Ancient History, Vol. XII. Cambridge, England: Cambridge University Press, 1961.

JONES, A. H. M., *The Decline of the Ancient World.* London: Longmans, 1966.

JONES, A. H. M., *The Later Roman Empire, 284–602: A Social, Economic, and Administrative Survey.* Oxford: Basil Blackwell, 1964.

LOT, FERDINAND, *The End of the Ancient World and the Beginnings of the Middle Ages.* London: Routledge and Kegan Paul, 1953.

MACMULLEN, RAMSEY, *Constantine.* New York: Dial Press, 1969.

MATTINGLY, HAROLD, *Roman Imperial Civilization.* London: Edward Arnold, 1957.

VOGT, JOSEPH, *The Decline of Rome.* New York: New American Library, 1967.

R. G. COLLINGWOOD

The Idea of History in Antiquity

◄§§► History has itself a history: this study is usually called historiography. Until about forty years ago, historiography was a largely neglected subject. Historians assumed that there was one absolute historical truth; if several historians offered different interpretations of an era or event, only one could be the truth, the others erroneous due to inadequate evidence or wrong assessment of the evidence. Historians at that time regarded themselves as scientists and they believed that in science there can be only one truth about a particular aspect of reality and that other views were simply false.

This "positivist" or scientific view of history is no longer adhered to by many, probably most, professional historians. We are, in any case, no longer so sure that history is a science in the sense that physics is a science. But be that as it may, the paradigm of scientific thought that historians applied to understand their own discipline has been superseded. We know now that scientific theories are only models of reality, intellectual constructs to fit the facts; and no scientific proposition can be said to be absolutely and eternally true.

This conceptual inconstancy and intellectual relativity, if meaningful for the exact sciences, is all the more the case with a human discipline like history. The study of histori-

FROM R. G. Collingwood, *The Idea of History* (New York: A Galaxy Book, Oxford University Press, 1956), pp. 10–52.

ography in the past four decades has come to be predicated on the proposition that an historical thesis is dependent not only upon the hard core of evidence, but also upon how this evidence is perceived by a mind, that is, by the historian's point of view. So conflicting interpretations may not be the consequence of one historian of the subject having more facts than another, but rather of the two historians looking on the problem, and its factual evidence, from quite different perspectives. The study of historiography, therefore, involves not only assessment of the historians' methods of handling source materials but also of their assumptions about human behavior and social experience which condition their points of view.

A scholar who made a very important contribution to this principle of historiographical perspective was R. G. Collingwood. His book *The Idea of History,* published in 1946, three years after his death, is still the best history of history in Western civilization, a truly seminal work of rare brilliance, learning, and subtlety. Collingwood understood, perhaps more clearly than any other historian of his generation, how much the power of the mind is involved in historical interpretation, how much input there is and must be from the historian's imagination. His history of history is a study of how varying intellectual assumptions have shaped historiographical development. This approach marks a decisive break with positivist or scientific history of the single-truth variety. It allows us to realize how strongly the philosophy—the assumptions about life and humanity —that the historian brings to his research affects the form that the interpretation finally takes.

Collingwood arrived at his approach and his historiographical views partly because he was an Oxford philosopher of the Neo-Hegelian Idealist school, which stressed the active role of mind and imagination in the creation of reality. He also arrived at his relativistic conclusions because he was himself a great researcher, the leading authority in his generation on Roman Britain; his work with the difficult archaeological and literary materials of this period, where the researcher must make sense and construct a pattern out of very fragmentary evidence, revealed to him how much the historian's mind contributes to the making of history.

Historical thought and literature begin with the ancient world, with contributions by Greek, Roman, and Christian writers. In the following selection from *The Idea of History* Collingwood assesses how classical and early Christian understanding of the cosmos, the world, deity, and human nature conditioned the historical interpretations the ancient writers developed, how the particular perspectives of ancient thinkers prompted them to develop the idea of history itself. And since the historical visions of antiquity left a profound impression on the whole subsequent history of history in Western civilization, this is a subject of the greatest importance—also the greatest complexity, requiring a philosopher-historian of Collingwood's transcendent genius to explicate.

❧

Historians nowadays think that history should be (*a*) a science, or an answering of questions; (*b*) concerned with human actions in the past; (*c*) pursued by interpretation of evidence; and (*d*) for the sake of human self-knowledge. But this is not the way in which people have always thought of history. For example, [Charles F. Jean] writes of the Sumerians in the third millennium before Christ:

'Historiography is represented by official inscriptions commemorating the building of palaces and of temples. The theocratic style of the scribes attributes everything to the action of the divinity, as can be seen from the following passage, one of many examples.

' "A dispute arises between the kings of Lagash and of Umma about the boundaries of their respective territories. The dispute is submitted to the arbitration of Mesilim, king of Kish, and is settled by the gods, of whom the kings of Kish, Lagash, and Umma are merely the agents or ministers:

' "Upon the truthful word of the god Enlil, king of the territories, the god Ningirsu and the god Shara deliberated. Mesilim, king of Kish, at the behest of his god, Gu-Silim, . . . erected in [this] place a stela. Ush, *isag* of Umma, acted in accordance with his ambitious designs. He removed Mesilim's stela and came to the plain of Lagash. At the righteous word of the god Ningirsu, warrior of the god Enlil, a combat with Umma took place. At the word of the god Enlil, the great divine net laid low the enemies, and funerary *tells* were placed in their stead in the plain." '

Monsieur Jean, it will be noticed, says not that Sumerian historiography *was* this kind of thing, but that in Sumerian literature historiography *is represented by* this kind of thing. I take him to mean that this kind of thing is not really history, but is something in certain ways resembling history. My comment on this would be as follows. An inscription like this expresses a form of thought which no modern historian would call history, because, in the first place, it lacks the character of science: it is not an attempt to answer a question of whose answer the writer begins by being ignorant; it is merely a record of something the writer knows for a fact; and in the second place the fact recorded is not certain actions on the part of human beings, it is certain actions on the part of gods. No doubt these divine actions resulted in actions done by human beings; but they are conceived in the first instance not as human actions but as divine actions; and to that extent the thought expressed is not historical in respect of its object, and consequently is not historical in respect of its method, for there is no interpretation of evidence, nor in respect of its value, for there is no suggestion that its aim is to further human self-knowledge. The knowledge furthered by such a record is not, or at any rate is not primarily, man's knowledge of man, but man's knowledge of the gods.

From the writer's point of view, therefore, this is not what we call an historical text. The writer was not writing history, he was writing religion. From our point of view it can be used as historical evidence, since a modern historian with his eye fixed on human *res gestae* [actions, things done] can interpret it as evidence concerning actions done by Mesilim and Ush and their subjects. But it only acquires its character as historical evidence posthumously, as it were, in virtue of our own historical attitude towards it; in the same way in which prehistoric flints or Roman pottery acquire the posthumous character of historical evidence, not because the men who made them thought of them as historical evidence, but because *we* think of them as historical evidence.

The ancient Sumerians left behind them nothing at all that we should call history. If they had any such thing as an historical consciousness, they have left no record of it. We may say that they must have had such a thing; to us, the historical consciousness is so real and so all-pervasive a feature of life that we cannot see how anyone can have lacked it; but whether we are right so to argue is very doubtful. If we stick to facts as revealed to us by the documents, I think we must say that the historical consciousness of the ancient Sumerians is what scientists call an occult entity, something which the rules of scientific method forbid us to assert on the principle of Occam's Razor that [entities should not be multiplied except when necessary].

Four thousand years ago, then, our forerunners in civilization did not possess what we call the idea of history. This, so far as we can see, was not because they had the thing itself but had not reflected upon it. It was because they did not possess the thing itself. History did not exist. There existed, instead, something which in certain ways resembled what we call history, but this differed from what we call history in respect of every one of the four characteristics which we have identified in history as it exists to-day.

History as it exists to-day, therefore, has come into existence in the last four thousand years in western Asia and Europe. How did this happen? . . .

THEOCRATIC HISTORY AND MYTH

By what steps and stages did the modern European idea of history come into existence? Since I do not think that any of these stages occurred outside the Mediterranean region, that is, Europe, the Near East from the Mediterranean to Mesopotamia, and the northern African coastlands, I am precluded from saying anything about historical thought in China or in any other part of the world except the region I have mentioned.

I have quoted one example of early Mesopotamian history from a document of about 2500 B.C. I say history, but I ought rather to say quasi-history, because, as I have pointed out, the thought expressed in this document resembles what we call history in making statements about the past, but differs from it, first, in that these statements are not answers to questions, not the fruits of research, but mere assertions of what the writer already knows; and secondly, that the deeds recorded are not human actions but, in the first instance at any rate, divine actions. The gods are conceived on the analogy of human sovereigns, directing the actions of kings and chiefs as these direct the actions of their human subordinates; the hierarchical system of government is carried upwards by a kind of extrapolation. Instead of the series: subject, lower official, higher official, king, we have the series: subject, lower official, higher official, king, god. Whether the king and the god are sharply distinguished so that the god is conceived as the real head of the community and the king as his servant, or whether the king and the god are somehow identified, the king being conceived as an incarnation of the god or at any rate as in some way or other divine, not merely human, is a question into which we need not enter, because, however we answer it, the result will be that government is conceived theocratically.

History of this kind I propose to call *theocratic history*; in which phrase 'history' means not history proper, that is scientific history, but a statement of known facts for the information of persons to whom they are not known, but who, as worshippers of the god in question, ought to know the deeds whereby he has made himself manifest.

There is another kind of quasi-history, of which we also find examples in Mesopotamian literature, namely the *myth*. Theocratic history, although it is not primarily the history of human actions, is nevertheless concerned with them in the sense that the divine characters in the story are the superhuman rulers of human societies, whose actions, therefore, are actions done partly to those societies and partly through them. In theocratic history humanity is not an agent, but partly an instrument and partly a patient, of the actions recorded. Moreover, these actions are thought of as having definite places in a time-series, as occurring at dates in the past. Myth, on the contrary, is not concerned with human actions at all. The human element has been completely purged away and the characters of the story are simply gods. And the divine actions that are recorded are not dated events in the past: they are conceived as having occurred in the past, indeed, but in a dateless past which is so remote that nobody knows when it was. It is outside all our time-reckonings and called 'the beginning of things'. Hence, when a myth is couched in what seems a temporal shape, because it relates events one of which follows another in a definite order, the shape is not strictly speaking temporal, it is quasi-temporal: the narrator is using the language of time-succession as a metaphor in which to express relations which he does not conceive as really temporal. The subject-matter which is thus mythically expressed in the language of temporal succession is, in myth proper, the relations between various gods or various elements of the divine nature. Hence myth proper has always the character of *theogony*.

For an example, let us consider the main outline of the Babylonian *Poem on the Creation*. We have it in a text of the seventh century B.C., but this professes to be, and doubtless is, a copy of very much older texts, probably going back to the same period as the document I have already quoted:

'The poem begins at the origin of all things. Nothing exists as yet, not even the gods. Out of this nothingness appear the cosmic principles *Apsu*, fresh water, and *Tiamat*, salt water.' The first step in the theogony is the birth of *Mummu*, the first-born son of Apsu and Tiamat. 'The gods increase and multiply. Then they become rebellious against [this original] divine triad. Apsu decides to destroy them. . . . But the wise *Ea* triumphs by the use of magic. He casts a powerful spell upon the waters, Apsu's element, puts his ancestor to sleep', and makes Mummu captive. Tiamat now 'plans to avenge the conquered. She marries Qingu, makes him head of her army, and confides to his care the tablets of fate.' Ea, divining her plans, reveals them to the ancient god Anshar. At first Tiamat triumphs over this coalition, but now arises Marduk, who challenges Tiamat to single combat, kills her, cuts her body in two 'like a fish', and makes out of one half the heavens, in which he places the stars, and out of the other the earth. Out of Marduk's blood, man is made.

These two forms of quasi-history, theocratic history and myth, dominated the whole of the Near East until the rise of Greece. For example, the Moabite Stone (ninth century B.C.) is a perfect document of theocratic history, showing that little change has taken place in that form of thought for between one and two millennia:

'I am Mesha, the son of Kemosh, king of Moab. My father was king over Moab thirty years and I became king after my father. And I made this high-place for Kemosh, for he saved me from my downfall and made me triumph over my enemies.

'Omri, king of Israel, was the oppressor of Moab for many long days because Kemosh was angered against his country. His son succeeded him, and he also said "I will oppress Moab". It was in my day that he said it. And I triumphed over him and his house. And Israel perished for ever.

'And Omri took possession of the land of Mehedeba and lived there during his life and half his sons' lives, forty years; but Kemosh restored it to us in my lifetime.'

Or again, here is a quotation from the account, put into the mouth of Esar-Haddon, king of Nineveh early in the seventh century B.C., of his campaign against the enemies who had killed his father Sennacherib:

'The fear of the great gods, my lords, overthrew them. When they beheld the rush of my terrible battle, they were beside themselves. The goddess Ishtar, goddess of battle and of fighting, she who loves my priesthood, remained at my side and broke their line. She broke their battle-line, and in their assembly they said "It is our king!" '

The Hebrew scriptures contain a great deal of both theocratic history and myth. From the point of view from which I am now considering these ancient literatures, the quasi-historical elements in the Old Testament do not greatly differ from the corresponding elements in Mesopotamian and Egyptian literature. The main difference is that whereas the theocratic element in these other literatures is on the whole particularistic, in the Hebrew scriptures it tends to be universalistic. I mean, the gods whose deeds are recorded in these other literatures are on the whole regarded as the divine heads of particular societies. The God of the Hebrews is certainly regarded as in a special sense the divine head of the Hebrew community; but under the influence of the 'prophetic' movement, that is, from about the middle of the eighth century onwards, they came to conceive Him more and more as the divine head of all mankind; and therefore expected Him no longer to protect their interests as against those of other particular societies, but to deal with them according to their deserts; and to deal with other particular societies in the same way. And this tendency away from particularism in the direction of universalism affects not only the theocratic history of the Hebrews but also their mythology. Unlike the Babylonian creation-legend, the Hebrew creation-legend contains an attempt, not indeed a very well-thought-out attempt (for every child, I suppose, has asked its elders the unanswerable question, 'Who was Cain's wife?'), but still an attempt, to account not only for the origin of man in general but for the origin of the various peoples into which mankind, as known to the authors of the legend, was divided. Indeed one might almost say that the peculiarity of the Hebrew legend as compared with the Babylonian is that it replaces theogony by ethnogony.

THE CREATION OF SCIENTIFIC HISTORY BY HERODOTUS

As compared with all this, the work of the Greek historians as we possess it in detail in the fifth-century historians, Herodotus [484?– 425? B.C.] and Thucydides [c.460–400 B.C.], takes us into a new world. The Greeks quite clearly and consciously recognized both that history is, or can be, a science, and that it has to do with human actions. Greek history is not legend, it is research; it is an attempt to get answers to definite questions about matters of which one recognizes oneself as ignorant. It is not theocratic, it is humanistic. . . . Moreover, it is not mythical. The events inquired into are not events in a dateless past, at the beginning of things: they are events in a dated past, a certain number of years ago.

This is not to say that legend, either in the form of theocratic history or in the form of myth, was a thing foreign to the Greek mind. The work of Homer is not research, it is legend; and to a great extent it is theocratic legend. The gods appear in Homer as intervening in human affairs in a way not very different from the way in which they appear in the theocratic histories of the Near East. Similarly, Hesiod has given us an example of myth. Nor is it to say that these legendary elements, theocratic or mythical as the case may be, are entirely absent even from the classical works of the fifth-century historians. F. M. Cornford in his *Thucydides Mythistoricus* (London, 1907) drew attention to the existence of such elements even in the hard-headed and scientific Thucydides. He was of course perfectly right; and similar legendary elements are notoriously frequent in Herodotus. But what is remarkable about the Greeks was not the fact that their historical thought contained a certain residue of elements which we should call non-historical, but the fact that, side by side with these, it contained elements of what we call history.

The four characteristics of history which I enumerated [are] (*a*) that it is scientific, or begins by asking questions, whereas the writer of legends begins by knowing something and tells what he knows; (*b*) that it is humanistic, or asks questions about things done by men at determinate times in the past; (*c*) that it is rational, or bases the answers which it gives to its questions on grounds, namely appeal to evidence; (*d*) that it is self-revelatory, or exists in order to tell man what man is by telling him what man has done. Now the first, second, and fourth of these characteristics clearly appear in Herodotus: (i) The fact that history as a science was a Greek invention is recorded to this day by its very name. History is a Greek word, meaning simply an investigation or inquiry. Herodotus, who uses it in the title of his work, thereby 'marks a literary revolution' (as Croiset, an historian of Greek literature, says). Previous writers had been . . . writers-down of current stories: 'the historian', say How and Wells, 'sets out to "find" the truth.' It is the use of this word, and its implications, that make Herodotus the father of history. The conversion of legend-writing into the science of history was not native to the Greek mind, it was a fifth-century invention, and Herodotus was the man who invented it. (ii) It is equally clear that history for Herodotus is humanistic as distinct from either mythical or theocratic. As he says in his preface, his purpose is to describe the deeds of men. (iii) His end, as he describes it himself, is that these deeds shall not be forgotten by posterity. Here we have my fourth characteristic of history, namely that it ministers to man's knowledge of man. In particular, Herodotus points out, it reveals man as a rational agent: that is, its function is partly to discover what men have done and partly to discover why they have done it. . . . Herodotus does not confine his attention to bare events; he considers these events in a thoroughly humanistic manner as actions of human beings who had reasons for acting as they did: and the historian is concerned with these reasons.

These three points reappear in the preface of Thucydides, which was obviously written with an eye on that of Herodotus. Thucydides . . . does not of course use the word [history], but he refers to it in other terms: to make it clear that he is no logographer but a scientific student, asking questions instead of repeating legends, he defends his choice of subject by saying that events earlier than those of the Peloponnesian War cannot be accurately ascertained. . . . He emphasizes the humanistic purpose and the self-revelatory function of history, in words modelled on those of his predecessor. And in one way he improves on Herodotus, for Herodotus makes no mention of evidence (the third of the characteristics mentioned above), and one is left to gather from the body of his work what his idea of evidence was; but Thucydides does say explicitly that historical inquiry rests on evidence . . . 'when I consider in the light of the evidence'. What they thought about the nature of evidence, and the way in which an historian interprets it, is a subject to which I shall return.

ANTI-HISTORICAL TENDENCY OF GREEK THOUGHT

In the meantime, I should like to point out how remarkable a thing is this creation of scientific history by Herodotus, for he was an ancient Greek, and ancient Greek thought as a whole has a very definite prevailing tendency not only uncongenial to the growth of historical thought but actually based, one might say, on a rigorously anti-historical metaphysics. History is a science of human action: what the historian puts before himself is things that men have done in the past, and these belong to a world of change, a world where things come to be and cease to be. Such things, according to the prevalent Greek meta-physical view, ought not to be knowable, and therefore history ought to be impossible.

For the Greeks, the same difficulty arose with the world of nature since it too was a world of this kind. If everything in the world changes, they asked, what is there in such a world for the mind to grasp? They were quite sure that anything which can be an object of genuine knowledge must be permanent; for it must have some definite character of its own, and therefore cannot contain in itself the seeds of its own destruction. If it is to be knowable it must be determinate; if it is de-terminate, it must be so completely and exclusively what it is that no internal change and no external force can ever set about making it into something else. Greek thought achieved its first triumph when it dis-covered in the objects of mathematical knowledge something that satis-fied these conditions. A straight bar of iron may be bent into a curve, a flat surface of water may be broken into waves, but the straight line and the plane surface, as the mathematician thinks of them, are eternal objects that cannot change their characteristics.

Following the line of argument thus opened up, Greek thought worked out a distinction between two types of thought, knowledge proper . . . and what we translate by 'opinion'. . . . Opinion is the empirical semi-knowledge we have of matters of fact, which are always changing. It is our fleeting acquaintance with the fleeting actualities of the world; it thus only holds good for its own proper duration, for the here and now; and it is immediate, ungrounded in reasons, incapable of demonstration. True knowledge, on the contrary, holds good not only here and now but everywhere and always, and it is based on demonstra-tive reasoning and thus capable of meeting and overthrowing error by the weapon of dialectical criticism.

Thus, for the Greeks, process could be known only so far as it was perceived, and the knowledge of it could never be demonstrative. An exaggerated statement of this view, as we get it in the Eleatics [some early philosophers], would misuse the weapon of dialectic, which is really valid only against error in the sphere of knowledge strictly so called, to prove that change does not exist and that the 'opinions' we have about the changing are really not even opinions but sheer illusions. Plato rejects that doctrine and sees in the world of change something not indeed intelligible but real to the extent of being perceptible, some-thing intermediate between the nullity with which the Eleatics had identified it and the complete reality and intelligibility of the eternal.

On such a theory, history ought to be impossible. For history must have these two characteristics: first it must be about what is transitory, and secondly it must be scientific or demonstrative. But on this theory what is transitory cannot be demonstratively known; it cannot be the object of science; it can only be a matter of . . . perception, whereby human sensibility catches the fleeting moment as it flies. And it is essential to the Greek point of view that this momentary sensuous perception of momentary changing things cannot be a science or the basis of a science.

GREEK CONCEPTION OF HISTORY'S NATURE AND VALUE

The ardour with which the Greeks pursued the ideal of an unchanging and eternal object of knowledge might easily mislead us as to their historical interests. It might, if we read them carelessly, make us think them uninterested in history, somewhat as Plato's attack on the poets might make an unintelligent reader fancy that Plato cared little for poetry. In order to interpret such things correctly we must remember that no competent thinker or writer wastes his time attacking a man of straw. An intense polemic against a certain doctrine is an infallible sign that the doctrine in question figures largely in the writer's environment and even has a strong attraction for himself. The Greek pursuit of the eternal was as eager as it was, precisely because the Greeks themselves had an unusually vivid sense of the temporal. They lived in a time when history was moving with extraordinary rapidity, and in a country where earthquake and erosion change the face of the land with a violence hardly to be seen elsewhere. They saw all nature as a spectacle of incessant change, and human life as changing more violently than anything else. Unlike the Chinese, or the medieval civilization of Europe, whose conception of human society was anchored in the hope of retaining the chief features of its structure unchanged, they made it their first aim to face and reconcile themselves to the fact that such permanence is impossible. This recognition of the necessity of change in human affairs gave to the Greeks a peculiar sensitiveness to history.

Knowing that nothing in life can persist unchanged, they came habitually to ask themselves what exactly the changes had been which, they knew, must have come about in order to bring the present into existence. Their historical consciousness was thus not a consciousness of agelong tradition moulding the life of one generation after another into a uniform pattern; it was a consciousness of violent [upheavals, transformations], catastrophic changes from one state of things to its opposite, from smallness to greatness, from pride to abasement, from happiness to misery. This was how they interpreted the general character of human life in their dramas, and this was how they narrated the particular parts of it in their history. The only thing that a shrewd and critical Greek like Herodotus would say about the divine power that ordains the course of history is that . . . it rejoices in upsetting and disturbing things. He was only repeating what every Greek knew: that the power of Zeus is manifested in the thunderbolt, that of Poseidon in the earthquake, that of Apollo in the pestilence, and that of Aphrodite in the passion that destroyed at once the pride of Phaedra and the chastity of Hippolytus.

It is true that these catastrophic changes in the condition of human life, which to the Greeks were the proper theme of history, were unintelligible. There could be no [philosophic knowledge proper] of them, no demonstrative scientific knowledge. But all the same history had for the Greeks a definite value. Plato himself laid it down that right opinion (which is the sort of pseudo-knowledge that perception gives us of what changes) was no less useful for the conduct of life than scientific knowledge, and the poets maintained their traditional place in Greek life as the teachers of sound principles by showing that in the general pattern of these changes certain antecedents normally led to certain consequents. Notably, an excess in any one direction led to a violent change into its own opposite. Why this was so they could not tell; but they thought it a matter of observation that it was so; that people who became extremely rich or extremely powerful were thereby brought into special danger of being reduced to a condition of extreme poverty or weakness. There is here no theory of causation; the thought does not resemble that of seventeenth-century inductive science with its metaphysical basis in the axiom of cause and effect; the riches of Croesus are not the cause of his downfall, they are merely a symptom, to the intelligent observer, that something is happening in the rhythm of his life which is likely to lead to a downfall. Still less is the downfall a punishment for anything that, in an intelligible moral sense, could be called wrongdoing. When Amasis in Herodotus broke off his alliance with Polycrates, he did it simply on the ground that Polycrates was too prosperous: the pendulum had swung too far one way and was likely to swing as far in the other. Such examples have their value to the person who can make use of them; for he can use his own will to arrest these rhythms in his life before they reach the danger-point, and check the thirst for power and wealth instead of allowing it to drive him to excess.

Thus history has a value; its teachings are useful for human life; simply because the rhythm of its changes is likely to repeat itself, similar antecedents leading to similar consequents; the history of notable events is worth remembering in order to serve as a basis for prognostic judgements, not demonstrable but probable, laying down not what will happen but what is likely to happen, indicating the points of danger in rhythms now going on.

This conception of history was the very opposite of deterministic, because the Greeks regarded the course of history as flexible and open to salutary modification by the well-instructed human will. Nothing that happens is inevitable. The person who is about to be involved in a tragedy is actually overwhelmed by it only because he is too blind to see his danger. If he saw it, he could guard against it. Thus the Greeks had a lively and indeed a naïve sense of the power of man to control his own destiny, and thought of this power as limited only by the limitations of his knowledge. The fate that broods over human life is, from this Greek point of view, a destructive power only because man is blind to its workings. Granted that he cannot understand these workings, he can yet have right opinions about them, and in so far as he acquires such opinions he becomes able to put himself in a position where the blows of fate will miss him.

On the other hand, valuable as the teachings of history are, their value is limited by the unintelligibility of its subject-matter; and that is why Aristotle said that poetry is more scientific than history, for history is a mere collection of empirical facts, whereas poetry extracts from such facts a universal judgement. History tells us that Croesus fell and that Polycrates fell; poetry, according to Aristotle's idea of it, makes not these singular judgements but the universal judgement that very rich men, as such, fall. Even this is, in Aristotle's view, only a partially scientific judgement, for no one can see why rich men should fall; the universal cannot be syllogistically demonstrated; but it approaches the status of a true universal because we can use it as the major premiss for a new syllogism applying this generalization to fresh cases. Thus poetry is for Aristotle the distilled essence of the teaching of history. In poetry the lessons of history do not become any more intelligible and they remain undemonstrated and therefore merely probable, but they become more compendious and therefore more useful.

Such was the way in which the Greeks conceived the nature and value of history. They could not, consistently with their general philosophical attitude, regard it as scientific. They had to consider it as, at bottom, not a science but a mere aggregate of perceptions. What, then, was their conception of historical evidence? The answer is that, conformably with this view, they identified historical evidence with the reports of facts given by eyewitnesses of those facts. Evidence consists of eyewitnesses' narratives, and historical method consists of eliciting these.

GREEK HISTORICAL METHOD AND ITS LIMITATIONS

Quite clearly, it was in this way that Herodotus conceived of evidence and method. This does not mean that he uncritically believed whatever eyewitnesses told him. On the contrary, he is in practice highly critical of their narratives. And here again he is typically Greek. The Greeks as a whole were skilled in the practice of the law courts, and a Greek would find no difficulty in applying to historical testimony the same kind of criticism which he was accustomed to direct upon witnesses in court. The work of Herodotus or Thucydides depends in the main on the testimony of eyewitnesses with whom the historian had personal contact. And his skill as a researcher consisted in the fact that he must have cross-questioned an eyewitness of past events until he had called up in the informant's own mind an historical picture of those events far fuller and more coherent than any he could have volunteered for himself. The result of this process was to create in the informant's mind for the first time a genuine knowledge of the past events which he had perceived but of which up till then he had [opinion] only, not [knowledge].

This conception of the way in which a Greek historian collected his material makes it a very different thing from the way in which a modern historian may use printed memoirs. Instead of the easy-going belief on the informant's part that his prima facie recollection was adequate to the facts, there could grow up in his mind a chastened and criticized recollection which had stood the fire of such questions as 'Are you quite sure that you remember it just like that? Have you not now contradicted what you were saying yesterday? How do you reconcile your account of that event with the very different account given by so-and-so?' This method of using the testimony of eyewitnesses is undoubtedly the method which underlies the extraordinary solidity and consistency of the narratives which Herodotus and Thucydides finally wrote about fifth-century Greece.

No other method deserving the name scientific was available to the fifth-century historians, but it had three limitations:

First, it inevitably imposed on its users a shortness of historical perspective. The modern historian knows that if only he had the capacity he could become the interpreter of the whole past of mankind; but whatever Greek historians might have thought of Plato's description of the philosopher as the spectator of all time, they would never have ventured to claim Plato's words as a description of themselves. Their method tied them on a tether whose length was the length of living memory: the only source they could criticize was an eyewitness with whom they could converse face to face. It is true that they relate events from a remoter past, but as soon as Greek historical writing tries to go beyond its tether, it becomes a far weaker and more precarious thing. For instance, we must not deceive ourselves into thinking that any scientific value attaches to what Herodotus tells us about the sixth century or to what Thucydides tells us about events . . . [in earlier Greek history]. From our twentieth-century point of view, these early stories in Herodotus and Thucydides are very interesting, but they are mere logography and not scientific. They are traditions which the author who hands them down to us has not been able to raise to the level of history because he has not been able to pass them through the crucible of the only critical method he knew. Nevertheless, this contrast in Herodotus and Thucydides between the unreliability of everything farther back than living memory and the critical precision of what comes within living memory is a mark not of the failure of fifth-century historiography but of its success. The point about Herodotus and Thucydides is not that the remote past is for them still outside the scope of scientific history but that the recent past is within that scope. Scientific history has been invented. Its field is still narrow; but within that field it is secure. Moreover, this narrowness of field did not matter much to the Greeks, because the extreme rapidity with which their own civilization was developing and changing afforded plenty of first-class historical material within the confines set by their method, and for the same reason they could produce first-rate historical work without developing what in fact they never did develop, any lively curiosity concerning the remote past.

Secondly, the Greek historian's method precludes him from choosing his subject. He cannot, like Gibbon, begin by wishing to write a great historical work and go on to ask himself what he shall write about. The only thing he can write about is the events which have happened within living memory to people with whom he can have personal contact. Instead of the historian choosing the subject, the subject chooses the historian; I mean that history is written only because memorable things have happened which call for a chronicler among the contemporaries of the people who have seen them. One might almost say that in ancient Greece there were no historians in the sense in which there were artists and philosophers; there were no people who devoted their lives to the study of history; the historian was only the autobiographer of his generation and autobiography is not a profession.

Thirdly, Greek historical method made it impossible for the various particular histories to be gathered up into one all-embracing history. Nowadays we think of monographs on various subjects as ideally forming parts of a universal history, so that if their subjects are carefully chosen and their scale and treatment carefully controlled they might serve as chapters in a single historical work; and this is the way in which a writer like Grote actually treated Herodotus' account of the Persian War and Thucydides' of the Peloponnesian. But if any given history is the autobiography of a generation, it cannot be rewritten when that generation has passed away, because the evidence on which it was based will have perished. The work that a contemporary based on that evidence can thus never be improved upon or criticized, and it can never be absorbed into a larger whole, because it is like a work of art, something having the uniqueness and individuality of a statue or a poem. . . . The rewriting of their histories, or their incorporation into the history of a longer period, would have seemed to [Thucydides and Herodotus] an absurdity. To the Greek historians, therefore, there could never be any such thing as a history of Greece. There could be a history of a fairly extensive complex of events, like the Persian War or the Peloponnesian War; but only on two conditions. First, this complex of events must be complete in itself: it must have a beginning, a middle, and an end, like the plot of an Aristotelian tragedy. Secondly, it must be . . . like an Aristotelian city-state. [That is, just] as Aristotle thought that no community of civilized men under a single government could exceed in size the number of citizens that could be within earshot of a single herald, the dimensions of the political organism being thus limited by a purely physical fact, so the Greek theory of history implies that no historical narrative could exceed in length the years of a man's lifetime, within which alone the critical methods at its disposal could be applied.

HERODOTUS AND THUCYDIDES

The greatness of Herodotus stands out in the sharpest relief when, as the father of history, he is set against a background consisting of the general tendencies of Greek thought. The most dominant of these was anti-historical, as I have argued, because it involved the position that only what is unchanging can be known. Therefore history is a forlorn hope, an attempt to know what, being transitory, is unknowable. But we have already seen that, by skilful questioning, Herodotus was able to elicit [knowledge] from his informant's [opinion] and thus to attain knowledge in a field where Greeks had thought it impossible.

His success must remind us of one of his contemporaries, a man who was not afraid, either in war or in philosophy, to embark on forlorn hopes. Socrates brought philosophy down from heaven to earth by insisting that he himself knew nothing, and inventing a technique whereby, through skilful questioning, knowledge could be generated in the minds of others as ignorant as himself. Knowledge of what? Knowledge of human affairs: in particular, of the moral ideas that guide human conduct.

The parallel between the work of the two men is so striking that I put Herodotus side by side with Socrates as one of the great innovating geniuses of the fifth century. But his achievement ran so strongly counter to the current of Greek thought that it did not long survive its creator. Socrates was after all in the direct line of the Greek intellectual tradition, and that is why his work was taken up and developed by Plato and many other disciples. Not so Herodotus. Herodotus had no successors.

Even if I conceded to an objector that Thucydides worthily carried on the Herodotean tradition, the question would still remain: Who carried it on when Thucydides had finished with it? And the only answer is: Nobody carried it on. These fifth-century giants had no fourth-century successors anything like equal in stature to themselves. The decay of Greek art from the late fifth century onwards is undeniable; but it did not entail a decay of Greek science. Greek philosophy still had Plato and Aristotle to come. The natural sciences were still to have a long and brilliant life. If history is a science, why did history share the fate of the arts and not the fate of the other sciences? Why does Plato write as if Herodotus had never lived?

The answer is that the Greek mind tended to harden and narrow itself in its anti-historical tendency. The genius of Herodotus triumphed over that tendency, but after him the search for unchangeable and eternal objects of knowledge gradually stifled the historical consciousness, and forced men to abandon the Herodotean hope of achieving a scientific knowledge of past human actions.

This is not a mere conjecture. We can see the thing happening. The man in whom it happened was Thucydides.

The difference between the scientific outlook of Herodotus and that of Thucydides is hardly less remarkable than the difference between their literary styles. The style of Herodotus is easy, spontaneous, convincing. That of Thucydides is harsh, artificial, repellent. In reading Thucydides I ask myself, What is the matter with the man, that he writes like that? I answer: he has a bad conscience. He is trying to justify himself for writing history at all by turning it into something that is not history. Mr. C. N. Cochrane, in his *Thucydides and the Science of History* (London, 1929), has argued, I think rightly, that the dominant influence on Thucydides is the influence of Hippocratic medicine. Hippocrates was not only the father of medicine, he was also the father of psychology, and his influence is evident not only in such things as the Thucydidean description of the plague, but in such studies in morbid psychology as the description of war-neurosis in general and the special instances of it in the Corcyrean revolution and the Melian dialogue. Herodotus may be the father of history, but Thucydides is the father of psychological history.

Now what is psychological history? It is not history at all, but natural science of a special kind. It does not narrate facts for the sake of narrating facts. Its chief purpose is to affirm laws, psychological laws. A psychological law is not an event nor yet a complex of events: it is an unchanging rule which governs the relations between events. I think that every one who knows both authors will agree with me when I say that what chiefly interests Herodotus is the events themselves; what chiefly interests Thucydides is the laws according to which they happen. But these laws are precisely such eternal and unchanging forms as, according to the main trend of Greek thought, are the only knowable things.

Thucydides is not the successor of Herodotus in historical thought but the man in whom the historical thought of Herodotus was overlaid and smothered beneath anti-historical motives. This is a thesis which may be illustrated by mentioning one familiar feature of Thucydides' method. Consider his speeches. Custom has dulled our susceptibilities;

but let us ask ourselves for a moment: could a just man who had a really historical mind have permitted himself the use of such a convention? Think first of their style. Is it not, historically speaking, an outrage to make all these very different characters talk in one and the same fashion, and that a fashion in which no one can ever have spoken when addressing troops before a battle or when pleading for the lives of the conquered? Is it not clear that the style betrays a lack of interest in the question what such and such a man really said on such and such an occasion? Secondly, think of their contents. Can we say that, however unhistorical their style may be, their substance is historical? The question has been variously answered. Thucydides does say (i. 22) that he kept 'as closely as possible' to the general sense of what was actually said; but how close was this? He does not claim that it was very close, because he adds that he has given the speeches roughly as he thought the speakers would have said what was appropriate to the occasion; and when we consider the speeches themselves in their context, it is difficult to resist the conclusion that the judge of 'what was appropriate' was Thucydides himself. Grote argued long ago that the Melian dialogue contains more imagination than history, and I have seen no convincing refutation of his argument. The speeches seem to me to be in substance not history but Thucydidean comments upon the acts of the speakers, Thucydidean reconstructions of their motives and intentions. Even if this be denied, the very controversy on this question may be regarded as evidence that the Thucydidean speech is both in style and in content a convention characteristic of an author whose mind cannot be fully concentrated on the events themselves, but is constantly being drawn away from the events to some lesson that lurks behind them, some unchanging and eternal truth of which the events are, Platonically speaking, [merely paradigms, images, or imitations].

THE HELLENISTIC PERIOD

After the fifth century B.C. the historian's outlook underwent an enlargement in time. When Greek thought, having attained a consciousness of itself and its own worth, set out to conquer the world, it embarked on an adventure whose development was too vast to fall within the view of a single generation, and yet its consciousness of its own mission gave it a conviction of the essential unity of that development. This helped the Greeks to overcome the particularism which had coloured all their historiography before the time of Alexander the Great. In their eyes history had been essentially the history of one particular social unit at one particular time:

(i) They were conscious that this particular social unit was only one among many; and, in so far as it came into contact, friendly or hostile, with others during the given space of time, these others put in an appearance on the stage of history. But although for this reason Herodotus has to say something about the Persians, he is interested in them not for their own sake but only as enemies of the Greeks: worthy and honourable enemies, but still enemies and no more. (ii) They were conscious in the fifth century, and even earlier, that there was such a thing as the human world, the totality of all particular social units; [the world inhabited by man] as distinct from . . . the natural world. But the unity of this human world was for them only a geographical, not an historical, unity. The consciousness of that unity was not an historical consciousness. The idea of oecumenical history, world-history, was still nonexistent. (iii) They were conscious that the history of the particular society in which they were interested had been going on for a long time. But they did not try to trace it back very far. The reason for this I have already explained. The only genuinely historical method hitherto invented depended on cross-questioning eyewitnesses; consequently the backward limit of any historian's field was dictated by the limits of human memory.

These three limitations were all overcome in what is called the Hellenistic period.

(i) The symbol of the parochial outlook of the fifth-century Greeks is the linguistic distinction between Greeks and Barbarians. The fourth century did not obliterate this distinction, but it abolished its rigidity. This was not a matter of theory, it was a matter of practice. It became a familiar fact about the contemporary world that Barbarians could become Greeks. This graecizing of Barbarians is called in Greek Hellenism (. . . to talk Greek, and, in a wider sense, to adopt Greek manners and customs); and the Hellenistic period is the period when Greek manners and customs were adopted by Barbarians. Thus the Greek historical consciousness, which for Herodotus had been primarily the consciousness of hostility between Greeks and Barbarians (the Persian Wars), becomes the consciousness of co-operation between Greeks and Barbarians, a co-operation in which Greeks take the lead, and Barbarians, by following that lead, become Greeks, heirs to Greek culture, and thus heirs to the Greek historical consciousness.

(ii) Through the conquests of Alexander the Great, whereby the [human world] or at least a very large part of it (and a part which included all the non-Greek peoples in whom the Greeks were specially interested) became a single political unit, the 'world' became something more than a geographical expression. It became an historical expression. The whole empire of Alexander now shared a single history of the Greek world. Potentially, the whole [human world] shared it. Any ordinarily well-informed person knew as a fact that Greek history was a single history that held good from the Adriatic to the Indus and from the Danube to the Sahara. For a philosopher, reflecting on this fact, it was possible to extend the same idea over the whole [human world]: 'The poet says, Dear city of Cecrops: wilt thou not say, Dear city of Zeus?' That is, of course, from Marcus Aurelius in the second century A.D.; but the idea, the idea of the whole world as a single historical unit, is a typically Stoic idea, and Stoicism is a typical product of the Hellenistic period. It was Hellenism that created the idea of oecumenical history.

(iii) But a world-history could not be written on the strength of testimony from living eyewitnesses, and therefore a new method was required, namely compilation. It was necessary to construct a patchwork history whose materials were drawn from 'authorities', that is, from the works of previous historians who had already written the histories of particular societies at particular times. This is what I call the 'scissors-and-paste' historical method. It consists in excerpting the required material from writers whose work cannot be checked on Herodotean principles, because the eyewitnesses who co-operated in that work are no longer alive. As a method, this is far inferior to the Socratic method of the fifth century. It is not a wholly uncritical method, because judgement can and must be exercised as to whether this or that statement, made by this or that authority, is true. But it cannot be used at all without the assurance that this or that authority is on the whole a good historian. Consequently, the oecumenical history of the Hellenistic age (which includes the Roman age) is based on a high estimate of the work done by the particularistic historians of the Hellenic age.

It was especially the vividness and excellence of the work done by Herodotus and Thucydides that re-created a lively idea of the fifth century in the minds of later generations and increased the backward scope of historical thought. Just as the past achievements of great artists gave people a sense that artistic styles other than that of their own day were valuable, so that a generation of literary and artistic scholars and dilettanti arose for whom the preservation and enjoyment of classical art was an end in itself, so there arose historians of a new type who could feel themselves imaginatively as contemporaries of Herodotus and Thucydides while yet remaining men of their own time and able to compare their own times with the past. This past the Hellenistic historians could feel as their own past, and thus it became possible to write a new kind of history with a dramatic unity of any size, so long as the historian could collect materials for it and could weld them into a single story.

POLYBIUS

The idea of this new kind of history is full-grown in the work of Polybius [203?–120 B.C.]. Like all real historians, Polybius has a definite theme; he has a story to tell, a story of notable and memorable things, namely the conquest of the world by Rome; but he begins that story at a point more than 150 years before the time of writing, so that the extent of his field is five generations instead of one. His ability to do this is connected with the fact that he is working in Rome, whose people had a kind of historical consciousness quite different from that of the Greeks. History for them meant continuity: the inheritance from the past of institutions scrupulously preserved in the form in which they were received; the moulding of life according to the pattern of ancestral custom. The Romans, acutely conscious of their own continuity with their past, were careful to preserve memorials of that past; they not only kept their ancestral portraits in the house, as a visible symbol of the continuing and watchful presence of their forefathers directing their own life, but they preserved ancient traditions of their own corporate history to an extent unknown to the Greeks. These traditions were no doubt affected by the inevitable tendency to project the characteristics of late Republican Rome into the history of her earliest days; but Polybius, with his critical and philosophical mind, guarded against the historical dangers of that distortion by only beginning his narrative where his authorities became, in his own opinion, trustworthy: and in using these sources he never allowed his critical faculty to go to sleep. It is to the Romans, acting as always under the tuition of the Hellenistic mind, that we owe the conception of a history both oecumenical and national, a history in which the hero of the story is the continuing and corporate spirit of a people and in which the plot of the story is the unification of the world under that people's leadership. Even here, we have not arrived at the conception of national history as we understand it: national history as the complete biography, so to speak, of a people from its very beginnings. For Polybius, the history of Rome begins with Rome already fully formed, adult, ready to go forth on her mission of conquest. The difficult problem of how a national spirit comes into existence is not yet tackled. For Polybius, the given, ready-made national spirit is the [reference point] of history, the unchanging substance that underlies all change. Just as the Greeks could not even contemplate the possibility of raising the problem which we should call the problem of the origin of the Hellenic people, so even for Polybius there is no problem of the origin of the Roman people; if he knew the traditions about the foundation of Rome, as he doubtless did, he silently cut them out of his field of vision as lying behind the point at which historical science, as he conceived it, could begin.

With this larger conception of the field of history comes a more precise conception of history itself. Polybius uses the word ἱστορία [in Latin, *historia*] not in its original and quite general sense as meaning any kind of inquiry, but in its modern sense of history: the thing is now conceived as a special type of research needing a special name of its own. He is an advocate of the claims of this science to universal study for its own sake, and points out in the first sentence of his work that this is a thing not hitherto done; he thinks of himself as the first person to conceive of history as such as a form of thought having a universal value. But he expresses this value in a way which shows that he has come to terms with the anti-historical or substantialistic tendency which, as I said before, dominated the Greek mind. History, according to this tendency, cannot be a science, for there can be no science of transitory things. Its value is not a theoretical or scientific value, it can only be a practical value—the kind of value which Plato had ascribed to [opinion], the quasi-knowledge of what is not eternal and intelligible but temporal and perceptible. Polybius accepts and emphasizes this notion. History, for him, is worth studying not because it is scientifically true or demonstrative, but because it is a school and training-ground for political life.

But a person who had accepted this notion in the fifth century (as no one did, because Herodotus still thought of history as a science and Thucydides, so far as I can see, did not raise the question of the value of history at all) would have inferred that the value of history lies in its power of training individual statesmen, a Pericles or the like, to conduct the affairs of their own community with skill and success. This view was held by Isocrates in the fourth century, but it had become impossible by the time of Polybius. The naïve self-confidence of the Hellenic age has disappeared with the disappearance of the city-state. Polybius does not think that the study of history will enable men to avoid the mistakes of their predecessors and surpass them in worldly success; the success to which the study of history can lead is for him an inner success, a victory not over circumstances but over self. What we learn from the tragedies of its heroes is not to avoid such tragedies in our own lives, but to bear them bravely when fortune brings them. The idea of fortune [tyche] bulks largely in this conception of history, and imports into it a new element of determinism. As the canvas on which the historian paints his picture grows larger, the power attributed to the individual will grow less. Man finds himself no longer master of his fate in the sense that what he tries to do succeeds or fails in proportion to his own intelligence or lack of it; his fate is master of him, and the freedom of his will is shown not in controlling the outward events of his life but in controlling the inward temper in which he faces these events. Here Polybius is applying to history the same Hellenistic conceptions which the Stoics and Epicureans applied to ethics. Both these schools agreed in thinking that the problem of moral life was not how to control events in the world around us, as the classical Greek moralists had thought, but how to preserve a purely inward integrity and balance of mind when the attempt to control outward events had been abandoned. For Hellenistic thought, self-consciousness is no longer, as it was for Hellenic thought, a power to conquer the world; it is a citadel providing a safe retreat from a world both hostile and intractable.

LIVY AND TACITUS

With Polybius the Hellenistic tradition of historical thought passes into the hands of Rome. The only original development it received there was from Livy [59 B.C.–17 A.D.], who conceived the magnificent idea of a complete history of Rome from her very beginning. A great part of Polybius' work had been done on the fifth-century method, in collaboration with his friends of the Scipionic circle who had achieved the culminating stages in the construction of the new Roman world. It was only the introductory phases of Polybius' narrative that had to depend by scissors-and-paste means on the work of earlier authorities. In Livy the centre of gravity is changed. It is no mere introduction, it is the whole body of his work, that is constructed by scissors and paste. Livy's whole task is to assemble the traditional records of early Roman history

and weld them together into a single continuous narrative, the history
of Rome. It was the first time anything of the sort had been done. The
Romans, serenely confident in their own superiority to all other peoples
and their monopoly of the only virtues deserving the name, thought
their own history the only one worth narrating; and hence the history
of Rome as narrated by Livy was to the Roman mind not one out of a
number of possible particular histories but universal history, the history
of the only genuinely historical reality: oecumenical history, because
Rome had now, like Alexander's Empire, become the world.

Livy was a philosophical historian; less philosophical no doubt than
Polybius, but far more philosophical than any later Roman historian.
His preface therefore deserves the closest study. I shall comment briefly
on a few points in it. First, he pitches the scientific claims of his work
very low. He makes no claim to original research or original method.
He writes as if his chance of standing out from the ruck of historical
writers depended chiefly on his literary qualities; and certainly these
qualities are, as all his readers have agreed, outstanding. . . . Secondly,
he emphasizes his moral purpose. He says that his readers will doubtless
prefer to be told about the recent past; but he wants them to read about
the remote past, because he wishes to hold up before them the moral
example of the early days when Roman society was simple and uncor-
rupted, and to show them how the foundations of Roman greatness
were laid in this primitive morality. Thirdly, he is clear that history is
humanistic. It flatters our conceit, he says, to think of our origins as
divine; but the historian's business is not to flatter his reader's conceit
but to paint the doings and manners of men.

Livy's attitude towards his authorities is sometimes misrepresented.
Like Herodotus, he is often charged with the grossest credulity; but, like
Herodotus, wrongly. He does his best to be critical; but the methodical
criticism practised by every modern historian was still not invented.
Here was a mass of legends; all he could do with them was to decide, as
best he could, whether or not they were trustworthy. Three courses
were open to him: to repeat them, accepting their substantial accuracy;
to reject them; or to repeat them with the caution that he was not sure
of their truth. Thus, at the outset of his history, Livy says that the traditions referring to events before the foundation of Rome, or rather to
events before those immediately leading up to that foundation, are
fables rather than sound traditions and can neither be affirmed nor criticized. He therefore repeats them with a caution, merely remarking that
they show a tendency to magnify the origins of the city by mingling

divine agencies with human; but once he comes to the foundation of Rome he accepts the tradition pretty much as he finds it. There is here only the very crudest attempt at historical criticism. Presented with a great wealth of traditional material, the historian takes it all at its face value; he makes no attempt to discover how the tradition has grown up and through what various distorting media it has reached him; he therefore cannot reinterpret a tradition, that is, explain it as meaning something other than it explicitly says. He has to take it or leave it, and, on the whole, Livy's tendency is to accept his tradition and repeat it in good faith.

The Roman Empire was not an age of vigorous and progressive thought. It did singularly little to advance knowledge on any of the paths that the Greeks had opened up. It kept alive for a time the Stoic and Epicurean philosophies without developing them; only in Neoplatonism did it show any philosophical originality. In natural science it did nothing to surpass the achievements of the Hellenistic Age. Even in applied natural science it was extremely weak. It used Hellenistic fortification, Hellenistic artillery, and arts and crafts partly Hellenistic and partly Celtic. In history its interest survived but its vigour failed. No one ever took up Livy's task again and tried to do it better. After him, historians either copied him or drew in their horns and confined themselves to a narrative of the recent past. So far as method goes, Tacitus [c.55–c.117 A.D.] already represents a decline.

As a contributor to historical literature, Tacitus is a gigantic figure; but it is permissible to wonder whether he was an historian at all. He imitates the parochial outlook of the fifth-century Greeks without imitating their virtues. He is obsessed with the history of affairs at Rome, neglecting the Empire, or seeing it only as refracted through the spectacles of a homekeeping Roman; and his outlook on these purely Roman affairs is narrow in the extreme. He is flagrantly biased in favour of the senatorial opposition; he couples a contempt for peaceful administration with an admiration for conquest and military glory, an admiration blinded by his remarkable ignorance of the actualities of warfare. All these defects make him curiously unfitted to be the historian of the early Principate, but at bottom they are only symptoms of a graver and more general defect. What is really wrong with Tacitus is that he has never thought out the fundamental problems of his enterprise. His attitude towards the philosophical groundwork of history is frivolous, and he takes over the current pragmatic view of its purpose in the spirit of a rhetorician rather than that of a serious thinker.

'His professed purpose in writing is to hold up signal examples of political vice and virtue for posterity to execrate or to admire, and to teach his readers, even through a narrative which he fears may weary them by its monotonous horrors, that good citizens may live under bad rulers; and that it is not mere destiny or the chapter of accidents, but personal character and discretion, dignified moderation and reserve, that best guard a senator of rank unharmed through time of peril, in which not only the defiant on one side, but almost as often the sycophant on the other, are struck down as the course of events or even the changing humours of the prince may prompt.' [Furneaux]

This attitude leads Tacitus to distort history systematically by representing it as essentially a clash of characters, exaggeratedly good with exaggeratedly bad. History cannot be scientifically written unless the historian can re-enact in his own mind the experience of the people whose actions he is narrating. Tacitus never tried to do this: his characters are seen not from inside, with understanding and sympathy, but from outside, as mere spectacles of virtue or vice. One can hardly read his descriptions of an Agricola or a Domitian without being reminded of Socrates' laugh at Glaucon's imaginary portraits of the perfectly good and the perfectly bad man: 'My word, Glaucon, how energetically you are polishing them up like statues for a prize competition!'

Tacitus has been praised for his character-drawing; but the principles on which he draws character are fundamentally vicious and make his character-drawing an outrage on historical truth. He found warrant for it, no doubt, in the Stoic and Epicurean philosophies of his age, to which I have already referred: the defeatist philosophies which, starting from the assumption that the good man cannot conquer or control a wicked world, taught him how to preserve himself unspotted from its wickedness. This false antithesis between the individual man's character and his social environment justifies, in a sense, Tacitus' method of exhibiting the actions of an historical figure as flowing simply from his own personal character, and making no allowance either for the way in which a man's actions may be determined partly by his environment and only in part by his character, or for the way in which character itself may be moulded by the forces to which a man is subjected by his environment. Actually, as Socrates urged against Glaucon, the individual character considered in isolation from its environment is an abstraction; not a really existing thing. What a man does depends only to a limited extent on what kind of man he is. No one can resist the forces of his environment. Either he conquers the world or the world will conquer him.

Thus Livy and Tacitus stand side by side as the two great monuments to the barrenness of Roman historical thought. Livy has attempted a really great task, but he has failed in it because his method is too simple to cope with the complexity of his material, and his story of the ancient history of Rome is too deeply permeated with fabulous elements to be ranked with the greatest works of historical thought. Tacitus has attempted a new approach, the psychological-didactic; but instead of being an enrichment of historical method this is really an impoverishment, and indicates a declining standard of historical honesty. Subsequent historians under the Roman Empire, instead of overcoming the obstacles by which Livy and Tacitus were baffled, never even equalled their achievement. As the Empire went on, historians began more and more to content themselves with the wretched business of compilation, amassing in an uncritical spirit what they found in earlier works and arranging it with no end in view except, at best, edification or some other kind of propaganda.

CHARACTER OF GRECO-ROMAN
HISTORIOGRAPHY: (I) HUMANISM

Greco-Roman historiography as a whole has firmly grasped one at least of the four characteristics [of genuine history]: it is humanistic. It is a narrative of human history, the history of man's deeds, man's purposes, man's successes and failures. It admits, no doubt, a divine agency; but the function of this agency is strictly limited. The will of the gods as manifested in history only appears rarely; in the best historians hardly at all and then only as a will supporting and seconding the will of man and enabling him to succeed where otherwise he would have failed. The gods have no plan of their own for the development of human affairs; they only grant success or decree failure for the plans of men. This is why a more searching analysis of human actions themselves, discovering in them alone the grounds for their success or failure, tends to eliminate the gods altogether, and to substitute for them mere personifications of human activity, like the genius of the Emperor, the goddess Rome, or the virtues represented on Roman Imperial coins. The ultimate development of this tendency is to find the cause of all historical events in the personality, whether individual or corporate of human agents. The philosophical idea underlying it is the idea of the human will as freely choosing its own ends and limited in the success it achieves in their pursuit only by its own force and by the power of the intellect which apprehends them and works out means to their achievement. This implies that whatever happens in history happens as a direct result of human will; that some one is directly responsible for it, to be praised or blamed according as it is a good thing or a bad.

Greco-Roman humanism, however, had a special weakness of its own because of its inadequate moral or psychological insight. It was based on the idea of man as essentially a rational animal, by which I mean the doctrine that every individual human being is an animal capable of reason. So far as any given man develops that capacity and becomes actually, and not potentially, reasonable, he makes a success of his life: according to the Hellenic idea, he becomes a force in political life and a maker of history; according to the Hellenistic-Roman idea, he becomes capable of living wisely, sheltered behind his own rationality, in a wild and wicked world. Now the idea that every agent is wholly and directly responsible for everything that he does is a naïve idea which takes no account of certain important regions in moral experience. On the one hand, there is no getting away from the fact that men's characters are formed by their actions and experiences: the man himself undergoes change as his activities develop. On the other hand, there is the fact that to a very great extent people do not know what they are doing until they have done it, if then. The extent to which people act with a clear idea of their ends, knowing what effects they are aiming at, is easily exaggerated. Most human action is tentative, experimental, directed not by a knowledge of what it will lead to but rather by a desire to know what will come of it. Looking back over our actions, or over any stretch of past history, we see that something has taken shape as the actions went on which certainly was not present to our minds, or to the mind of any one, when the actions which brought it into existence began. The ethical thought of the Greco-Roman world attributed far too much to the deliberate plan or policy of the agent, far too little to the force of a blind activity embarking on a course of action without foreseeing its end and being led to that end only through the necessary development of that course itself.

CHARACTER OF GRECO-ROMAN HISTORIOGRAPHY: (II) SUBSTANTIALISM

If its humanism, however weak, is the chief merit of Greco-Roman historiography, its chief defect is substantialism. By this I mean that it is constructed on the basis of a metaphysical system whose chief category is the category of substance. Substance does not mean matter or physical substance; indeed many Greek metaphysicians thought that no substance could be material. For Plato, it would seem, substances are immaterial though not mental; they are objective forms. For Aristotle, in the last resort, the only ultimately real substance is mind. Now a substantialistic metaphysics implies a theory of knowledge according to which only what is unchanging is knowable. But what is unchanging is not historical. What is historical is the transitory event. The substance to which an event happens, or from whose nature it proceeds, is nothing to the historian. Hence the attempt to think historically and the attempt to think in terms of substance were incompatible.

In Herodotus we have an attempt at a really historical point of view. For him events are important in themselves and knowable by themselves. But already in Thucydides the historical point of view is being dimmed by substantialism. For Thucydides the events are important chiefly for the light they throw on eternal and substantial entities of which they are mere accidents. The stream of historical thought which flowed so freely in Herodotus is beginning to freeze up.

As time goes on this freezing process continues, and by the time of Livy history is frozen solid. A distinction is now taken for granted between act and agent, regarded as a special case of substance and accident. It is taken for granted that the historian's proper business is with acts, which come into being in time, develop in time through their phases, and terminate in time. The agent from which they flow, being a substance, is eternal and unchanging and consequently stands outside history. In order that acts may flow from it, the agent itself must exist unchanged throughout the series of its acts: for it has to exist before this series begins and nothing that happens as the series goes on can add anything to it or take away anything from it. History cannot explain how any agent came into being or underwent any change of nature; for it is metaphysically axiomatic that an agent, being a substance, can never have come into being and can never undergo any change of nature. We have already seen how these ideas affected the work of Polybius.

We have sometimes been taught to contrast the unphilosophical Romans with the philosophical Greeks, and we may thus have been led to think that if the Romans were as unphilosophical as all that they would not allow metaphysical considerations to affect their historical work. Nevertheless it was so. And the completeness with which the practical and hard-headed Romans adopted the substantialistic metaphysics of the Greeks does not appear in the Roman historians alone. It appears with equal clarity in the Roman lawyers. Roman law, from beginning to end, is constructed on a framework of substantialistic metaphysical principles which influence its every detail.

I will give two examples of how this influence appears in the two greatest Roman historians.

First, in Livy. Livy set himself the task of writing a history of Rome. Now, a modern historian would have interpreted this as meaning a history of how Rome came to be what it is, a history of the process which brought into existence the characteristic Roman institutions and moulded the typical Roman character. It never occurs to Livy to adopt any such interpretation. Rome is the heroine of his narrative. Rome is the agent whose actions he is describing. Therefore Rome is a substance, changeless and eternal. From the beginning of the narrative Rome is ready-made and complete. To the end of the narrative she has undergone no spiritual change. The traditions on which Livy relied projected such institutions as augury, the legion, the Senate, and so forth, into the very first years of the city, with the assumption that they remained thereafter unchanged; hence the origin of Rome, as he describes it, was a kind of miraculous leap into existence of the complete city as it existed at a later date. For a parallel, we should have to imagine an historian of England assuming that Hengist created a parliament of Lords and Commons. Rome is described as 'the eternal city'. Why is Rome so called? Because people still think of Rome, as Livy thought of her: substantialistically, non-historically.

Secondly, in Tacitus. Furneaux pointed out long ago that when Tacitus describes the way in which the character of a man like Tiberius broke down beneath the strain of empire, he represents the process not as a change in the structure or conformation of a personality but as the revelation of features in it which had hitherto been hypocritically concealed. Why does Tacitus so misrepresent facts? Is it simply out of spite, in order to blacken the characters of the men whom he has cast for the part of villains? Is it in pursuance of a rhetorical purpose, to hold up awful examples to point his moral and adorn his tale? Not at all. It is because the idea of development in a character, an idea so familiar to ourselves, is to him a metaphysical impossibility. A 'character' is an agent, not an action; actions come and go, but the 'characters' (as we call them), the agents from whom they proceed, are substances, and therefore eternal and unchanging. Features in the character of a Tiberius or a Nero which only appeared comparatively late in life must have been there all the time. A good man cannot become bad. A man who shows himself bad when old must have been equally bad when young, and his vices concealed by hypocrisy. . . . Power does not alter a man's character; it only shows what kind of man he already was.

Greco-Roman historiography can therefore never show how anything comes into existence; all the agencies that appear on the stage of history have to be assumed ready-made before history begins, and they are related to historical events exactly as a machine is related to its own movements. The scope of history is limited to describing what people and things do, the nature of these people and things remaining outside its field of vision. The nemesis of this substantialistic attitude was historical scepticism: events, as mere transitory accidents, were regarded as unknowable; the agent, as a substance, was knowable indeed, but not to the historian. But what, then, was the use of history? For Platonism history could have a pragmatic value, and the idea of this as the sole value of history intensifies from Isocrates to Tacitus. And as this process goes on it produces a kind of defeatism about historical accuracy and an unconscientiousness in the historical mind as such.

THE LEAVEN OF CHRISTIAN IDEAS

Three great crises have occurred in the history of European historiography. The first was the crisis of the fifth century B.C. when the idea of history as a science, a form of research, . . . came into being. The second was the crisis of the fourth and fifth centuries A.D. when the idea of history was remodelled by the revolutionary effect of Christian thought. I have now to describe this process and to show how Christianity jettisoned two of the leading ideas in Greco-Roman historiography, namely (i) the optimistic idea of human nature and (ii) the substantialistic idea of eternal entities underlying the process of historical change.

(i) The moral experience which Christianity expressed contained as one of its most important elements a sense of human blindness in action: not a fortuitous blindness due to individual failure of insight, but a necessary blindness inherent in action itself. According to Christian doctrine, it is inevitable that man should act in the dark without knowing what will come of his action. That inability to achieve ends clearly conceived in advance, which in Greek is called . . . missing one's mark, is no longer regarded as accidental but as a permanent element in human nature, arising out of the condition of man as man. This is the original sin upon which St. Augustine laid such stress, and which he connected psychologically with the force of natural desire. Human action, on this view, is not designed in view of preconceived ends by the intellect; it is actuated . . . by immediate and blind desire. It is not only the uninstructed vulgar, it is man as such, that does what he wants to do instead of thinking out a reasonable course of action. Desire is not the tamed horse of Plato's metaphor, it is a runaway horse, and the 'sin' (to use the technical term of theology) into which it leads us is not a sin which we deliberately choose to commit, it is an inherent and original sin proper to our nature. From this it follows that the achievements of man are due not to his own proper forces of will and intellect, but to something other than himself, causing him to desire ends that are worth pursuing. He therefore behaves, from the point of view of the historian, as if he were the wise architect of his own fortunes; but the wisdom displayed in his action is not his, it is the wisdom of God, by whose grace man's desires are directed to worthy ends. Thus the plans which are realized by human action (such plans, I mean, as the conquest of the world by Rome) come about not because men have conceived them, decided on their goodness, and devised means to execute them, but because men, doing from time to time what at the moment they wanted to do, have executed the purposes of God. This conception of grace is the correlative of the conception of original sin.

(ii) The metaphysical doctrine of substance in Greco-Roman philosophy was challenged by the Christian doctrine of creation. According to this doctrine nothing is eternal except God, and all else has been created by God. The human soul is no longer regarded as a past existence *ab aeterno* [from eternity], and its immortality in that sense is denied; each soul is believed to be a fresh creation. Similarly, peoples and nations considered collectively are not eternal substances but have been created by God. And what God has created He can modify by a reorientation of its nature towards fresh ends: thus by the operation of His grace He can bring about development in the character of a person or a people already created. Even the substances, so called, which were still tolerated by early Christian thought were not really substances as substances had been conceived by the thinkers of antiquity. The human soul is still called a substance, but it is now conceived as a substance created by God at a certain time and depending on God for its continued existence. The natural world is still called a substance, but with the same qualification. God Himself is still called a substance, but His character as substance is now regarded as unknowable: not only undiscoverable by unaided human reason, but not even capable of being revealed. All we can know about God is His activities. By degrees, as the leaven of Christianity worked, even these quasi-substances disappeared. It was in the thirteenth century that St. Thomas Aquinas threw overboard the conception of divine substance and defined God in terms of activity. . . . In the eighteenth, Berkeley jettisoned the conception of material substance, and Hume the conception of spiritual substance. The stage was then set for the third crisis in the history of European historiography and for the long-delayed entrance of history as, at last, a science.

The introduction of Christian ideas had a threefold effect on the way in which history was conceived:

(a) A new attitude towards history grew up, according to which the historical process is the working out not of man's purposes but of God's; God's purpose being a purpose for man, a purpose to be embodied in human life and through the activity of human wills, God's part in this working-out being limited to predetermining the end and to determining from time to time the objects which human beings desire. Thus each human agent knows what he wants and pursues it, but he does not know why he wants it: the reason why he wants it is that God has caused him to want it in order to advance the process of realizing His purpose. In one sense man is the agent throughout history, for everything that happens in history happens by his will; in another sense God is the sole agent, for it is only by the working of God's providence that the operation of man's will at any given moment leads to *this* result, and not to a different one. In one sense, again, man is the end for whose sake historical events happen, for God's purpose is man's well-being; in another sense man exists merely as a means to the accomplishment of God's ends, for God has created him only in order to work out His purpose in terms of human life. By this new attitude to human action history gained enormously, because the recognition that what happens in history need not happen through anyone's deliberately wishing it to happen is an indispensable precondition of understanding any historical process.

(b) This new view of history makes it possible to see not only the actions of historical agents, but the existence and nature of those agents themselves, as vehicles of God's purposes and therefore as historically important. Just as the individual soul is a thing created in the fullness of time to have just those characteristics which the time requires if God's purpose is to be fulfilled, so a thing like Rome is not an eternal entity but a transient thing that has come into existence at the appropriate time in history to fulfil a certain definite function and to pass away when that function has been fulfilled. This was a profound revolution in historical thinking; it meant that the process of historical change was no longer conceived as flowing, so to speak, over the surface of things, and affecting their accidents only, but as involving their very substance and thus entailing a real creation and a real destruction. It is the application to history of the Christian conception of God as no mere workman fashioning the world out of a pre-existing matter but as a creator, calling it into existence out of nothing. Here, too, the gain to history is immense, because the recognition that the historical process creates its own vehicles, so that entities like Rome or England are not the presuppositions but the products of that process, is the first step towards grasping the peculiar characteristics of history.

(c) These two modifications in the conception of history were derived, as we have seen, from the Christian doctrines of original sin, grace, and creation. A third was based on the universalism of the Christian attitude. For the Christian, all men are equal in the sight of God: there is no chosen people, no privileged race or class, no one community whose fortunes are more important than those of another. All persons and all peoples are involved in the working out of God's purpose, and therefore the historical process is everywhere and always of the same kind, and every part of it is a part of the same whole. The Christian cannot be content with Roman history or Jewish history or any other partial and particularistic history: he demands a history of the world, a universal history whose theme shall be the general development of God's purposes for human life. The infusion of Christian ideas overcomes not only the characteristic humanism and the substantialism of Greco-Roman history, but also its particularism.

CHARACTERISTICS OF CHRISTIAN HISTORIOGRAPHY

Any history written on Christian principles will be of necessity universal, providential, apocalyptic, and periodized.

(i) It will be a *universal* history, or history of the world, going back to the origin of man. It will describe how the various races of men came into existence and peopled the various habitable parts of the earth. It will describe the rise and fall of civilizations and powers. Greco-Roman oecumenical history is not universal in this sense, because it has a particularistic centre of gravity. Greece or Rome is the centre round which it revolves. Christian universal history has undergone a Copernican revolution, whereby the very idea of such a centre of gravity is destroyed.

(ii) It will ascribe events not to the wisdom of their human agents but to the workings of *Providence* preordaining their course. The theocratic history of the Near East is not providential in this sense, because it is not universal but particularistic. The theocratic historian is interested in the doings of a particular society, and the God who presides over these doings is a God for whom that particular society is a chosen people. Providential history, on the other hand, treats history indeed as a play written by God, but a play wherein no character is the author's favourite character.

(iii) It will set itself to detect an intelligible pattern in this general course of events, and in particular it will attach a central importance in this pattern to the historical life of Christ, which is clearly one of the chief preordained features of the pattern. It will make its narrative crystallize itself round that event, and treat earlier events as leading up to it or preparing for it, and subsequent events as developing its consequences. It will therefore divide history at the birth of Christ into two parts, each having a peculiar and unique character of its own: the first, a forward-looking character, consisting in blind preparation for an event not yet revealed; the second a backward-looking character depending on the fact that the revelation has now been made. A history thus divided into two periods, a period of darkness and a period of light, I shall call *apocalyptic* history.

(iv) Having divided the past into two, it will then naturally tend to subdivide it again: and thus to distinguish other events, not so important as the birth of Christ but important in their way, which make everything after them different in quality from what went before. Thus history is divided into epochs or *periods,* each with peculiar characteristics of its own, and each marked off from the one before it by an event which in the technical language of this kind of historiography is called epoch-making.

All these four elements were in fact consciously imported into historical thought by the early Christians. We may take Eusebius of Caesarea, in the third and early fourth century, as an example. In his *Chronicle* he set himself to compose a universal history where all events were brought within a single chronological framework instead of having events in Greece dated by Olympiads, events in Rome dated by consuls, and so on. This was compilation; but it was a very different thing from the compilations of pagan scholars under the late Empire, because it was inspired by a new purpose, the purpose of showing that the events thus chronicled formed a pattern with the birth of Christ in its centre. It was with this end in view that Eusebius composed another work, the so-called *Praeparatio Evangelica,* in which he showed that the history of the pre-Christian world could be regarded as a process designed to culminate in the Incarnation. Jewish religion, Greek philosophy, Roman law, combined to build up a matrix in which it was possible for the Christian revelation to take root and grow to maturity; if Christ had been born into the world at any other time, the world would not have been able to receive Him.

Eusebius was only one of a large number of men who were struggling to work out in detail the consequences of the Christian conception of man; and when we find many of the Fathers like Jerome, Ambrose, and even Augustine speaking of pagan learning and literature with contempt and hostility it is necessary to remind ourselves that this contempt arises not from lack of education or a barbarous indifference towards knowledge as such, but from the vigour with which these men were pursuing a new ideal of knowledge, working in the teeth of opposition for a reorientation of the entire structure of human thought. In the case of history, the only thing with which we are here concerned, the reorientation not only succeeded at the time, but left its heritage as a permanent enrichment of historical thought.

The conception of history as in principle the history of the world, where struggles like that between Greece and Persia or between Rome and Carthage are looked at impartially with an eye not to the success of one combatant but to the upshot of the struggle from the standpoint of posterity, became a commonplace. The symbol of this universalism is the adoption of a single chronological framework for all historical events. The single universal chronology, invented by Isidore of Seville in the seventh century and popularized by the Venerable Bede in the eighth, dating everything forward and backward from the birth of Christ, still shows where the idea came from.

The providential idea became a commonplace. We are taught in our school text-books, for example, that in the eighteenth century the English conquered an empire in a fit of absence of mind: that is, they carried out what to us looking back on it appears as a plan, though no such plan was present in their minds at the time.

The apocalyptic idea became a commonplace, although historians have placed their apocalyptic moment at all sorts of times: the Renaissance, the invention of printing, the scientific movement of the seventeenth century, the Enlightenment of the eighteenth, the French Revolution, the Liberal movement of the nineteenth century, or even, as with Marxist historians, in the future.

And the idea of epoch-making events has become a commonplace, and with it the division of history into periods each with its own peculiar character.

All these elements, so familiar in modern historical thought, are totally absent from Greco-Roman historiography and were consciously and laboriously worked out by the early Christians.

Suggestions for Further Reading

BUTTERFIELD, HERBERT, *Man On His Past*. Boston: Beacon, 1960.

CANTOR, NORMAN F. and RICHARD I. SCHNEIDER, *How to Study History*. New York: Thomas Y. Crowell Company, 1967.

COCHRANE, C. N., *Thucydides and the Science of History*. London: Oxford University Press, 1929.

CORNFORD, F. M., *Thucydides Mythistoricus*. London: 1907, reprinted by Greenwood Press, Westport, Conn.: 1970.

GARDINER, PATRICK, ed., *Theories of History*. New York: The Free Press, 1959.

GRANT, MICHAEL, *Ancient Historians*. New York: Charles Scribner's Sons, 1970.

TOYNBEE, ARNOLD J., *Greek Historical Thought*. New York: Mentor, 1952.

R. R. BOLGAR

The Classical Heritage: Its Formation and Transmission

꿐꿐 A hundred or even eighty years ago no university-educated person in the Western world would need to have the classical heritage defined for him; now one cannot be so sure that the nature of the classical heritage is self-evident. So far have we come from the traditional literate culture of European society. At the end of the nineteenth century the classical heritage still dominated the secondary school and university curricula all the way from the snows and forests of Wisconsin to the snows and forests of Siberia. It is not easy to state simply what dominates the curricula of educational institutions over this vast area today; but it is not the classical heritage.

The classical heritage, defined as simply as possible, is the literature of ancient Greece and Rome—of pagan antiquity. Stated in a more complex and subtle way, the classical heritage comprises the rhetorical forms, linguistic structure, and thought-patterns that predominate in this ancient Greco-Roman literature. The classical heritage was characterized by, first, a tendency to believe that there was a "right" and a "wrong" way to speak and write, and the right way involved the complex grammar and highly sophisticated sentence structure of Greco-Roman belletristic literature. Secondly, the classical heritage meant a predilection to think in terms of abstractions and generalities rather

FROM R. R. Bolgar, *The Classical Heritage and Its Beneficiaries* (Cambridge: Cambridge University Press, 1958), pp. 13–26, 45–58.

than particulars, nuances, and specific detailed qualities of things, whether of societies, individuals, or nature. A fancy way of putting this is to say that classical culture was strongly typological rather than empirical. Thirdly, the classical literature viewed persons and societies in moral and political terms; it had nothing significant (and often nothing at all) to say about the world in its economic and technological aspects or about men in their psychological makeup. Fourthly, the classical heritage was elitist both in origin and doctrine—it was the culture of the ruling class of Greece and Rome. It did not express either the language or the attitudes of the common man (not even the middle class, let alone the poor and downtrodden).

Given these severe limitations, why should anyone in modern democratic, industrial society—except for reactionaries and antiquarians—give a damn about the classical heritage today? Well, as a matter of fact not many people, even educated people, even professional intellectuals and most college teachers, do give much thought nowadays to the classical heritage. But there are two very important reasons why we should know the *history* of the classical heritage, if there is only limited justification (largely aesthetic) for close study of classical literature itself in this day and age.

First, the classical heritage dominated—indeed it virtually *was*—Western culture down to about 1890. If we want not only to know the intellectual history of the West but also to understand the public and private behavior of educated men in Western society, we have to comprehend the assumptions, attitudes, and ideals that were drummed into their minds as children in the schools whose curricula were entirely or almost entirely classical culture. Secondly, while our own literate culture, in its philosophies, ideologies, and scientific doctrines, has departed enormously from classical culture, in terms of rhetoric, language, articulated communication, it has not greatly departed from the literary culture of a hundred years ago. We are not as far beyond classical culture as we like to think. Listen to a politician's speech or a news commentator—the sentence structure, the imagery, the heavily moral categories are strongly reminiscent of the speeches of the Roman orator-politician Cicero, in the late first century B.C. We must become conscious of the meaning of classical culture if only to transcend it—and of course there is still a little band of humanists around who think that classical literature and philosophy are the fount of wisdom.

The best book ever written about the classical heritage is by the Cambridge scholar R. R. Bolgar. He tried to show who were "the beneficiaries" of classical culture—what was socially useful in classical literature in various eras so as to explain why Greco-Roman literature for so long dominated Western consciousness. In the following selection he analyzes the emergence of the classical heritage and how it faced its first great challenge, Christianity.

THE CHARACTER OF THE CLASSICAL HERITAGE

No one has ever brought together on the shelves of a single library all that has been written in Latin and ancient Greek. The collection would be imposing even by modern standards; and for quality as well as for quantity. But its most remarkable feature would have nothing to do with its size or even with the great number of masterpieces it contained. More has been written in English alone; and the best of English writers can take their place without question alongside their classical predecessors. No, the noteworthy and indeed unique characteristic of such a collection would be the space of time it covered, extending from Homer to the present day. For although ancient Greek has been truly a dead language for almost two centuries, Latin is still used by scholars and by the Roman Catholic Church.

The question therefore arises as to how much of this monumental array we can regard as the proper subject-matter of classical studies. No one has ever suggested that the latest Papal encyclicals should be read by classicists alongside Livy and Virgil. But men have wondered about Psellus, and the superiority of Petrarch to Cicero has been seriously maintained. There have been teachers prepared to include Alan of Lille in the curriculum, just as there have been others who were prepared to exclude Tacitus.

We shall find, however, that in practice modern students of the classics tend to regard any work written after the close of the sixth century A.D. as falling outside their proper field of study; and they also tend to neglect the theologians and other specifically Christian authors who flourished before that date. There exist, in short, certain conventions governing the classical curriculum which command the tacit support of the majority of scholars; and they would seem to have their roots in an intuitive judgement that the pagan writers of the period before A.D. 600 had some important characteristic in common which their Christian contemporaries and medieval successors manifestly lacked. For if there was no common element to distinguish the writings we call classical, if the literary productions of ancient times had no bond of union other than their date, there could be no good reason for feeling that one must exclude St Augustine and St Gregory while including Symmachus and Boethius.

Such a common element would be nothing unusual. It is widely recognised that there have been numerous examples of the literature—and even of the whole artistic output—of a society, possessing at a given period a marked unity of character. For a proof of this we need look no further than eighteenth-century England. Between the verses of Pope, the cynicism of Chesterfield, the embattled periods of Gibbon, the façade of Blenheim, Brown's gardening and the geometrical design of an Adam ceiling, there exists a link whose precise nature is difficult to define, but whose impact remains undeniable. The impossibility of finding an adequate description has given rise to the habit of talking in vague terms about an eighteenth-century spirit.

The same phenomenon can be observed in the case of other periods. Romanticism set a recognisable stamp on literature and art, so did seventeenth-century Classicism, so—we are beginning to discover—did the late nineteenth century. The fact that these broad similarities cannot be described in satisfactorily positive terms need not trouble us. We are not dealing with something altogether intangible. There is a line of approach to the puzzle which does provide a clear-cut answer.

Suppose we abandon all attempts at description and turn our attention instead to the origins of this curious impression of unity which meets us in the classics, in eighteenth-century literature and elsewhere. When we do this, various possibilities present themselves, some of which can be speedily eliminated. Language, or to be precise, the more obvious elements of linguistic usage, would appear to be largely irrelevant. *La Princesse de Clèves* makes use of the same vocabulary and the same classical French syntax as *Les Liaisons Dangereuses*; yet there is a world of difference between the impressions produced by the two books. On the other hand, *Pantagruel* and the *Moriae Encomium*, written the first in French, the second in Latin, belong manifestly together. Form in its broader aspects is similarly unimportant. The sonnets of Mallarmé have more in common with the free verse of Laforgue than they have with the sonnets of Du Bellay or Ronsard. The impression gained by the reader cannot be associated with the utilisation of a particular genre or group of genres. It seems to attach itself, like some pervasive scent, to every kind of writing within a period. It derives not from the literary forms themselves, which we may find elsewhere used with a different impact, not from niceties of construction, metaphors, epithets or tricks of speech, but rather from the kind of choice which is made with regard to each of these separate elements of style. It is the perfume of the personality behind the writing.

A work of art reflects the landscape of its creator's mind. It enshrines some aspects of his sensibility, some of his attitudes to experience. The picture it gives is incomplete. A single poem or even a group of poems never contains more than a sample of the poet's mental world. But at the same time it never adds successfully to the content of that world from alien sources. The personality of the creative artist sets the limits within which his art can move.

What is true of art applies more or less to all forms of writing. The limiting factor is always the mind of the writer. But the human mind bears the stamp of society. It is moulded by the education, the language, the experience which each individual shares with a larger or smaller group of his contemporaries. Man is culturally conditioned; and those indefinable common characteristics, which we note for example in all the productions of the eighteenth century, are nothing else than the reflection at the level of creative activity of the coherent eighteenth-century culture pattern.

This relationship between literature and culture is of primary importance for our purposes; and we shall do well to take a closer look at the concepts involved. Many of them are self-explanatory, but they need to be kept in mind. Each society has its own way of life, its particular apparatus of practical and intellectual techniques. Some of these techniques may be the private endowment of individuals, but most are held in common, either in the sense that they are used simultaneously by a great number, or in the sense that they are handed down from generation to generation for the performance of specific tasks. In a tribe, this common stock of cultural techniques is shared by nearly everybody. Where we have a large society, made up of several distinct social groups, each group has of course its own stock and the several traditions merge more or less successfully into an overall pattern. In the latter instance, the concept of cultural coherence needs a more subtle analysis than we can appropriately discuss in this context. But the essential point is clear enough. Whether we have in mind a social group, or a simple, or a complex society, the common way of life, to which its members subscribe, must be one which they can comfortably follow. Otherwise, there are disruptive conflicts. So except in the case of societies which are undergoing rapid change or stand on the verge of collapse, the common patterns of living will possess what we might call a psychological coherence. The institutions on which they are based, the economic and social activities which they require, the forms of sensibility which they favour and the ideas whose spread they advance, will be in harmony one with another; or at least the oppositions between them will not provoke conflict. In short, there will be a real pattern whose ultimate principle is the spiritual comfort of the individual.

It would appear therefore that we ought to look for an explanation of that similarity, which by general consent marks Greek and Latin literature from Homer to Boethius, in the existence of a common classical culture. But here we come up against an obvious difficulty. The world of Homer was not the world of Demosthenes, Rome was not Greece, the Republic was not the Empire. The semi-tribal societies at the dawn of Greek history were replaced by the city-states which in turn yielded before the megalopolitan civilisation of the Hellenistic Age. These sank into a world empire; and uneasy prosperity was succeeded by a disintegration full of incidental horrors. The history of the period offers us a spectacle of restless social change. How then could there be cultural unity?

We shall find the answer to this question if we consider in detail under what circumstances, and with what aims in view, the various sections of ancient literature came to be written. The conditions of the time did not favour what we have come to regard as the normal relationship between literature and culture. Their intimate connection was disturbed by a series of accidents.

The scene of the Homeric poems is set in the Heroic Age of tribal warfare, when noble birth and prowess in personal combat were the highroads to social eminence, and man moved in a world he did not try to understand, content to see himself as the plaything of supernatural forces beyond his ken. The *Iliad* and the *Odyssey* describe this primitive epoch with considerable accuracy. The space allotted to accounts of hand-to-hand fighting and to the fantasy life of Olympus reflects in the very construction of the poem the overriding importance which these elements had for Achaean culture. Nevertheless, the description for all its faithful detail is not from the inside. We know that these epics were composed originally to amuse the great men of the post-tribal period, and that they were not given their final form until the recension of Peisistratus, by which time the city-state was a social reality. Consequently, they lay an understandable emphasis on those traits which the pictured past shared with the emergent civilisation of the *polis*, on the popular assembly, the interplay of prestige and eloquence, and the reasoned exploitation of practical possibilities. At the same time, specifically primitive themes, such as the struggles in Olympus which have their effects on earth, are depicted with a slightly cynical exuberance in which the absence of belief is manifest. Culturally speaking, the Homeric poems belong rather to the beginnings of the city-state than to the heroic period of Mycenae and Troy. Moreover, throughout Greek history, but in particular during the golden age of Athens, they played the same role as the Authorised Version [of the Bible] later did in England. They formed the source-book of the educated imagination; and their intellectual magnetism exerted a constant pull to bring Greek civilisation back through all its changes into nearer contact with its first origins. As a result, the Homeric world picture is much more closely integrated into the later Greek tradition than at first sight appears; and what has been said about Homer applies with almost equal force to the rest of the early epic literature.

The period from the seventh to the fourth century B.C. saw the rise, the glory and the political eclipse of the city-states. Unhampered by the rigours of climatic extremes, sheltered (at least during the critical hundred and twenty years that followed Salamis) from the interference of outside powers, and predisposed to enterprise by the rewards of an expanding economy, their citizens lived in a world whose problems were for once not beyond man's power to solve. They developed as children develop to whom a wise teacher sets tasks within their capacity, learnt to observe and to plan, to make use of facts and reason, to be self-reliant and persevering; for they had no need to be discouraged, as so many have been since the beginning of time, by habitually losing the fruits of their vigour and sagacity through the operation of agencies outside their control.

The city-states provided Europe with its first concept of a reasonable society, as man would run it if nature did not interfere by setting him insoluble problems. Their example, idealised, was to serve future generations as an inspiring myth. But perhaps their finest achievement was to bring into existence the earliest written literature. Other civilisations had discovered the practical value of writing and had employed it to preserve notices of laws, details of ownership or financial transactions and chronicles of events, as well as the songs, legends and rituals of religion, but these early written memorials had been in the main innocent of artistic intention. The Greeks were the first to record compositions intended to give aesthetic pleasure. They seem to have been exceptional among the societies which knew how to write, in possessing a lively poetic tradition. Accustomed to the Homeric recitations of the rhapsodes, the epinicean odes and the dramatic contests, they placed a high value on the songs and verse narratives which their ancestors had handed down verbally from one generation to the next, with the result that they were the people to take the decisive step of entrusting poetic material to those written records which until then had been used for utilitarian purposes.

This practice, which by the middle of the fifth century had gone some way towards the creation of a written literature, then received a violent stimulus from the popularity of rhetoric, a development directly due to the political conditions of the city-state. Gorgias and others worked out rules for public speaking, exact techniques for making an impression. Experts trained in these methods travelled from city to city vending their intellectual wares; and soon no orator dared to trust to spontaneous inspiration. This movement had a double effect. It made men more conscious that composition was an art; and at the same time it led to the increased use of writing. Speeches had to be prepared in advance and then reproduced with great verbal exactitude. Even if you made them up yourself you were grateful for a record to which you could refer; but eventually most plain men did not trust their own skill, they employed professionals to provide them with a brief, and then a written memorial was indispensable. So between 450 and 350 B.C. writing and reading which had been rare accomplishments became the necessary instruments of every-day living.

By the birth of Alexander, Athens had produced a literature in which the principles of artistic composition were applied to tragedy and comedy in addition to several other poetic genres, to the numerous forms of oratory, to history and to the philosophical dialogue. Nothing like it was known at the time; and its uniqueness was to have a most remarkable influence.

In Asia and Africa, Hellenisation was confined to the larger towns, where the inhabitants lived in a way which differed in every essential from the old city-state pattern. They had not even the beginnings of independence and security. Few of them owned land; fewer still possessed any controlling interest in the production of necessary raw materials. They depended for all their requirements on the military dominance of the rulers they served, on the subservience of a peasantry they met only as customers and on the hazards of distant markets. Their physical surroundings emphasised their helplessness. Crowded in their tenements, they were peculiarly susceptible to the ravages of disease, to mass starvation if supplies should fail and to the shocks of mass hysteria, while the heavy monuments of royal and military power were there in the midst of their streets as a daily reminder of the arbitrary will which cut across their destinies. Such people could not have either self-respect or self-reliance. What use had they for observing reality or measuring means to ends? They were the playthings of circumstances; and their only god was Luck.

At the same time, on the mainland of Greece and the islands the old world still survived though without much of its vitality. Men still lived in small and largely self-subsistent cities over which they could feel to have some control. But the national economy was no longer expanding and a general restriction of life was the order of the day. So there were no new advances, but enough remained of the old conditions to make the fifth-century patterns of thought still acceptable. The old values of self-development, rational action and public service still made sense.

That is the background against which we must set the work of the Alexandrian scholars and poets; and then we shall not be tempted to deride them as pedants or to accuse them of living in an ivory tower. They may have been pedants, and they may have been obscure. But they were not remote from the world. If anything, they erred in the opposite direction. They had their practical aims too persistently in view. How else would they have had the patronage of Philadelphus and Euergetes who were not men to be fooled by academic fashions?

Philetas came from Cos, Zenodotus from Ephesus, Lycophron from Calchis, and the polymath Eratosthenes had studied long at Athens. Drawn from these areas where the old culture still lingered, and paid to pass their lives among the products of an imperfect Hellenisation, it would have been strange if they had not regarded themselves as the representatives of the fifth-century tradition; and they were encouraged in this attitude by their masters who had sound political reasons for desiring that tradition to be glorified. The interpretation which Philetas and his successors gave to their task, led them to open several fields of activity which were to prove of the greatest importance for the history of Greek literature and indirectly for the history of the world. They tried to establish and explain the texts of the great Greek authors, starting significantly enough with the ones their contemporaries must have found the most difficult, namely the great epic cycles, the lyric poets, and the tragedians. They prepared to this end recensions, commentaries and lists of difficult words, and to reinforce their academic teachings, filled their own verse with a plethora of mythological allusions. Like the rest of their work this cult of mythology served the ultimate purpose of keeping intact their contemporaries' links with the past, and at the same time, they attacked also from another quarter. Producing lexicons and later grammars of Attic usage, and imitating the established genres, they inaugurated a linguistic, as well as an antiquarian, revival.

Thus, Greek ambitions, Greek patriotism and the natural wish not to lose touch with a unique and glorious past led to the breaking of the links which had existed until then between the language of artistic composition and the spoken idiom; and simultaneously the content of literature was dissociated from everyday interests. The prose writers of the golden age had used the language of their contemporaries, ornamenting it perhaps by occasional phrases from epic poetry which was after all a popular possession, and if the poets had employed a more elevated style, they had similarly drawn upon the familiar Homeric heritage. These writers had produced their works for public occasion, for religious festivals, for the celebration of athletic victories, for drama competitions, for the hustings or the law courts. Unless they aspired to be historians or philosophers, all their masterpieces were composed with reference to some social event. But with the Alexandrians the connection between literature and life came to an end. Literature stopped being the artistic expression of contemporary culture and became instead an instrument of education.

This development was of the greatest importance; and since it has often been attacked on the ground that it distorted the natural growth of Greek culture, certain points might reasonably be made in its defence. We shall do well to remind ourselves first of all that if the Alexandrian scholars had not produced their imitations of existing genres, there would in all probability have been no Hellenistic literature at all. For the Hellenistic societies did not provide their writers with the stimuli that had called into being the odes of Pindar or the drama of Athens. Places like Alexandria and Antioch had little in common with the fifth-century states. They resembled rather the great urban agglomerations of the Orient which through the many centuries of their existence produced no literary work of merit. They were commercial entrepôts, wasteful of human energy, and we should be foolish to regard them as potential breeding grounds for art. Furthermore, if local literatures had managed to arise and if by some strange chance a school of Egyptian or Syriac writers had come to reflect faithfully the outlook and sensibility of Hellenistic man, it is necessary to remember that the emergence of these new literatures written in the new forms which the Greek language was taking, would have led to the neglect and eventually to the loss of the fifth-century heritage. In that case, too, posterity would have suffered.

Thanks to the efforts which had for their centre the library at Alexandria, the Greek writers of the four centuries that followed the death of Alexander remained faithful to the old tradition. Their imitations were admittedly not exact. They did not know enough about style or language. They lacked as yet the necessary apparatus of grammars and lexicons which would have enabled them to reproduce Homer or Demosthenes without a fault; and so their works show traces of the new Hellenistic idioms and of the new Hellenistic sensibility. But these traces are slight. The main pattern of thought, feeling and expression is that of the Golden Age.

These writers (and the educated men who read them) saw their world through the spectacles of the fifth century. Using the language of the past, they thought to a large extent in the categories of the past, neglecting much and distorting even more of the experience that was directly and personally theirs. This ordering of their world within the framework of outmoded perspectives came easily to them because the city-state culture still persisted in a weakened form. Most of them came from regions where a local autonomy still preserved the trappings of the old freedom; and in any case the new ways of life were repellent. The *douceur de vivre* pleaded strongly for a revival of the Periclean Age.

The inordinate sweep of Alexander's conquests was the original cause which first dissociated literature from contemporary culture in the Greek-speaking world. But single upheavals, however notable, are rarely sufficient to achieve long-lasting results, and the survival of the dissociation was due to another influence. During the second century B.C. the cult of the past was given an added sanction through the rise of Roman power. Rome, admittedly, had never been a democratic city-state as Greeks understood the term; and after the Punic Wars it was fast losing even its original oligarchic structure. But although by the time of the Eastern Wars the senate had shed much of its authority, the credit of its members as individuals remained considerable. They were still the most powerful men in the commonwealth. They were the élite whom all admired and they set the tone which was to be reflected in the general orientation of Roman culture. These senators of the decaying republic who were prepared one and all to exploit to the full the opportunities of a dictatorial age, who intrigued unceasingly for personal power, continued at the same time to hitch their waggon to the star of the old republican ideals. They vaunted Cincinnatus going back to his plough and Regulus going back to Carthage. Cicero seems to have believed without any doubt that all his political allies would have preferred to live in those primitive times when a public-spirited self-abnegation was habitual.

It is clear enough of course that this cult of the early republican virtues owed some of its popularity to the fact that the losing party whose ambitions were frustrated could use it with good effect as a weapon against their successful opponents. Nevertheless, its influence must not be underrated. The well-to-do senatorial circles who gave Roman society its pattern did maintain throughout the storms of the late Republic and the Empire a theoretical preference for the past as against the present. For whatever motives, they were in the habit of judging everything they saw around them according to a scale of values based on the much more limited experience of their remote ancestors; as if the improvident Roman mob was still a body of prudent farmers and craftsmen, as if finance was still a matter of driving away a few cows from a neighbouring city.

This preference led them to embrace enthusiastically the Greek city-state tradition and the literature in which it was embodied. Their enthusiasm moreover was reinforced by the usefulness of Greek rhetoric for pleading in the law courts and for the debates which cloaked the intrigues that really decided politics. So captive Greece enjoyed its intellectual triumph; and the works of Cicero, Livy and Virgil were written.

Thus, Roman literature started at the point which Greek literature reached only with the Hellenistic Age. Traditional in spirit and imitative in technique, it was never a direct expression of contemporary experience. Its language was from the first an artistic confection ordered by scholarship and remote from ordinary speech.

By the second century of the Empire, the literary traditions of both Greece and Rome were firmly linked to the past. The writers of the Alexandrian school had not imitated the language or the techniques of their models with an absolute precision. They had not yet been conscious of a need for such exactitude; nor had they yet possessed the means to achieve exact results. The road of plagiarism requires to be paved with more than intentions. The would-be imitator who relies on his memory alone will find that he reproduces little beyond an occasional phrase or turn of thought typical of his model. To do more requires a systematic approach.

When the Alexandrians had tried to write in the established tradition, to assimilate their epics and hymns to Homeric and their prose to Attic models, they had soon become conscious of a need for systematic guides to these various forms of the literary language. So Philetas had produced a glossary of difficult poetic words and Zenodotus a glossary to Homer; a certain Philemon had written on Attic nouns and Aristophanes of Byzantium had collected the Attic and Laconian terms covering all the usual social relationships. Their work had been continued by their successors of the second and first centuries B.C., by Dionysius Thrax, the founder of systematic grammar, by the fantastically industrious Didymus who produced vast tomes on metaphors and on comic and tragic diction, and by Tryphon who appears to have written on synonyms, on musical terms and on the names of animals and plants. With the passage of time, more and more aspects of the traditional written language had been explored in greater and greater detail, until by the second century A.D, the scene was set for a final systematisation.

It is important to realise that the Atticists came at the end of this long tradition. In effect, they were no more responsible for their programme than is the soldier for the shot he fires. Aelius Dionysius, Pausanias and Phrynichus merely completed a process when they sorted out the component parts of literary Attic in their huge dictionaries and grammars and enunciated the principle that any usage which differed from those they had noted was a damnable barbarism. Here at last were the necessary instruments for a perfect imitation. Intending writers had merely to study them, to digest them thoroughly; and the great wind of Attic glory would blow again. That the categories of language set limits upon thought, that using only the expressions sanctioned by the past forces one's experience on to a procrustean bed, cutting it down in effect to those elements which the present and the past have in common, did not enter their heads. The final absurdity of the prison they prepared for genius was hidden from them. They were concerned only with imitation.

In the meantime, Latin had undergone a similar development. Its rules had been formulated by a succession of learned grammarians from Stilo to Palaemon; and the techniques of imitation, the habit of reading notebook in hand to collect telling words and phrases, metaphors, parts of speech and arguments and the desirability of memorising this material until it became part of the natural furniture of one's mind were all regularly taught in the rhetorical schools.

Thus, during the last centuries of the Empire, the imitative tendency which had characterised all literature since the death of Alexander was sharply intensified. The well-organised educational system of the Empire had for its main aim to teach the two literary languages and to inculcate in the minds of all its pupils the established methods and desirability of imitation.

Moreover, just as the difficulties of the Diadochi [Alexander's successors] had originally helped to preserve the fifth-century Greek heritage and the thwarted ambitions of the Roman Senate had led its members to idealise the city-state, so once again political considerations intervened to further the spread of what had become the official Graeco-Roman tradition. As the protective might of the legions weakened, so the imperial government came to rely to an ever greater extent on its intangible assets; and the excellence of Graeco-Roman culture was turned into a useful bait for retaining the loyalty of the uncertain provincials. Steel was in short supply. So the provinces were to be grappled to the soul of Rome by hoops of a different make. Literature was taught with great zeal as an introduction to the Roman way of life; but what it introduced men to was in the last analysis the old life of the city-states.

Enough has been said perhaps to indicate why the classical literatures are unified as to their cultural reference in spite of the obvious social changes which occurred during the period of their composition. Among the reasons why the Empire failed we ought probably to number the intellectual failure of its educated class. Hampered by their traditionalism and by the strict linguistic discipline which they imposed upon their minds, the members of that class could not solve their immediate problems. They could not for a start suddenly invent after centuries of neglect the terms in which these problems might have been properly posed. But while they suffered in consequence, we, the recipients of the heritage they preserved, have on our side immeasurably gained.

This traditionalism which we have described did not carry all before it. There were exceptions to the general trend; and now and then in the later authors we catch glimpses of the horrors of megalopolitan culture. Theocritus has left some suggestive pieces; and there are passages of subtle understanding in Polybius. The novelists who wrote without the guidance of traditional models benefited from this liberty to produce some vivid sketches of contemporary life, while Philo and the Neo-platonists went a long way towards giving philosophical form to the longings and beliefs of the contemporary urban population. But in all these cases, the contemporary response was still to some extent clothed in the accepted traditional categories, as in the haunting rhythms of the *Pervigilium Veneris* [second or third century A.D.] the longing for a magical rebirth, that external salvation which had always been the comfort of the helpless, finds expression through the etiolated pretti-ness of the familiar worship of Love. The emotion which sprang from a deep contemporary need and the shop-worn trappings which poets had used for centuries with no background of feeling sit uneasily together. The result is a work of art which leaves the reader with a slight discom-fort, as if he were suspended between two worlds.

The life of the great urban populations was characterised, as we have said, by an acute sense of personal helplessness. Crowded conditions and the spread of endemic malaria multiplied the common dangers of death and disease. The supply of food was erratic, dependent on the dubious success of large-scale feats of organisation, while war, lawless-ness and the incidental ferocities of arbitrary governments were an ever present threat. Add to this the fact that the great numbers of slaves and freedmen were constantly exposed to suffering from the cruelty or ir-responsibility of their masters, and the general picture becomes one that we cannot contemplate without feeling outraged. The idleness, dishonesty and deep-seated corruption which the historians of the time proclaim to have been the characteristics of the urban populace, its avowed preference for living on charity and its delight in the public sufferings of others were but the natural outcome of the appalling conditions under which it was forced to exist.

With this chaos around him, man could not have had any confidence in his power to mould his destiny. The old beliefs in the value of effort and calculation vanished; and the insecure turned for help and solace to the supernatural. In the failure of reason, magic was invoked as a means of controlling events. The idea that everything might be determined by the operation of forces outside of the material universe which the initiate could influence, provided no doubt a certain measure of comfort. At the same time, the Orphic mysteries and the cults of the Magna

Mater and Mithras gave in their emotional rites moments of heightened experience with the promise of similar happiness in the future. Placing the goal of life outside of a sordid and insecure reality, they made daily commerce with that reality more tolerable.

These cults and religions, though they satisfied the longings of millions, had not the moral and intellectual content which would have enabled them to leave their mark on literature. That role was reserved for Christianity; and the Christian literature of the patristic age contains the most detailed expression we possess of the human mind during the later phases of ancient culture. The evidence it offers is limited in scope, for every topic is treated from a strictly religious viewpoint; and even the best of its products are not entirely free from the stamp of the traditional Graeco-Roman outlook, for the Fathers made their own the categories in which the Greeks habitually interpreted their experience. But all the same it offers us a concept of man and his fate which differs considerably from earlier formulations.

Thus, we shall find it convenient to divide the writings of antiquity into two groups. All the pagan works, with the possible exception of the novels, have their roots primarily in the culture which grew up in the city-states. The Christian literature, on the other hand, in spite of its affinities with this pagan tradition, belongs in its deepest essence to that later world of rabbit-warren towns and monster autocracies, to despair born of chaos.

If we were therefore to make a sharp chronological division and were to set ourselves the task of describing the influence on later ages of all that had been written before A.D. 600, we should have to treat our subject under two heads between which there would be only the arbitrary connection of temporal coincidence. [And only the] pagan group of writings . . . constitute what is normally meant by the classical heritage, whose most perfect expression is found in the masterpieces of Athens and Augustan Rome.

*   *   *   *   *

THE PATRISTIC TRADITION

Among the various factors which decided the fortunes of the classical heritage, the influence of Christianity holds an obvious pride of place. By the end of the sixth century, the Christian religion not only commanded the faith and ultimate hopes of millions. It had set the impress of its principles on all the more important spheres of human activity, in the number of which the acquisition of knowledge was naturally included; and it had come to dominate the field of affairs through an institution which disposed of an authority greater than that of any prince.

For the contemporaries of St Gregory the Great [c. 540–604], the literary heritage of the past was already something outside of their own world, which they could accept because of its usefulness, or reject because of the dangers it might bring in its train. The predominance of Christianity had therefore the effect of making the views of the Christian community extremely influential when it came to determining how the classical heritage was to be studied. Was the conscience of the time to sponsor the rebuilding of the ancient world with a wholehearted approval? Or was it to oppose such an effort? There was no unanimous answer.

This uncertainty had good reasons to excuse it. The Christian and classical patterns of life possessed many traits in common; but equally there was much to divide them. The former had developed originally within the culture where the latter was supreme, and was bound to it by the strongest ties of affiliation. The nature of the debt which the dogma, discipline, law and ritual of the patristic Church owed to pagan Greece and Rome cannot be described in detail without impinging on abstruse and controversial issues. But its great extent remains beyond dispute. Equally indisputable, however, is the importance of the differences which sundered that pagan order from its Christian successor, the Rome of the Forum from the Rome of the Popes. The Faith which had built the catacombs and sustained the tortures of the arena had its roots in experiences of which its persecutors were necessarily ignorant; and religion was a lion unlikely in any case to lie down in peaceful concord with the lamb of sweet reason.

The result was that the two traditions presented a strange variety of similarities and discords which now drew them together, now forced them bitterly apart; and of these one example may perhaps be given. Both the Hellenic and the Christian outlook laid a notable stress on personal responsibility. This trait was for each the keystone of its special values, and served to distinguish them both from those creeds and cultures that made man a helpless or a worthless pawn. But the best of the Greeks had sought to be responsible in the wise assessment and control of material circumstances for the purpose of achieving a worldly happiness. The Christians on the contrary were concerned with the choice between the road of salvation and the road of evil. The former had held themselves accountable for rational conduct in the natural sphere. The latter measured all things, responsibility among them, by the yardstick of an eternal law. Compromise between these two attitudes was admittedly possible. The Christian view can without being inconsistent admit worldly happiness as a permissible secondary aim, and it is not difficult to find support for a similar hierarchy of values in the writings of the most eminent Greek philosophers. But a compromise of that nature could not be permanent. Ideological enthusiasm affords such a convenient outlet for human aggressiveness that no complex attitude which depends on accepted principles *not* being carried to their logical extremes, has ever enjoyed a long lease of life; and in this instance the chances of survival were less than usual since the extreme positions, both on the Christian and on the Humanist side, had a strong attraction for certain temperaments. The unconditional service of Heaven was a comfort to those who were inhibited from enjoying the pleasures of this world, while Hedonism had its charms for those compulsively attracted to luxury or lust.

We must keep in mind however that the men of the early Middle Ages did not try to settle these problems of conflict and compromise from first principles. They did not think for themselves to any great extent. Their attitude to the classical heritage was determined by the history of the preceding six centuries; and if we are to understand Gregory I or Alcuin, we must take into account the opinions of the patristic age.

The majority of early Christians entertained ambivalent feelings about the Roman world. Passionately resenting some of its aspects, they were prepared to cling with equal passion to the rest. They hated the immoralities they saw around them. They wanted paganism destroyed; but they would have been horrified by the thought that the civilisation they knew might not be preserved. After the Christian religion had spread to include vast numbers of converts, most of its adherents were normal men and women, busy about everyday things; and their normality prevented them from visualising life independent of society, or society constituted otherwise than its familiar setting of rabbit-warren cities and an undermanned countryside. They wanted to be Christians, but amid the usual appurtenances of Roman life.

Similarly they were in two minds about the pagan literature which, as the basis of grammar and rhetoric, formed the staple subject-matter of the schools. If we can still be moved by the beauty of these works which spring from a world separated from us in some cases by more than two thousand years, and which are written in languages we have never heard spoken, how great must have been the spell they exercised over the minds of those who knew them as their national heritage. In spite of the intense hatred of all pagan practices and beliefs which the persecutions and the social depravity of the age naturally aroused, there were many educated Christians whose devotion to the poets and orators nothing could shake. We shall be discussing the case of Jerome in some detail; but he was not alone in his attitude. Even during the period when the imperial power was doing its best to stamp out Christianity, we find Arnobius and Lactantius upholding as zealously as any pagan rhetor the conventional values of linguistic exactitude and style; and it is evident from the dismay aroused by Julian's edict which forbade Christians to lecture on authors with whom they did not agree, as also from the number of the professors who resigned, that by the middle of the fourth century the representatives of the new religion were well entrenched in the schools and their academic work was sufficiently after the normal pattern to earn the respect of their colleagues. They could not have differed from these colleagues in the value they set upon their common subject-matter.

The ancient literatures, beside their aesthetic charm, embodied the best aspects of the pagan tradition; and so they could not be rejected by anyone who was not at the same time prepared to cut himself off from the whole of existing civilisation. Indeed many who were prepared to reject all else, many who had nothing but contempt for the world around them, still retained in their hearts a liking for Cicero or Virgil which no prejudice could dispel.

This ambivalence which characterised the outlook of the Christian in the street also affected the most eminent and influential of the Fathers. An Augustine, a Jerome, a Basil of Caesarea had not the kind of outlook which enables its possessors to consider life from a narrow angle as an assemblage of purely personal problems. The difficulties that engaged their attention and could mobilise the vigour of their feelings were present to their consciousness in the wider involvement of a social context. Their temperaments were such that they sought spontaneously for solutions which presupposed the noise and turmoil of men living together, which accordingly accepted civilisation and all its works. They were prepared to assume that in the new Christian society of the future numerous traits of the pagan world would be preserved although paganism itself would need to be purged away. Fundamentally, their attitude, which had the implicit support of the majority of their co-religionists was one of compromise.

But side by side with the tolerant majority there existed also a small and highly articulate minority who contended that the faithful ought to sever all contact with a degraded and degrading paganism. These zealots argued from premisses well-grounded in Christian belief that the world in general was evil, and that a world dominated by pagan ideas must in consequence be doubly damned; that life in society was no preparation for the judgement to come; that the satisfaction of bodily needs, the improvement of property and the peaceful production of wealth and children had no real importance in the eyes of a jealous God; and that the prayer and vacant contemplation which are man's right true end were most effectively practised in the decent untroubled solitude of a desert cell.

The fervour of these extremists, the prevalence of the evils they combated and the ruthless logic of their ideas had the effect of installing them as the keepers of the Christian conscience. Their single-mindedness was a powerful asset. For during these dislocated centuries which preceded the Dark Ages, no man could gauge the extent of the calamities which so plainly threatened. None therefore could feel confidence in his own sober judgement of what action was expedient or good; and the wisest Fathers of the Church had their fearful and uncertain moments. The ways of wisdom appear to us so complicated, so awkward to sum up in formulae, that even in easy times we find it hard to believe their worth. When difficulties threaten, they are quickly relinquished. In crises men are emotionally prepared to grasp at any panacea provided that it is firmly enough offered; and here the panacea had certain merits of its own. For that abandonment of the world, which the zealots were preaching, presented itself, on the one hand, as an escape from formidable moral and practical problems and so appeared desirable to the weary. On the other hand, being a mortification of the flesh it provided simultaneously with rest a welcome relief from anxiety. Its self-inflicted punishment anticipated the dreaded punishments of fortune. Thus, we find the Fathers every so often driven from the citadels of their common sense into a more or less whole-hearted acceptance of a policy of flight, from which, and on calmer occasions, they again withdraw, to put forward with their usual hesitations the balanced views of compromise.

We have talked so far as if patristic literature gave expression to a common outlook, and that is perhaps legitimate. For the opinions of the Fathers do add up to a unified tradition. But all the same they differed as individuals in the degree of their respect for the non-Christian past. The Greek Church supplied distinguished champions of the liberal policy which recommended imitating the best in paganism. Clement of Alexandria, who died early in the third century, had never felt the need to apologise for his wide reading. He had spread the legend that Greek literature went back to Jewish sources and had then cheerfully drawn on the Greek authors for argument and illustration. He was the first to propound the view, which was to gain considerable currency later, that the pagan literature was a propaedeutic to the Scriptures; and unlike most of those who repeated his remark, he had in mind not the information the Greek writings contained but what he was pleased to describe as their power to dispel prejudice.

Clement had been prepared to admit that he was influenced by Hellenism. Others had felt the same influence, but failed to make the same admission. Origen, whose theology was expressed in Neo-Platonic terms, scorned the thinkers whose ideas he had borrowed. And there were many who followed Origen's pattern. But the spirit, which lends dignity to the utterances of Clement, inspired, a hundred and fifty years later, a brilliant generation of young men who grew up at the precise point of time when the old traditions were still strong, but Christianity was already respectable. St Basil of Caesarea and his friend St Gregory Nazianzen had studied under Himerius in Athens, Theodore of Mopsuestia had sat at the feet of Diodorus in Antioch, while St John Chrysostom had been the favourite pupil of Libanius. All four possessed an expert knowledge of the ancient classics. Theodore spent his life in ardent controversies in the course of which he tried to persuade his fellow theologians to apply to the Scriptures the interpretative methods traditional in Greek scholarship. The other three were primarily stylists. Trained by the most eminent of contemporary Atticist scholars, they expressed Christian beliefs in the language, and therefore within the system of ideas, which Athens had bequeathed to the world. They were all zealous litterateurs as was also that lesser figure Bishop Synesius. But Basil and Gregory were also the boldest and most open protagonists of a Christian Humanism who had ever dared to make their voices heard. They went beyond the position taken up by Clement that pagan philosophy had the power of dispelling prejudices meaner than itself, and suggested that it would actually ennoble the minds of its readers. After their death the learning of the Greek theological schools took a different turn and ran dry in the aridities of sectarian conflict. But their writings had a great influence and the mantle of their sanctity was always there to protect and sanction in the Greek Church a reasoned tolerance of the pagan past.

The literature of ancient Greece was largely philosophic in tone. That of Rome contained a much higher proportion of the merely lascivious. Thus, it was in the West that paganism wore its most immoral, repellent and anti-Christian face; and for that reason, the Latin Fathers, while accepting the dependence of a future Christian society upon the old culture, were more inclined than their Greek compeers to treat that culture with suspicion, to play down its usefulness, and even for moments to condemn it altogether.

So we find Tertullian most reluctant to see Christian children in the pagan schools, but permitting their attendance because he realises that they must master reading and writing with at least a modicum of general knowledge, and realises too that the conventional grammar schools afford the only means to that end. He then straightaway cancels out this concession by forbidding Christians to teach. Pagan education may have been indispensable. All the same it was not to be countenanced.

Tertullian was a pioneer, theologically suspect, and his influence was therefore never great. Jerome and Augustine were the men who decided the educational future of the West. They were the contemporaries of Basil and Gregory, but they inhabited a different and more alarming world than was visible to the placid East. Their countries were torn by dissension and war; and the impermanence of all civil power was plainly manifest to their eyes. There must have been moments when they thought that civilisation could not survive. Since men's interest in pagan literature derived from their hope for an ordered and civilised future, this greater uncertainty of life in the West will perhaps account for the hectic fluctuations of mood and judgement which can be observed in the writings of the two Latin Fathers. For sometimes they are as broadly Humanist as Basil himself; but sometimes they turn quite the other way and, victims of some urgent anxiety, take refuge in the emotional extreme of an absolute rejection.

St Jerome had studied under Donatus and adored beauty of language with a passion which it is not easy for our more literate age to imagine. When he was already a mature man and a scholar whose reputation had been safely established, he fell ill during a trip to the East. In a dream at the crisis of his fever he pictured himself before the judgement seat of God and heard a plangent voice accuse him of being no Christian but a Ciceronian. This experience left him shaken as after a profound shock.

He immediately abjured all profane studies. Following the current ascetic custom he fled to the desert; and there he stayed for the full five years of a slow spiritual convalescence, first lying on the sand black with dust and eating uncooked food, then working with his hands, then copying books and finally undertaking the study of Hebrew. By 380 he was back in Constantinople and back too at his old habits, reading Greek books under the benevolent eye of Nazianzen; and it was a little while later that he began his great Latin version of the Bible [the Vulgate]. His old age was spent in a cloister near Bethlehem, busy with his translating, with his book of biographical sketches after the manner of Suetonius, with lecturing on the pagan authors to a class of boys. During the Middle Ages his example came to inspire both the partisans and the opponents of the studies he loved. The legend of his dream was used to deter the studious. But the Vulgate was always there to remind the Church of the blessings which accrue when a saint is inconsistent in his contempt for mundane beauty.

St Jerome was an artist. A graceful style filled him with keen delight. He was prepared to read the pagan writers, and to see his fellow Christians read them. He was prepared to tolerate even the morally dubious Comedians and the Satirists because they wrote correctly and rhythmically, because there was beauty in their imagery and aptness in their figures of speech, and because personally he never looked much beyond their literary qualities. Their content did not interest him. To the inattentive all things are pure; and those Christians whose love of pagan literature was based on a genuine failure to see that literature whole, whose interest was focused on its formal elements and who were nearly blind to all else, the writers in short and the connoisseurs, found in his sanctity and in his great service to Christian letters an unshakeably convincing justification of their attitude; and during the long Middle Ages that justification was to be sorely needed.

His example was, however, supplemented for Christendom by the teachings of St Augustine. The Bishop of Hippo was in many ways the antithesis of his aesthetically perceptive contemporary; and that he should have left written precepts where Jerome left a legend, a fact unimportant in itself, is an interesting symbol of the differences which divided the two men. Augustine was an intellectual for whom every sphere of knowledge and experience resolved itself into a collocation of definable details. It has been remarked that he considered the art of writing to be no more than the cunning use of literary devices, and that he treated systems of philosophy as if they had been mathematical theories. He had the scientific approach before the days of science. His intellect moreover was one of exceptional power. It could impose a clear mental pattern on the most complicated and most refractory of subjects. There were no limits to its span, and nothing dismayed its unflagging energy.

This vigour of mind, so far above the normal as to constitute a veritable prodigy of genius, shaped Augustine's outlook in a way which was to have great importance for his treatment of educational problems. Since it cost him no trouble to envisage elaborate and subtle relationships interacting over a wide field, he was not tempted to blind himself to the difficulties which arise because man is a social animal. When he considered the human condition, he thought naturally in terms of communities and not of individuals. Salvation as far as he was concerned presupposed the City of God and not merely the divine vision granted to an artificially isolated anchorite.

Thus, Augustine was admirably fitted to provide a reasoned explanation of that attitude to the pagan heritage which the majority of Christians inarticulately shared. He could understand those social pressures and needs which the ordinary man felt but could not put into words. Convinced that the virtues of the elect ought to find social expression, and that it was the duty of every Christian to facilitate such social improvements as could be achieved, he put forward a single solution to the problem of how to preserve civilisation without preserving paganism. Giving free play to his curious talent for splitting up organic wholes into artificial but easily definable parts, he envisaged the separation of all that was useful in the pagan legacy from its impious, immoral, or merely dispensable accompaniments. Christian culture could then take the first and jettison the second with a clear conscience. The analogy he used to illustrate his principle was the looting of the Egyptians by the people of Israel. Rome was laden with heterogeneous treasures, distinct and quickly recognisable, which the hosts of Christendom might appropriate and employ without prejudice for their own purposes.

Besides formulating this general principle, which was so attractive in its simplicity, and which minds familiar with the procedures of war found easy to comprehend, Augustine also made certain suggestions of a more specific character.

He advised the use of summaries. As a young man, round about the time of his conversion, he had begun a systematic survey of the liberal arts; and though he failed to complete this work a passage in his *Retrac-*

tationes shows that he continued to consider it of potential value. It was evident that such compendia, where Christian teachers brought together the essential facts on a number of important topics, could give the young safe access to information which they would otherwise need to seek from dangerous sources: and within a limited sphere, Augustine had no doubts about their efficacy.

Another suggestion he made was concerned with the teaching of rhetoric. In that all-important subject, text-books had only a limited value. Rules could be systematically stated, but as everyone knew, a bald statement was not sufficient. Pupils required examples. They could remember only what they had seen a hundred times embodied in an actual text: and where except in the established classics could suitable texts be found? The general attitude of Christian teachers on this point was that of Lactantius, who had bewailed the supremacy of the pagans but had firmly refused to consider any alternatives to their use. Augustine, who was deeply concerned about religious needs and whom the aesthetic beauties of a Virgil or a Cicero did not move as deeply as they moved Jerome, saw an alternative and had no hesitation in putting it forward. The Christian preachers, he pointed out, would find all the rules of rhetoric illustrated in the Scriptures. If they had a technical treatise to tell them what to look for, and a Bible in which to search out their examples, they would be adequately equipped.

These incidental suggestions are of more considerable import than might at first appear. A pillaging of the classical heritage, whose spoils were then gradually embodied in new technical and literary works to the replacement of their pagan predecessors, was likely to have very different results in the long run from a pillaging which had always to begin afresh so that each generation came into direct contact with the masterpieces of the past. Augustine wrote so much and expressed so great a variety of opinions that one cannot venture on any hard and fast judgement about what he may have thought on a point that he did not specifically develop. But the probability is that he did not envisage the replacing of pagan literature at least for many generations to come. His remark about the Bible occurs in a treatise where he is dealing specifically with the education of the clergy; and even in that context it was only for the study of rhetoric that he had in his own opinion proved the pagan authors redundant: though this is in the very field where according to Jerome they were indispensable. As regards content, he realised that there was material of great value in both poets and prose writers which could not be excerpted and would need to be gathered from the

original texts so that Christians would always have to rely on the firm-
ness of their principles to enable them to retain the good and to give the
bad no foothold in their memory.

Augustine represented in this matter the midpoint of the Christian
attitude. Those Greek Fathers who were humanistically inclined like
Basil and Gregory Nazianzen were prepared to allow pagan literature
to be taught in the schools to Christian children because they regarded
it—the obviously gross writers apart—as a suitable introduction in both
form and subject-matter to the study of theology. Jerome was prepared
to allow it to be taught, because of its beauty; and blinkered by his
artist's viewpoint he too failed to make any clear distinction as regards
subject-matter. These writers stood at one end of the scale. Against
them were arrayed men like Ennodius and Claudius Victor who were
ready to blame all the misfortunes of the age on the reading of Virgil
and Ovid, and men who like Paulinus of Nola were prepared to flee
into solitude. Augustine took up a position half-way between the con-
tending parties. He never considered the possibility of a sudden break
with Graeco-Roman culture, but he dismissed the arguments of Jerome
and attenuated those of Basil, making it clear that while a limited
amount of borrowing from paganism was vitally necessary, the amount
could be limited. Bringing to bear on the problem that cut and dried
simplifying spirit which was his notable contribution to the development of his age, he worked out a solution which ordinary men could
easily accept.

The next theologian whose opinions were to count for much in the
future was Gregory the Great. During the two centuries which separate
him from Augustine, certain important developments had taken place.
Martianus Capella had composed his playfully pedantic treatise on the
Seven Arts, which had proved popular, and had been revised a hundred
years or so after its original appearance by the Christian rhetorician,
Memor Felix. Cassiodorus had written his *Institutiones* with the avowed
purpose of providing an easy and safe equivalent of traditional education
for his monks. These works, along with the comprehensive and monumental encyclopedia of Isidore, the brother of Gregory's friend Leander,
were to become the favourite text-books of the early Middle Ages; and
it is reasonable to assume that they owed their popularity to the circumstance that they did summarise more or less adequately the most basic
and most obvious material that the Christian world wanted from the
pagan. They implemented to a great extent the first part of that programme which we saw sketched out in the fourth century.

At the same time, Christian literature had grown in volume and dignity. Christian poets used the classical metres with skill. The monk who was interested in verse could study Prudentius, Paulinus or Sidonius instead of Ovid or Virgil, and they would teach him all he might want to know about rhythm and poetic language. In prose, there was the Vulgate and there were the stylists among the early Fathers. Salvian, educated in Gaul during the fifth century, already knew his Lactantius better than his Cicero and was a skilled rhetorician for all that. The Christian writings of the first four centuries have been studied for the most part as theology and not as literature; and scholarship has not yet revealed how much they owed to their models. But the debt was certainly great enough for them to fulfil one function. They supplied an adequate set of illustrations for the rules contained in the textbooks.

To see the relationship in which the Christian culture of the late Empire stood to its predecessors, we need to take another look at the written language. By the fifth century there had developed independently in the East and in the West those variations on the official idioms, which we now call ecclesiastical Greek and Latin. These differed from their classical norms both by omissions and additions. They lacked those subtleties which derive from the involved possibilities of an elaborate and logical syntax, the classical usage having been in many cases replaced by a cruder one drawn from current speech. And what was perhaps more important, their vocabulary was smaller. A good number of the less common words of antiquity appear to have escaped the notice of the patristic writers altogether, while many others retained only the simplest of their several shades of meaning. These losses were to some extent compensated by the addition of numerous theological terms, technical in character and cautiously defined, but nevertheless capable of arousing strong feeling. In their sentimental balance at least the two ecclesiastical idioms differed markedly from their secular counterparts. Less vivid on the whole, they had a great emotive power concentrated in their newly-coined religious terminology.

These were the observable differences; but what really counted was not that the ancient languages had altered, but that men's attitude to them had changed. Your second-century Atticist—and for that matter your second-century Ciceronian—wanted his writings to form an integral part of the literature of an earlier age. He tried therefore to familiarise himself with the language of that age and thus gained through a thousand casual clues a very full picture of its ways of thought, its habits and its sensitivity. The Christian aims affecting the literary field were simpler and less organic. The faithful of the fifth century were not interested in sharing the literary skill of their earlier brethren, but only in sharing their beliefs. They consulted their authorities for accounts of certain events, for the explanation of certain doctrines and for encouragement to observe the moral standards arising out of these doctrines. To achieve these limited purposes, it was not necessary to maintain an exact correspondence between the idioms they used and those of their most respected texts. A general correspondence was sufficient provided that the technical terms remained fixed. In ecclesiastical Greek and Latin we get a falling away from the strict classical standards, which fluctuates in its extent but never goes beyond a certain point. With linguistic change kept within these bounds, the records of traditional Christianity never lost their value. The main features of the ideology set down in them were never obscured, and the subtleties did not matter. Indeed, there were no subtleties except those of doctrine which were guarded by the careful definition of the theological terms. Christian literature did not mirror the Christian culture pattern. It dealt with the legends and beliefs which formed the focal point of that pattern; but how their influence manifested itself, for different men in different walks of life, does not seem to have been known at this point and certainly passed unrecorded.

Given these circumstances, it is easy to see how a highly intelligent man like Gregory I could regard ancient literature as outmoded and the effort to write correct Latin as pointless. He did not see any good reason why he should avoid solecisms and barbarisms; and he was right. In his case, no reason existed. For he did not set any value upon that underlying purpose which had prompted men in earlier times to be Atticists or Ciceronians. He wrote to Bishop Desiderius of Vienne calling him to order for instructing boys in the pagan classics. Such activities were scarcely suitable for laymen; and they were shocking in the case of a bishop. Gregory was definite in his opinion that enough had been taken over from pagan sources. He did not believe that the Christian world would benefit from further contact with pagan literature. He had Prudentius. He could do without Ovid.

St Jerome, St Augustine, St Gregory the Great in the West, St Basil of Caesarea and St Gregory Nazianzen in the East, these were the oracles to which the future was to turn for guidance. The opinions they had advanced on pagan studies had been conditioned, as we have seen, by their temperaments and interests, by the specific needs of the societies in which they lived, and sometimes, as with Augustine and Gregory I, by the limited requirements of some particular situation. In reading Jerome it is necessary to keep in mind that he is vividly aware of form in literature almost to the exclusion of content. When Augustine advised the use of the Bible as a source-book for rhetoric, he had no one in mind but the preachers whose education he was planning, and there is no evidence of his wishing to suggest that the Bible rendered all ancient literature redundant from every point of view. Nor can we suppose that Gregory, when he trounced Desiderius, meant his words to apply outside their context. He was concerned primarily with the conduct of bishops, secondarily perhaps with the usefulness of pagan authors in grammar teaching. It is unlikely that he would have denied the value of classical writings as a source of general information, or that he would have looked with anything but favour upon the great enterprise of Isidore's encyclopedia.

Very little attention was paid, however, to these modifying circumstances by the generations that were to govern their conduct by the prescripts of the Fathers. Each saying was elevated into a principle of wide application and indiscriminately applied. The results were somewhat confusing. Patristic authority could be quoted for almost any attitude between a complete rejection and a very generous acceptance of the classical heritage. Every Humanist and every anti-Humanist could find a text to support his case.

In general, however, in spite of the opportunities which Jerome and the Greek Fathers gave to those enthusiasts for ancient letters who wanted to plead their special case, the main influence of the patristic tradition was against the free study of the classical authors. All the Fathers envisaged some restrictions, and a few, as for example the extremely influential Gregory the Great, could be interpreted to recommend that pagan authors were best avoided. Since Latin was the indispensable official language of the Church, and since the classical heritage contained so much to forward the growth of European civilisation, neither the prohibitions attributed to Gregory I nor the moderate limitations proposed by Augustine could gain general acceptance even in the West. In the East, where the views of Basil and Gregory Nazianzen set the tone, the Hellenists anyway enjoyed a fair modicum of ecclesiastical support.

The study of the ancient literatures could not be stopped. It could not even be restricted within set limits as Augustine had hoped. The suspicion with which they were regarded by certain Christians could not do much to hinder their spread. Yet, although it is clear that the tide of learning flowed with an ever increasing vigour from the sixth century to the sixteenth, we should do wrong to dismiss as unimportant that opposition it aroused and which had its origins in the Fathers' distrust of all things pagan. For if this opposition could not hinder the movement, it nevertheless could and did serve to canalise it into specific channels, so that certain types of study were preferred to others, and the assimilation of classical material proceeded unequally.

Suggestions for Further Reading

BOWRA, C. M., *The Greek Experience*. London: Weidenfeld and Nicholson, 1957.

COCHRANE, C. N., *Christianity and Classical Culture*. London: Oxford University Press, 1957.

DUDLEY, DONALD R., *The Civilization of Rome*, 2nd ed. New York: New American Library, 1962.

GRANT, MICHAEL, *The World of Rome*. New York: Praeger Publishers, Inc., 1970.

HIGHET, GILBERT, *The Classical Tradition*. London: Oxford University Press, 1949.

KITTO, H. D. F., *The Greeks*. Baltimore, Md.: Penguin Books, 1960.

MOMIGLIANO, ARNALDO, ed., *Conflict Between Paganism and Christianity in the Fourth Century*. New York: Oxford University Press, 1963.